Lois Marshall

Lois Marshall
~ A Biography

JAMES NEUFELD

DUNDURN PRESS
TORONTO

Copy Editor: Cheryl Hawley
Designer: Jennifer Scott
Printer: Webcom

Library and Archives Canada Cataloguing in Publication

Neufeld, James E., 1944-
         Lois Marshall : a biography / by James Neufeld.

ISBN 978-1-55488-469-8

         1. Marshall, Lois, 1925-1997. 2. Sopranos (Singers)--Canada--Biography. I. Title.

ML420.M368N48 2009   782.0092   C2009-902461-6

1   2   3   4   5   14   13   12   11   10

Conseil des Arts du Canada   Canada Council for the Arts   Canadä   ONTARIO ARTS COUNCIL CONSEIL DES ARTS DE L'ONTARIO

We acknowledge the support of the **Canada Council for the Arts** and the **Ontario Arts Council** for our publishing program. We also acknowledge the financial support of the **Government of Canada** through the **Book Publishing Industry Development Program** and **The Association for the Export of Canadian Books**, and the **Government of Ontario** through the **Ontario Book Publishers Tax Credit program**, and the **Ontario Media Development Corporation**.

Care has been taken to trace the ownership of copyright material used in this book. The author and the publisher welcome any information enabling them to rectify any references or credits in subsequent editions.

J. Kirk Howard, President

Printed and bound in Canada.
www.dundurn.com

FSC
Mixed Sources
Product group from well-managed
forests and other controlled sources
Cert no. SW-COC-002358
www.fsc.org
© 1996 Forest Stewardship Council

Dundurn Press
3 Church Street, Suite 500
Toronto, Ontario, Canada
M5E 1M2

Gazelle Book Services Limited
White Cross Mills
High Town, Lancaster, England
LA1 4XS

Dundurn Press
2250 Military Road
Tonawanda, NY
U.S.A. 14150

TABLE OF CONTENTS

Acknowledgements   11
Introduction: In the Archives   17

Chapter One: 19
    1925 to 1939 — On Ellerbeck Street

Chapter Two: 41
    1939 to 1947 — The Conservatory and Weldon Kilburn

Chapter Three: 69
    1947 to 1950 — Bach, Handel, and Sir Ernest MacMillan

Chapter Four: 95
    1950 to 1953 — With Toscanini at Carnegie Hall

Chapter Five: 125
    1953 to 1957 — Beecham's Protégée

Chapter Six: 155
    1957 to 1960 — To Russia with Love

Chapter Seven: 187
    1960 to 1967 — Wagner and the Vocal Crisis

Chapter Eight: 221

1967 to 1975 — On the Road with the Bach Aria Group

Chapter Nine: 249

1975 to 1997 — Home Again at the Faculty of Music

Appendix A   283

Notes   287

Selected Bibliography   317

Index   319

For John W.

I think of myself as a singer. I'm not a great intellectual, but I can sing and I know that. So I think I'm just a singer. And if I am remembered at all I guess I would like to be remembered for bringing people some pleasure.

— Lois Marshall

ACKNOWLEDGEMENTS

In her lifetime, Lois Marshall resisted the idea of a biography. She was, as she often put it, "just a singer," not a celebrity, and that was fine by her. She preferred to keep her private life private. After she died, her family and friends honoured her wishes, even as the public grief at her death belied her basic premise: for almost fifty years, Lois Marshall had been a defining presence in Canada's cultural life. Thus, private wishes and public interest stood at loggerheads, until chance intervened. Lois's sister, the late Rhoda Scott, received some advice from a casual acquaintance about the merits of a biography just at the time I proposed this book to her. Now convinced of its importance, she agreed to participate in the project.

Her co-operation opened the doors to Lois's friends and associates, who accepted my intrusions patiently over more than ten years of research and writing. Rhoda gave me hours of her time, during which she reminisced extensively about Marshall family life. Rhoda's daughter, Kim Scott, responded to further questions from me after her mother's death. Among Lois's many friends, three in particular gave me valued support and access to important memorabilia — Stuart Hamilton, Carl Morey, and Cindy Townsend. Doreen Uren Simmons championed the idea of a biography of her dear friend from the first moment I broached it, gave me many important contacts from among Lois's wide circle of acquaintance, read an early draft of the manuscript, and remained loyal to the project, and to me, when many others would have lost hope.

In order to write about Lois Marshall, it was essential that I have her voice in my ears. I needed recordings to remind me of the sound I had experienced live in the concert hall. That was a tall order, given that she recorded very little for an artist of her stature, and that most of the recordings she did make have long been unavailable. Fortunately, the CBC came to my rescue. Lois broadcast regularly on the CBC for thirty-six years, from 1947 through to her appearance at the National Arts Centre in *Eugene Onegin* in 1983, and the CBC archives contain a wealth of material, to which the corporation generously gave me access. I want to thank Gale Donald for granting me permission to listen to those recordings, and Ken Puley, who interrupted his working days in order to retrieve them for me and set me up with listening facilities in his own workspace. Stephen Clarke, an old friend and an expert collector of vocal rarities, supported this project from the outset. He provided invaluable help in tracking down a hitherto unknown Marshall performance and in obtaining crucial recording data from HMV concerning Marshall's British recordings. Ellen Shenk drew my attention to a notable CBC broadcast that documented, with recordings, Lois's Moscow debut. I had met Mary McDonald, for many years the principal pianist for the National Ballet of Canada, when I was writing *Power to Rise: The Story of the National Ballet of Canada*. Mary, who had been a parishioner at Holy Name Roman Catholic Church in Toronto when Lois was a young girl singing in the choir, arranged for me to tour the church and get a sense of the atmosphere of this important place in Lois's development. She also provided the beautiful photograph of the interior of Holy Name as it was in the 1940s, taken from the choir loft from which Lois sang.

Establishing the Kilburn family background would have been a daunting task had it not been for the assistance of Peter Kilburn, the family genealogist, who shared with me his extensive research into the Kilburns' British origins and emigration to Canada. Finding out Lois's family history posed an even more difficult challenge, one which Glenn Wright, formerly of Library and Archives Canada, cheerfully accepted. A skilled genealogist who refuses to believe there are any unanswerable genealogical questions, Glenn traced Lois's family tree back through three generations, and in the process gave me a basic education in how to research vital statistics in a variety of Canadian and American sources.

Despite the rich resources of information now available on the Internet, our country's cultural record still depends on the collections of our various libraries and archives, and on the archivists and library staff who keep them running. Research for this book has involved me, either by correspondence or through in-person visits, with the following archives and collections: Library and Archives Canada, Ottawa; Audio Archives of the Canadian Broadcasting Corporation, Toronto; University of Toronto Archives and Records Management Service; the Toronto Reference Library; Archives of the National Arts Centre, Ottawa; the New York Public Library for the Performing Arts at Lincoln Center; Clara Thomas Archives and Special Collections, York University, Toronto; the Canadian Opera Company Archives; Trent University Archives, Peterborough; Archives and Special Collections of the University of Calgary Library; Special Collections, Georgetown University, Washington; Rosenthal Archives of the Chicago Symphony Orchestra; Archives of the San Francisco Symphony; Archives of the Cincinnati Symphony Orchestra; Archives of the Cleveland Orchestra; the Minnesota Symphony Education Division. At each of these institutions, friendly and efficient staff made my searches and enquiries both easy and fruitful. I want to thank by name three of the wonderful archivists and staff of the Music Division of Library and Archives Canada, where Lois Marshall's papers are housed: Florence Hayes, Maureen Nevins, and Marlene Wehrle. Marnee Gamble, of the University of Toronto Archives and Records Management Service, provided expert help in locating the cover portrait and some of the photographs that appear in this biography. Wendy Watts, of *GetStock. com*, gave cheerful and efficient assistance in tracking down the rare photo of Marshall as the Queen of the Night. Kris Sieber, of Lazer Graphics Peterborough, did an expert job of scanning images and archival materials for the illustrations. And thanks also to Debbie Keith, of Columbia Artists Management International in New York, for providing archival information even though her organization does not maintain an archive for public access.

I was unable to travel to Russia for information on Lois's tours of the Soviet Union, but I was lucky to have the co-operation of Alexander Tumanov, of Edmonton, who was present at Lois's Russian debut and managed to bring tape recordings of her Moscow performance with him to Canada. I also recruited a friend, Benjamin Tromly, who was then a graduate student in Russian history, to conduct research for me on one of his trips to Moscow. Both he and his wife, Ekaterina Peshkova, translated Russian programs and documents for me, as, before his death, did Peter Roberts, a former Canadian Embassy official in Moscow, who played host to Lois on her first Moscow appearance and who later returned as Canada's ambassador to Russia. Another friend, Maria Setya, provided translations from the Dutch of the reviews of Lois's appearances in the Netherlands.

Much of the most valuable material in this book came from interviews with friends and colleagues of Lois. I took it as testimony to their admiration and respect for her that every person I approached agreed willingly to be interviewed for the project. I am grateful to them all for their candour and for their initiative in referring me to others when they themselves could not answer some of the questions I posed. The following individuals, some of whom have died since I spoke with them, have contributed their knowledge and memories of Lois to the making of this book: Dianne Ball, Roberta Clough, Doris Crowe, Marshall Crowe, Gayle Donald, Robert Donald, Mary Lou Fallis, Ute Gerbrandt, Nicholas Goldschmidt, Théa Gray, Stuart Hamilton, Walter Homburger, Nicholas Kilburn, Paul Kilburn, Ilona Kombrink, Greta Kraus, Anton Kuerti, Mary Lee, Joanne Mazzoleni, Irene McLellan, Carl Morey, Mary Morrison, Larry Pfaff, Naomi Roberts, Peter Roberts, William H. Scheide, Kim Scott, Rhoda Scott, Doreen Simmons, Jan Simons, Cindy Townsend, Alexander Tumanov, Becky Voth, Monica Whicher, Yehudi Wyner.

Research of this kind takes money as well as time, and I gratefully acknowledge the financial support I have received. The Trent University Internal Research Grants Committee provided me with two separate awards, in 1999 and in 2002, that enabled me to undertake the travel necessary for interviews and archival research. I also received generous sabbatical leaves from Trent University that freed me from other duties to be able to pursue this project. In 2007, the Symons Trust for Canadian Studies of Trent University awarded me a grant that enabled me to work with a professional editor in revising and improving the manuscript for this book, prior to submission to a publisher. The Estate of John Stratton supported some of the pre-publication costs for this project. For all of this financial support I am deeply grateful.

The grant from the Symons Trust brought me once again into close collaboration with Ramsay Derry, who had edited my previous book, *Power to Rise*. Ramsay has been a sensitive, demanding editor, but much more, he has been a trusted advisor and advocate for this project from its inception. Without his help, this book would not have its present form.

At Dundurn Press, I have benefited from Cheryl Hawley's patient and careful editorial suggestions and from Michael Carroll's expert guidance. To both of them, and to all the staff at Dundurn, my grateful thanks.

My wife, Lynn, has given me constant moral support throughout the years I have been working on *Lois Marshall: A Biography*, and has acted as unpaid research assistant and volunteer proofreader on the final galleys. Her many other gifts to me are beyond acknowledgement.

INTRODUCTION

In the Archives

Filed away somewhere in the depths of the closed stacks of Library and Archives Canada in Ottawa sits Video ISN 55060, a video transcript of a 1980 CBC television show called *Spectrum*. The program is a tribute to the Canadian soprano Lois Marshall in the waning days of her professional career. Since I am systematically reviewing all the archival holdings on Marshall, I page the video from the stacks. By this time, I've heard a lot of Marshall, and I'm not expecting any surprises.

The retrieval process takes its usual slow course. Finally, today, among the materials waiting for me at the service desk, here it is. I take it out of the busy, sunlit main reading room, with its tables of researchers and panoramic views of the Ottawa River and Gatineau beyond, into one of the dark, enclosed viewing cubicles, adjust my earphones, and insert the tape into the VCR. Here, there are no distractions. It's just me and the video. Even though I'm a diehard Marshall fan, I am completely unprepared for the impact that this piece of electronically recorded history has on me.

Television was never Lois Marshall's medium. The screen was too small-scale to accommodate the grandeur of her artistic personality, too intimate and personal for the serious formality of her style. By these late days of her career she had learned to erect countless little barriers that kept the audience at a respectful distance, slightly removed from her person, focused on her music. As the tape unrolls, I am struck once again by the strangeness of the stage picture she creates. Her dress, a deep blue affair covered in large, glistening sequins, shields her ample frame like a metallic breastplate, shimmering under the studio lighting. Her hair is piled high and lacquered to an artificial sheen (I will learn later in my research that it is the wig she wore at all times, both in private and in public, to conceal her greying hair). She is highly made up. Her round, matronly face peers hesitantly at the camera, as though overwhelmed by all the makeup and coiffure. As she prepares to sing, the sense of discomfort grows. The editors have cut the tape to eliminate her laborious progress across the set and into position by the piano, so the viewer doesn't see the pronounced limp, remnant of her childhood battle against polio, but the facial close-up exposes mercilessly the sheer physical effort required for her to breathe deeply enough to produce the full sound of the concert singer.

Then, with only a sparse piano accompaniment, she begins to sing a simple four-stanza setting of Robbie Burns's "Ae Fond Kiss," and all the artifice of television studio and concert hall presentation melts away. She has sung this song literally hundreds of times, in concert and recital halls across Canada and throughout the world. Briefly, I am tempted to hear in the plaintive lament echoes of Marshall's own unhappy love life, but the face on the screen forbids such facile equating of life with art. Her performance is heart-rending, not because it speaks of her experience, but because it speaks to mine. The bond she creates is intimate with self-surrender, the surrender of the listener to the power of a simple song. There is nothing confessional or autobiographical about Lois Marshall's art. She is a throwback to an earlier time, something like an ancient bard, emptying herself to sing for her people the songs they need to hear. Even this electronic vestige of Lois Marshall burns with the furious passion of that mysterious artistry. Her image and recorded sound have transformed a darkened cubicle in the archives' reading room into a world of heartbreak and splendour. Once again, I know why I must write her biography. There is no singer like her before the public today.

CHAPTER ONE

1925 to 1939 —
On Ellerbeck Street

Lois Marshall, born into a large Toronto family of no particular artistic leanings, learned early on to muster the determination, confidence, and *sang-froid* of the consummate professional. She walked, with physical difficulty and supreme resolution, onto the most prestigious stages in the world, tackled some of the most challenging vocal music ever written, and worked with the greatest of international conductors, some as renowned for their fierce tempers as for their musical accomplishments. All the while she accepted gruelling travel and concert schedules that would have exhausted an artist without her physical disability. She did so at a time when only a handful of Canadian classical musicians — pianist Glenn Gould, violinist Betty-Jean Hagen, singers Maureen Forrester, Jon Vickers, Léopold Simoneau, and James Milligan — were registering on the international musical scene. Yet when international commitments could have called her away from home full-time, Lois maintained her presence in Canada, through constant touring and CBC radio broadcasts so frequent she became a national fixture.

As centennial celebrations approached, anyone advancing an argument for Canada's cultural significance on the world stage would routinely invoke her name. Although she almost never did crossover repertoire, she achieved a status virtually unique in her time, a respected classical artist of the first rank who became a popular national figurehead. Lois sailed into international stardom and into the hearts of Canadians as though by birthright.

That impression couldn't have been farther from the truth.

Lois's father, David Marshall, was born in 1883 in the village of Riversdale, in Bruce County, Ontario, not far from Walkerton. His father, James Marshall, originally from Scotland, was the only one of Lois's grandparents not born in Canada. By the time David was a young man, his parents had moved the rest of their family to Saskatchewan, but David stayed behind, working for CPR steamships in Owen Sound, then briefly trying his luck in Detroit. He met Florence O'Brien during his time in Owen Sound, when she visited an aunt and uncle there.

Florence (Floss or Flossie, as she was known in her youth) was born in 1886, probably in Barrie. By 1901 she had moved with her family to Toronto, where, at age fifteen, she was already working as a "tailoress" according to the census for that year. In 1909, four or five years after they first met, David Marshall and Florence O'Brien married in Toronto. They remained there for the rest of their lives.

Even though the economic hardships of the Depression still lay in the future, life was far from easy for them in January 1925, when Lois was born. By then, Florence and David already had five children, the youngest of them, Rhoda, not yet two years old. It was a constant struggle to provide for them. David, the sole breadwinner, now worked as a salesman in linens and dry goods at the Queen Street location of Eaton's Department Store in downtown Toronto.

As was common for large families of slender means, David and Florence had lived with relatives for the first few years of their marriage. Off and on throughout the years of Lois's childhood, during times of need, they would share their home with various family members. Starting out in rented houses on Ellerbeck Street, the family moved frequently, once to a larger home on Langley Avenue, and then, when they experienced financial reversals, to a much smaller house on Millbrook Crescent. They lived always in the district bounded by Riverdale Park on the east and Withrow Park on the west, never too far from Danforth Avenue, the commercial and community spine of the neighbourhood. Florence, a staunch Irish Catholic, saw to it that all her children participated regularly in the life of their local parish, the Church of the Holy Name on the Danforth, near Pape Avenue.

Lois was born on January 29, 1925, in the bedroom of her parents' rented house at 102 Ellerbeck Street. Before Lois there were four girls and one boy, Fred (born in 1912), Mary, Jean, Ruth, and Rhoda, born in that order, at two or three year intervals. They were followed by Lois, Rita, and Patricia. Florence bore seven of her eight children at home. One year after Lois's birth, the family settled into another rented house just down the road, at 107 Ellerbeck Street. This childhood home of Lois's was a cramped, semi-detached house, less than a mile's walk from Holy Name Church. With only three bedrooms at their disposal, one for the parents and the most recent baby, one for Fred (the eldest, and the only boy), and one for the rest of the girls as they came along, the Marshall children grew up knowing family togetherness, family intimacies, and family jockeying for position. It was an old-fashioned family, in which Florence deferred to David as the disciplinarian, the older children helped out with the younger ones, and all were expected, when their time came, to contribute to the communal finances.

When Lois was only one and a half years old, the family suffered great hardship. In 1926, Ruthie, her father's darling, came down with measles. The doctor was called, but could provide little help. On July 24, 1926, after ten days of illness, Ruthie died at home. She was five years and eight months old.

Though Lois was too young to have any recollection of Ruthie at all, her death established a natural division of the Marshall children into two groups that defined the family as Lois knew it all her life. The three oldest, Fred, Mary, and Jean, made up the senior group, almost adults in the eyes of the younger children. Fred, after all, was twelve years older than Lois. After the gap caused by Ruthie's death, came the four younger girls, closer contemporaries, Rhoda, Lois, Rita, and Pat. The sleeping arrangements in the crowded girls' bedroom reflected this division by seniority, with Jean and Mary in one double bed, Lois on a cot, and Rhoda, Rita, and Pat jammed into the remaining double bed. There was hardly room to turn around, let alone keep a secret. Freddie, luxuriating in the privacy of his own bedroom, gradually acquired distance and independence from his sisters, even an air of mystery, while the four younger girls developed a hardy camaraderie, affectionate, competitive, irreverent, and intimate.

In the summer of 1927, with the death of Ruthie only a year behind them, serious childhood illness again disturbed the normal routines of family life. Lois fell ill. The doctor diagnosed tonsillitis, but the emergency tonsillectomy he performed only delayed the correct, and more alarming, diagnosis: Lois had contracted polio.

Poliomyelitis is caused by one of three different polioviruses, which usually result in a mild infection confined to the gastrointestinal tract. The virus can, however, invade the nervous system and attack the spinal cord, in which case muscular weakness, paralysis, or even death can occur. Treatment for polio in the 1920s consisted mainly of isolating the patient during the communicable stages of the disease and of strict immobilization in the hopes of allowing some recovery of the affected muscles. Before the discovery of an effective polio vaccine, the disease was universally feared as a scourge and killer of children.

Because so little was known about polio's cause, treatment, or prevention, families felt helpless under its onslaught. Canada had experienced a serious outbreak of polio in 1910 and had been affected by the American epidemic of 1916, which, of course, recognized no borders. Nineteen twenty-seven marked the outbreak, in western Canada, of another terrifying epidemic of the disease, which worked its way eastward across the country over the next five years. Lois was among the earliest of the Ontario cases.

David Marshall had been a gregarious man, full of stories, a great dancer, devoted to his family, a canny Scot with his money, who worked tirelessly and uncomplainingly to provide for his family's needs and his wife's small extravagances. However, the death of one child and life-threatening illness of another released the "black Celt" in his personality. (The phrase is Margaret Laurence's, from her novel *The Diviners*.) The outgoing, exuberant, fun-loving family man gradually receded, to be replaced by someone more distant, severe, and melancholy. To his credit, his devotion to his family never wavered. Throughout Lois's lengthy battle with polio, it was David who massaged her legs with cocoa butter every night and heard her prayers before bed. It was David who somehow managed to support his burgeoning family while shouldering many of the additional expenses that Lois's illness occasioned. But he did it all from an emotional distance. As Lois knew him, there was always an essential reserve about her father. His younger children approached him with respect mixed with fear. Years later, when Lois's touring took her to Regina, she finally made contact with two aunts and an uncle on her father's side, who were still living there. The stories they told of the demonstrative, effervescent, and affectionate young man they remembered reassured her, but amazed her too. She had known only the black Celt, never this other David Marshall.

In Lois's earliest childhood, illness pushed her family into the background. Grief at Ruthie's death had distanced her father from Lois, and polio replaced normal family life with the interminable routine of doctors and hospitals. For the next ten years the Hospital for Sick Children, on Elizabeth Street in Toronto, became her second home, and its medical staff her surrogate family, which she had to share with every other patient there. The unnecessary tonsillectomy, of course, had subjected Lois's already weakened system to additional strain and given the virus added opportunity to attack. It was remarkable that she survived the onslaught of polio at all. But survive she did — not only the disease, but also the punishing treatment favoured at the time.

After her initial hospital stay, the doctors entrusted Lois to her parents' care, sending her home trussed to a device called a Bradford frame, with strict instructions that she be kept confined to it at all times, in order to allow her muscles to regenerate. The frame resembled an instrument of torture, with restraints at the wrists, waist, abdomen, thighs, shins, ankles, and toes. Lois had all the natural stubbornness and determination of her nearly three years. According to family lore, despite her mother's pleading with her to lie still, she patiently awaited her opportunity, and the moment she was left alone started wriggling her wrists until she could free them from the straps. Then, through painstaking effort, she somehow learned to undo the remaining knots and buckles, thereby gaining some freedom, however limited. Florence, harried beyond measure, despaired of her. The doctors could not believe that a young child could get out of a Bradford frame without help, and suspected Florence of neglecting the prescribed treatment out of pity for her daughter. Florence's completely unnecessary feelings of guilt compounded the stress of the medical crisis and of nursing her sick child.

In the course of the next year, exercise, massage, twice-weekly visits to the Hospital for Sick Children, and much hard work and determination achieved a partial miracle. Lois regained full use of her right leg, but the muscles of the left leg did not respond to treatment. They remained atrophied, unable to provide the strength and control necessary for walking. By the time she was four, she was ready for the leg brace and orthopaedic shoe that would enable her to walk again. The day came for the contraption to be fitted, and Florence Marshall took her daughter to the appointment, her high hopes mixed with trepidation. She told the story of what happened next many times, to Lois and others, as testimony to her remarkable daughter's determination and strength. Once the cumbersome metal brace was on and suitably adjusted, Lois, who had had limited mobility at best for the past year and a half, walked immediately, without having to relearn the skill, as though there had been no interruption to her normal childhood development. As an adult, Lois believed she could still remember the sense of euphoria she felt at the freedom of walking again.

Her freedom was relative, of course. The brace constricted her left leg uncomfortably, and at the end of the day Lois revelled in taking it off and massaging and manipulating "little lefty," as she referred to her leg, for much-needed relief. During the night, if she had to go to the bathroom, instead of waking one of her sisters for help she simply bent over and loped along on "all threes," getting about as efficiently as her circumstances allowed.

As an adult, Lois recognized that her childhood encounter with polio had had a fundamental influence on every aspect of her life, but she refused to dwell on it, be depressed by it, or feel sorry for herself. Like the little four-year-old with a new leg brace, she was much more interested in getting on with life, on her own terms.

But polio hadn't finished with Lois Marshall yet. Public health concerns and a vigorous program of research into the disease kept polio at the forefront of medical attention. Lois was monitored regularly, and offered opportunities for treatment as they emerged. After a few years, when the restrictions of the leg brace began to outweigh the limited mobility it offered, the Marshalls' orthopaedic surgeon suggested that Lois might consider a complicated and risky surgery to her left leg that, if success-ful, would enable her to walk without a brace. After much consideration, Lois and her mother agreed to take the risk, and Lois found herself back again in the Hospital for Sick Children.

Hospital protocol in the late 1920s and early 1930s was severely effi-cient, and strikes modern sensibilities as needlessly inhumane. Only par-ents, no other family members, were allowed to visit children who were patients, and then only for one hour a week, on Sunday afternoon. As an exception for children undergoing surgery, one parent was allowed to be on hand when the child came out of anaesthetic. Otherwise, the children lived in an enclosed, ordered environment, run principally with an eye to adult medical efficiency rather than a child's emotional needs. When the weekly visiting hour was over, the silence in the ward seemed bleak, and the next week's visit, to a child's imagination, immeasurably far away.

These spartan regulations only increased the stress of recovery from surgery. Lois endured much pain, and a succession of heavy casts on her left leg. When the last cast was finally removed, and Lois was ready to attempt walking once again, she saw that her left leg, instead of being straight, was now bent at the knee, in a position intended to provide support as she transferred her body weight from the right side to the left while walking. But the bent knee made the body's balance extremely precarious, and the left leg had no muscular ability to adjust for any mis-calculation in the transfer of weight. It was still a passive partner in the exercise, the point of the surgery being to place the left leg in a position that could more efficiently be exploited by the working right leg. Lois tried to take her first step but miscalculated her balance and fell, crashing down on her left knee. The pain was excruciating, and the fall actually seemed to force the knee further out of its strange alignment. Over and over again she tried, with the same devastating results. Despite her best efforts, Lois could not learn to walk after the surgery on which she had pinned such hopes. As far as she was concerned, it was an abject, painful, humiliating failure.

After this terrible setback, she recovered her spirits slowly, but with them she gradually formed new hopes of finding a solution that would avoid returning to the dreadful brace, which would only become more uncomfortable as her body grew. The surgeon now proposed a series of operations that would permanently fuse Lois's left knee and ankle, thereby providing rigidity and stability to enable her to walk without an artificial brace. There would be five operations in total, spread over a period of about three years, many more casts on her leg, and at the end of it all, Lois would never be able to bend her knee again. The choice was hers.

And so was the decision — at least that's how Lois, as an adult, remembered her eight-year-old self. Her father kept his own counsel, and her mother simply did not know how to advise her. (Finances seem not to have entered into the decision. It was common at the time for service clubs to pay for surgery like this one for disabled children whose families could not bear the cost, and perhaps they did so in Lois's case. Certainly David Marshall's salary was too small for him to shoulder that kind of expense himself.) Lois brought a child's intuitive responses to bear on this impossible task. After days of uncertainty, she woke up one morning simply knowing that she would go ahead. She acted on her feelings, and took responsibility for her own actions. Three more years of hospital life stretched before her.

If she never got used to it, Lois nevertheless got to know the medical round only too well. Leaving the family house, where she became an infrequent visitor rather than a regular member, she would be admitted to the girls' surgical unit at the Hospital for Sick Children. There she was prepped and underwent each of the surgeries in the series. After she came out of anaesthetic, greeted briefly by one or the other of her parents, she would be transferred to the Round Ward, which housed other children recovering from the critical stages of their surgeries. From there, she would be moved to the Long Ward, a much larger unit, for prolonged convalescence, which, for Lois, always involved adjustment to the most recent cast on her leg. Eventually, she would be sent home, on crutches if she was lucky, until her cast could be removed and her leg had healed enough to undergo the next round of surgery. Five times between the ages of eight and twelve Lois endured this cycle, her childhood's best years lost to interminable medical procedures.

The intervals at home could be disorienting too, for Lois and for the rest of the family. On one of her earliest returns, Florence, sitting with Lois in the rocking chair in which she had nursed each of her children, faced some curious questioning. Rhoda demanded to know who that strange child in her mother's lap might be. "Why she's your sister!" Florence replied indignantly. The story became a funny anecdote in the family history, but it spoke less comically to the degree of disruption that polio could cause. Lois, who longed to return home after every operation, discovered that home felt strange and that she felt out of place in it, at least initially. Her sisters were strangers to her, but more than that, the crowded house was chaos. By now used to the order and quiet of hospital routine, she had trouble claiming her place in all the activity, bustle, and general noise that constituted life in the rambunctious Marshall household. On every return, it required a period of adjustment before the shy and slightly reserved child of the hospital ward could again feel comfortable in her own home. Her mother's devotion provided the emotional constant Lois so desperately needed through these years. During the days, when the rest of the family was out of the house, Florence stole time from her own responsibilities to create a little private life, just for the two of them. The bonds created then lasted a lifetime. Though Lois's career eventually separated her from her mother for long periods of time, she never forgot Florence's patience and constancy.

Hospital life, though severe, was not cruel, and even had little pleasures of its own. Medical staff, like the young Dr. William Mustard, who was just beginning what was to be a brilliant career at the Hospital for Sick Children, took time out of their rounds to try to cheer the young patients up. Over the years, nurses at the hospital heard Lois singing to herself, and she eventually became known as "the girl who sings." They made a pet of her, and regularly asked her to sing for a new doctor or a visitor to the hospital. If she felt like it, Lois would sit up in bed and oblige. But she didn't always feel like it, and resented being coaxed and cajoled. She later remembered that when she did give these little impromptu hospital performances, she experienced an intense concentration and removal from the world of the hospital ward to one in which only the sound of her voice and the music itself mattered. "That probably sounds exaggerated for the reaction of a young girl," she recalled, "but it was like that then and for most of my singing life, when I have relied upon this compelling urge to take me to a state of utter concentration where my awareness is of everything pertaining to the music and nothing else."

Between operations, her intervals of recuperation at home gave her the enforced leisure to explore that inner life further. On one of them, laid up on the veranda to take advantage of the fresh air, she heard music drifting out from the family radio playing indoors. It was Schubert's Eighth Symphony, the "Unfinished," and she was hearing it for the first time in her life. Still less than twelve years old, Lois fastened on to this music with all the wonder and imaginative concentration of an impressionable, intelligent, and slightly bored child who had been denied the distractions of a normally active childhood. Her sister Rhoda recalled, "She said when she first heard that kind of music it was almost like it was all inside of her. She said sometimes she could hardly stand it, it was so powerfully uplifting to her."

Lois poured all of herself into this encounter with Schubert's Eighth, and it marked for her the beginning of her lifelong commitment to music. "I was affected by that more profoundly than by anything I ever heard and I knew then that some day and in some way I would be a musician."

The decision to be a musician came first; the decision to be a singer sprang from her natural talents and from expediency. Lois knew her family had no money for music lessons, let alone for an expensive musical instrument. Her instrument had been given to her free of charge, and that eliminated one financial problem. She would tackle the other in due course. It was fundamentally significant that Lois dated her love affair with music from the revelation provided to her by an orchestral work, not from some example of vocal virtuosity. She saw herself as a musician first and a singer second, a distinction that would eventually win her the admiration of some of the great chamber and orchestral instrumentalists of her day. There is a breed of singers, many wonderful musicians among them, whose first love is the sound of their own voices. Lois's first love was the sound of the music.

By the time she was twelve, when the relentless series of operations had finally come to an end, Lois Marshall was formed in two fundamental ways: she knew what she wanted to do with her life and she knew that her left leg would be of no help to her in doing it. She would always walk with a pronounced limp and her left leg would remain rigid, at a noticeably odd angle, even when she sat down. For a concert artist, whose appearance and stage presence are integral parts of her professional image, these are not negligible considerations. In Lois's own mind the second knowledge had no significant bearing on the first. She would simply have to deal with those who thought it did.

Eventually, despite the inevitable, frequent interruptions of her scheduled operations, the time came to enrol Lois in school. The Toronto Board of Education had, in 1926, established the first school in Canada for children with physical disabilities, using two rooms of Wellesley Public School at Bay and Wellesley (the present site of the Sutton Place Hotel) in downtown Toronto. In 1931, the school had expanded at that site, and included physiotherapists and occupational therapists, a lunchroom, and a school dietician, as well as academic staff. The Wellesley Orthopaedic School followed the practice of consolidating children with disabilities into a group, rather than distributing them throughout the regular school system, and bringing the services they needed to them. At the time, it was forward-thinking simply to recognize the needs of children with disabilities and invest in meeting them effectively. Lois clearly needed the resources available at the Wellesley School, and there was little choice but to accept the *de facto* segregation that went with the provision of them. The beginning of Lois's schooling, already late because of her medical condition, was further delayed by a bureaucratic snag created because her parents were Roman Catholic ratepayers opting to send one of their children to a school administered by the public school board. So another year slipped by before Lois could be enrolled. A January baby, she was eight years old when the special school bus for the Wellesley children rolled up to the front door in the fall of 1933 to take Lois to her first day of classes.

Being sent to a special school was no hardship as far as Lois was concerned. For starters, her sisters envied her. She got picked up and bused to school instead of having to walk, and received a hot lunch every day into the bargain. This seemed to the others to be the height of luxury. Then there was the environment itself. Whatever the disadvantages of separating students with disabilities from the rest of their peers, Lois enjoyed the camaraderie at the school, which she found in the unlikeliest of places — even on the baseball diamond, where, like the rest of her friends at the school, she simply adapted the rules of the game to her own abilities.

But special programs and resources can do no more than create a good environment for learning. The learning happens when a willing student encounters an inspiring teacher and her life is transformed. Many people never meet such teachers, or meet them at the wrong time in their lives. Lois was luckier than most. At Wellesley Orthopaedic she encountered two such teachers, just when she needed them most.

One was Jean Hampson. Her official position was as school physiotherapist, but really, in Lois's words, she was the school's "heart and soul." Every student at Wellesley Orthopaedic had daily private sessions with Miss Hampson, and additional group sessions with her as well. Whatever her skills as a physiotherapist, and they must have been considerable, her skills as communicator and confidante far outweighed them. She talked with her students and, by her attentiveness and sympathy, she encouraged them to talk to her. For Lois, used to the impersonal regimen of hospital life and the crowded family atmosphere at home, real conversation with Miss Hampson overcame her natural shyness and allowed her to speak of the things that mattered most. She could open up, confident that she was being heard.

Heard, but never mollycoddled. Miss Hampson, as Lois remembered her, exemplified the brisk, no-nonsense approach of old-school teaching. Her sympathy and sense of humour never diminished the rigorous demands she placed on every student in her charge. She was tough. If parents complained that the bar had been set too high, she held her ground, and insisted that their child would clear the current hurdle soon, and even higher ones over time. Lois loved the challenge and loved Miss Hampson for challenging her. It was exactly the kind of conditioning she needed as she formed her own extraordinarily ambitious goal for her life.

But it was Miss Hutchinson, the music teacher at Wellesley Orthopaedic, who helped Lois take the first steps towards the realization

Lois with Elsie Hutchinson, her teacher from Wellesley Orthopaedic School, at a reception given by the Toronto Board of Education after Lois's New York debut, December 1952.

Credit: Courtesy of GetStock.com.

of that goal. Surviving photos of Elsie Hutchinson show a round-faced, high-browed woman with a prominent nose and an obliging smile, given to large heavy glasses and extraordinary hats. She looks comfortable and motherly, and could easily pass for a small-town Ontario piano teacher of great enthusiasm and moderate abilities. However, according to her peers her musical abilities were formidable. Foremost among them was an ear astute enough to recognize the potential of the shy, dark-haired little girl with the rather large voice who appeared in her classroom whenever she wasn't in the hospital for one or another of her frequent operations. With a teacher's instinct for encouragement and assistance, Elsie Hutchinson went into action.

Just like the nurses at the Hospital for Sick Children, Miss Hutchinson liked to show off her young discovery. Any visitor to the school was trotted off to the music room, where Lois was expected to perform. But, as in the hospital, Lois's desire to sing came into conflict with her reluctance to attract attention to herself. She was just too shy to stand up readily in front of her classmates and the visitor of the day, and break into song. Ever practical, Miss Hutchinson worked out a solution. She would accompany from the upright piano in the classroom while Lois withdrew to the privacy of the cloakroom and sang from there, a disembodied voice. The whole school knew about it. Teachers were still telling the story to their pupils a decade and a half later, after Wellesley Orthopaedic had moved and changed its name to Sunny View Public School.

Lois vividly remembered the claustrophobic atmosphere of the cloakroom, stuffed with winter coats and mufflers, as her "first experience of having to battle against ghastly acoustics." Singing in that cloakroom was like being huddled up and stifled in the dark. Lois knew she needed the resonance of a good performance space in order to give her voice its full bloom, long before she had the courage to stand up on a stage and let it out.

Elsie Hutchinson's ambitions for her talented student extended beyond the classroom. As Lois matured and conquered some of her shyness, Miss Hutchinson sent other performance opportunities her way, at meetings of the Wellesley Orthopaedic Home and School Association (Miss Hutchinson accompanied Lois, as well as the community singing that followed) and functions of the Toronto Board of Education. When Lois was fourteen, she got her first taste of public performance on a larger scale. In the spring of 1939, Miss Hutchinson entered her in the annual vocal competition for the Toronto Public Schools. In the days before the Kiwanis Music Festival, which did not begin in Toronto until 1944, this was a major event, exposure on a city-wide basis.

The test piece was of the kind favoured for competitions and festivals, a pedestrian little number called "The Fairy's Lullaby." Thought by adults to be appropriate for a young child, it only offended Lois's well-developed musicality. She conceived a deep and abiding hatred for it. But there was no choice; against all her taste and musical better judgement, perform it she must. The day of the competition dawned inauspicious. Lois had had a run-in that morning with her father, over a small matter of a broken window, and she left the house under a cloud. In an effort to forestall too great a disappointment, Miss Hutchinson held a last-minute conversation with Lois about the merits of one of the other contestants, and cautioned her not to expect too much. Cast down as she was by her father's anger and her distaste for the test-piece, Lois had no expectations at all. When, in the time-honoured tradition of competitions, the winners were announced in reverse order, Lois stopped paying attention after the announcement of third place. Miss Hutchinson had to nudge her to check her competitor's number and get up to accept first prize.

The rest was a blur. She telephoned her mother, at home, and gave her the good news. Miss Hutchinson was elated. Back at the school, all the teachers crowded round Lois to hug her and congratulate her. They even took her to a celebratory lunch at the Round Room, in Eaton's College Street store. But all the excitement finally got the better of Lois. A fussy eater from her prolonged exposure to hospital food, she turned her nose up at the chicken salad and could only be consoled by a hot fudge sundae. When she got home and told her father about her achievement, she recalled that he showed no enthusiasm. She tried to tell herself it was just to prevent her from getting a swelled head, but she went to sleep heavy-hearted rather than elated.

On May 13, 1939, "Miss Lois Marshall, partially crippled pupil of Wellesley school," had her picture in the *Toronto Star* as winner of the girls' gold medal in the annual schools' competition. Her image peered out from above this caption unsmiling, sweet, and very serious, in a head-and-shoulders shot that need not have called for any comment on the state of her legs. The accompanying photo of the winner of the boys' division noted his church choir work, rather than his physical condition. It was just the first of countless references that would unthinkingly link her achievement to her disability in the years to come.

On May 16, another milestone: Lois appeared, for the first of many times, on the stage of Toronto's Massey Hall, home to the Toronto Symphony Orchestra and all the great visiting artists of the day, the most prestigious concert venue in the city. She performed as one of the two gold medal winners at the annual schools' concert, dressed in pink taffeta and this time with her mother in the audience. But again, her joy was muted. With Miss Hutchinson at the piano, under the bright stage lights of Massey Hall, she was forced once again to sing the song she had come to hate, "The Fairy's Lullaby."

Despite her father's reserve and the disruptions caused by hospital stays and attendance at a special school, in her later life Lois cherished an idyllic picture of her childhood, coloured, she admitted, by the poetry she encountered during her singer's training. She especially remembered summer evenings in the backyard on Ellerbeck Street, where she and her sisters played while her father tended the garden.

> Years later I studied the wonderful poem by James Agee, *Knoxville, Summer of 1915*, where he wrote, "It has become that time of evening when people sit on their porches, rocking gently and talking gently," and later, "They are not talking of much and the talk is quiet — of nothing in particular — of nothing at all." Whenever I think of those words [set to music by the American composer Samuel Barber], I am carried back to those hushed evenings at home so long ago when my father and mother seemed at peace.

Rhoda, on the other hand, painted a less sentimental picture, of their father as a strict man who rarely yielded to his daughters' requests for small treats when they summoned up the courage to interrupt his summer evenings, as he sat on the veranda, having a beer and trading stories with the neighbour.

Her sisters' complete indifference to her disability, and their refusal to give her any special treatment on account of it, strengthened the self-reliance and resolve that the programs of Wellesley Orthopaedic instilled. Lois was just one of the kids fending for herself in the rough and tumble of growing up in a large and sometimes unruly family. Like the rest, she hid under the covers when the bedtime shouting and pillow fights got too noisy and their father sternly mounted the stairs, strap in hand, to deal with matters. Blessed with a robust imagination, she developed into the family storyteller, regaling her sisters late into the night with stories she made up and acted out herself, stopping in frustration only when the last of her listeners had drifted off to sleep.

Her extravagant imagination imparted a theatrical intensity to her

childhood observance of the Roman Catholic faith. As she later told
her good friend, Doreen Uren Simmons, she made her confession every
two weeks, contemplating and embroidering her childish failings in her
own mind for days beforehand. On the day of confession, she worked
herself up from the moment she awoke, dressing as slowly as possible,
then delaying her walk to Holy Name Church by studying the shop
windows as she passed, watering the sidewalk of the Danforth with her
tears every step of the way. By the time she entered the confessional, she
was out of control, and sobbed her confession with much weeping and
self-reproach to the startled priest.

The celebration of Christmas, both at home and at church, figured prominently in Lois's childhood memories. Florence Marshall,
high-spirited, outgoing, proudly Irish, loved people, celebrations,
and small luxuries, a few of which she somehow managed, even on
David Marshall's limited salary. Together, no matter how financially
pressed they might be, David and Florence always provided a festive
Christmas celebration that struck the children as abundant, with good
food for the large family dinners, presents for all, a Christmas tree
decorated with painstaking care, family singing, and the obligatory
attendance at Christmas Eve mass. Lois and her sisters, Jean, Rhoda,
and Rita, who all sang in the Holy Name choir, started their approach
to Christmas around the beginning of the month, belting out all of
the repertoire for the midnight mass nightly in the kitchen, as they
cleared away the supper dishes. The choirmaster at Holy Name was
taciturn, and stingy with his praise. Lois recalled how he toyed with
her, never letting her know she was doing a solo until just before the
service. On Christmas Eve, she would toil up the steep, narrow flight
of stairs to the choir loft underneath the vaulted ceiling to be greeted
by, "O.K. girlie, you will sing 'Ave Maria' tonight." She could over-
look the demeaning "girlie" and the thoughtlessness of the "surprise"
announcement, transported now by the musical pleasures that lay
ahead. The choir loft at Holy Name was a far cry from the cloakroom
at Wellesley Orthopaedic School.

The architecture of the Church of the Holy Name has been designed
to exalt an impressionable imagination and a responsive spirit into

The interior of Holy Name Church, circa 1947, before alterations to the chancel area in response to Vatican II. Taken from the choir loft, where Lois sang as soloist and a member of the choir.

Credit: From the collection of Mary McDonald.

worlds far removed from the commercial bustle of Danforth Avenue, just outside. The striking south façade, all Indiana cut stone and modelled on the Church of Santa Maria Maggiore in Rome, draws worshippers into a monumental cruciform space. The eye travels first down the full 170-foot length of the nave, where, in Lois's day, an elaborately decorated high altar stood at the very end, then is pulled upwards to the crossing of the transepts, sixty dizzying feet above. From the altitude and anonymity of the choir loft, Lois could send her voice soaring out along the length of that nave, burnished by the church's wonderful acoustics. Singing in these conditions was perfect. She tasted happiness as great as any she had ever known.

Then there was the family carol singing, with Fred on tenor and Lois holding up the alto by herself, against the strong soprano section made up of all the rest of her sisters. Lois's mother had sung lullabies to each of her babies in a distinctive, full-throated voice. All the children took their mother's voice for granted, but Lois later recognized how unusual it was, and considered the fine voices that all the Marshall children had as an inheritance from the O'Brien gene pool. But they were all amateurs. Most of the girls favoured the pop music of the day; only Jean and Fred encouraged Lois to explore the classical repertoire in which she found her home.

Before the outbreak of the Second World War in 1939, while he was still living at home, Fred Marshall was an aspiring tenor. He studied voice at the Toronto Conservatory of Music, sang in the choir at St. Alban's Anglican Church, and performed occasionally at weddings and community events. Much to his sisters' consternation, who considered it an unwarranted luxury when the family could barely make ends meet, he found the money to buy a record player, and brought home records of Italian opera that Lois listened to whenever she got the chance. Jean, seven years older than Lois, recognized her sister's passion for serious music and became her family advocate, interceding with their father so that Lois was allowed to stay up late to listen to "The Voice of Firestone," "The Ford Sunday Evening Hour," and the regular radio show of the popular American tenor, Richard Crooks. She didn't need special dispensation to listen to the Metropolitan Opera on Saturday afternoons, or the New York Philharmonic on Sundays. Once Jean was earning money, she spent some of it on Lois's musical education, bringing home records for her to listen to and taking her to concerts, first to the popularly priced Promenade Concerts that were a summer fixture at Varsity Arena on Bloor Street, later to hear visiting recitalists like Heifitz, Horowitz, Milstein, and Serkin at Massey Hall.

By the time Lois was fourteen, she had her gold medal and her dreams of becoming a singer, but no clear way of realizing them. In addition to a promising voice, she already possessed imaginative and emotional resources that would be invaluable to her as an interpretive artist. Her childhood encounter with polio had awakened in her all the strength and determination needed for a career in music. Her family was musical enough to understand and support her, but too poor to afford the music lessons she absolutely required. She needed a fairy godmother, and found one in the familiar, matronly figure of Elsie Hutchinson.

Lois, circa 1940, with one of her sisters in Toronto.

Credit: From the collection of Cindy Townsend.

In her ongoing promotion of her star pupil, Miss Hutchinson had arranged for Lois to entertain at the annual Rotary Club Christmas party for disabled children at the Royal York Hotel in Toronto. Members of the club learned that this extraordinarily promising young singer had never had a singing lesson, and furthermore would never be able to afford lessons on her own. She needed a benefactor. The Rotarians stepped forward, and through Miss Hutchinson, made the offer. They would pay for Lois to begin formal training. Miss Hutchinson and the family colluded in breaking the news to Lois. On Christmas morning of 1939, after all the presents had been opened, Florence Marshall gave her daughter the momentous news. In the new year, Lois would begin singing lessons at last. Lois received the news quite solemnly, but inwardly, her excitement knew no bounds. Lois was fourteen years old, about to turn fifteen.

The year of her first formal vocal training would bring about another fundamental change in Lois's life. On September 6, 1940, Florence Marshall would answer a knock at the door of 32 Millbrook Crescent, where the family now lived. A strange man stood on the doorstep and Florence, who had acquired something of a reputation as the family psychic, said instantly, "Dave is dead and you've come to tell me." She was right. David Marshall, making his way home from work, had suffered a massive coronary attack and died on the streetcar. Fred and Rhoda went to St. Michael's Hospital to identify the body.

Lois had to be summoned home from the camp for crippled children at Blue Mountain, where the children of Wellesley Orthopaedic School were taken annually. The counsellors said nothing to her themselves, so Lois took the train back to Toronto not knowing what news awaited her. Mary and Jean met her at the station and took her home in a cab. On the way home, they finally broke the news to her. Then they took Lois into the house, where her father's body was already laid out in the living room.

Later, when Florence Marshall had the time to go through the contents of her husband's wallet, she showed Lois something he had apparently carried with him every day. It was the newspaper photograph of Lois when she won her gold medal for singing.

CHAPTER TWO

1939 to 1947 —
The Conservatory and Weldon Kilburn

Having her voice lessons financed was one thing; choosing the right teacher was quite another. In 1940, the Toronto Conservatory of Music was the first recourse for anyone seeking serious musical instruction in the city. The Conservatory was then located on the southwest corner of College Street and University Avenue, now the site of the Ontario Hydro building. It would not move to its present location, on Bloor Street, until 1963, long after Lois's student days were over. The Con, as it was known to its students, offered a choice of vocal instructors. Each ran an independent studio in the Conservatory's building, with devoted students and sometimes in an atmosphere of intense rivalry. Choosing a teacher was a daunting business, especially for a neophyte, but it was the most important decision an aspiring singer could make. The wrong teacher could ruin a voice and destroy an ego, and mistakes were hard to correct. Changing from one teacher to another in the hothouse, gossipy atmosphere of the Con, required enormous reserves of independence and strength. Best not to make a mistake in the first place. Fortunately, Lois received guidance from within her own family.

In 1940, Fred Marshall, not yet serving in the war, still had his sights set on a career in music. Like virtually all aspiring singers of the period he was getting a start by doing church choir work. With church attendance substantially higher than it is today, many of Toronto's churches still mounted ambitious music programs, with professional directors of music and sometimes with paid choristers, or at least a core of paid soloists to inspire the amateur singers. Among such churches, the Anglicans took the lead, drawing on the treasury of service music provided by the British choral tradition. An ambitious young singer had to set personal religious affiliation aside. You sang where the standards were high; with luck, where the money was good; and, more often than not, where your teacher was the choirmaster. Fred therefore abandoned his home church of Holy Name and joined the choir of St. Alban the Martyr Cathedral Church, an Anglican church and one of the most interesting relics of Toronto's ecclesiastical and architectural history.

Built on Howland Avenue in an area known as the Annex, St. Alban's had been planned as the Anglican Cathedral for the diocese of Toronto. Construction began according to grandiose plans appropriate to a large cathedral. At one point Ralph Cram, who worked on New York's mammoth Cathedral of St. John the Divine, was the architect in charge. But reversals of fortune and complicated church politics scuppered the project. In 1936, St. James' church on King Street East, was officially designated as Toronto's Anglican cathedral. The unfinished St. Alban's struggled on as a local parish church, housed in the chancel — the only part of the cathedral building to reach completion. But it maintained musical ambitions suitable to its origins, and employed as its organist and choirmaster a talented and versatile member of the Toronto Conservatory's piano faculty, a man named Weldon Kilburn, who also coached advanced vocal students. Fred had found his way to Kilburn's studio, and eventually, into Kilburn's choir.

Fred was emphatic in his advice to Lois. She must study with his teacher. No one else would do. Since no other family member had an informed opinion, the matter rested with Elsie Hutchinson. She decided to go to the top, and take it up with the Principal of the Conservatory, Sir Ernest MacMillan, organist, music educator, Dean of the Faculty of Music at the University of Toronto, and Director of the Toronto Symphony Orchestra (though not yet of the Toronto Mendelssohn Choir) — altogether the most prominent figure in Canadian music at that time. At Miss Hutchinson's request, and bowing reluctantly to her teacher's choice of repertoire, Lois sang for Sir Ernest "The Fairy's Lullaby," one last time. Lois remembered Sir Ernest as being polite, rather than bowled over by her talent, that he characterized her voice as "promising, but small," and that he mentioned as possibilities some of the senior voice teachers on the faculty at the time, people like George Lambert, Albert Whitehead, and Dorothy Allan Park. When Miss Hutchinson brought up Weldon Kilburn's name, Sir Ernest expressed some surprise. Kilburn was on the piano faculty, not, despite his position as a vocal coach, on the singing faculty. He did not, to MacMillan's knowledge, teach voice production or vocal technique.

Normally, only students with a secure grounding in technique, the mechanics of producing the voice, sign on with a vocal coach, who is typically concerned more with matters of interpretation and style than with the basics of voice production. As the senior vocal coach listed in the Conservatory's annual Yearbook, Kilburn would normally work only with experienced singers, concentrating on fine points of interpretation. Lois was clearly not yet at such an advanced stage. When Sir Ernest politely asked Lois her own opinion in the matter, Lois, despite all her adolescent diffidence, made her feelings known. Her brother thought that Kilburn was a very good teacher of voice production, as well as an excellent vocal coach. Sir Ernest decided that no harm could be done by starting Lois out with Mr. Kilburn.

Weldon Kilburn was nearly nineteen years Lois's senior. Born on September 9, 1906, in Lloydminster, on the Alberta–Saskatchewan border, he traced his distinguished musical pedigree back to County Durham in the northeast of England, where his family originated. Dr. Nicholas Kilburn, his great-uncle, had been a successful businessman there, but more importantly a distinguished musician and church organist, who enjoyed the friendship and respect of the eminent composer Sir Edward Elgar. Dr. Nicholas's nephew (Weldon Kilburn's father) emigrated to Saskatchewan to take up farming, but proved more successful as a businessman, settling eventually in Edmonton.

After initial training in Edmonton, Weldon went to Toronto in 1927 for further studies in both piano and organ. For organ studies, there was only one possible teacher: Healey Willan, who taught organ and theory at the Conservatory. At that time, as choirmaster of the Church of St. Mary Magdalene, Willan was establishing that choir's reputation as the city's foremost interpreter of the finest in liturgical music, including his own compositions. Willan, who would become the dean of Canadian church music, was also one of its great, roistering eccentrics. As he famously characterized his pedigree: "I am English by birth, Irish by extraction, Canadian by adoption, and Scotch by absorption." When Weldon Kilburn became Willan's student, he also joined his choir. Singing at St. Mary Magdalene for one year, Kilburn received training in the choir loft as well as the classroom. By the time he was twenty-two, he had left Willan's choir, though not his circle, to become the organist at St. Alban's. Willan described him as "the youngest cathedral organist in captivity," a claim that was technically true, at least until St. James was officially designated as Toronto's cathedral in 1936.

Weldon became a member of the piano faculty at the Conservatory in 1930 and was listed as a vocal coach for the first time in 1932. In 1941 he joined a popular performing group called the Five Piano Ensemble, whose other members at the time were his close friend Reginald Godden, Alberto Guerrero (Glenn Gould's teacher), Scott Malcolm, and Ernest Seits. In addition to these activities, Kilburn was also a frequent accompanist of singers and instrumentalists. In the 1930s and early 1940s, Kilburn seemed to be everywhere on the Toronto musical scene. A serious professional musician with conducting and performing experience to his credit, he inhabited a world Lois had only dreamed of entering. In appearance, he was handsome — tall, imposing, and rather stern, with a firm chin and an aquiline nose. He might well have intimidated a more robust and experienced soul than fourteen-year-old Lois, nervously approaching studio 18 in the exalted Toronto Conservatory of Music. For her first lesson, Fred escorted her up the stairs and made the introductions, but after that, Lois was on her own.

It started out very badly. As she used to do on her prolonged approaches to the confessional, Lois had worked herself into a nervous state before she even entered the building. Kilburn asked her to sing a few scales, just to let him hear her voice. She positioned herself by the piano, took a deep breath, opened her mouth, and made no sound. After a few more fruitless attempts, she felt tears welling up and by then it was game over. She was too distraught and too ashamed to be able to sing for her new teacher.

Seeing her distress, Kilburn sat her down and spent most of the lesson just talking to her about the human voice and about music in general. As this conversation caught her interest, Lois gradually calmed down. Once she had herself more or less under control, Kilburn asked if she had brought anything along that she would like to sing for him. As soon as she handed him the music, he went to the piano and launched into the spirited introduction, without giving her the chance to become nervous once again. Lois had chosen "Il Bacio," a Victorian era display piece by Luigi Arditi that includes complicated syncopations and tricky chromatic runs, rising coquettishly to a high B flat at its conclusion. It used to be standard encore fare for virtuoso coloratura sopranos, but was an unusual choice for a beginner, about as far away from "The Fairy's Lullaby" as Lois could get. She thought she sang it well and Kilburn seemed pleased. He promised much hard work for them both in the future. The first lesson was over.

"Much hard work" turned out to be an understatement. In her early lessons with Kilburn, Lois suffered the special torments reserved for the sensitive and diffident personality encountering the intractable demands of a strong and aggressive one. Unsure of herself in the studio and easily distracted, Lois could not produce the sound that Kilburn wanted from her. He lost his temper, shouted at her, accused her of being stupid, then, when she broke down and cried, tried to repair the damage with a few kind words, sometimes with hot chocolate in the Conservatory cafeteria, before sending her home. But Lois's determination trumped her sensitivity. Returning home in tears, she simply redoubled her efforts, studying the notes she had made at her last lesson and trying to find an opportunity to put Kilburn's ideas into practice. It never occurred to her, despite the indignation of her sister, Rhoda, to abandon Kilburn for a gentler, more sympathetic teacher.

Just finding the opportunity to practise presented a challenge. Whatever Lois's hesitancies in the studio might have been, at home she had to make noise, and make it in resonant surroundings. She favoured the kitchen, when it was empty after dinner, or the bathroom with all the sound-absorbent towels and bathmats removed, as places where she could let loose. Her appropriation of these rooms caused enormous inconvenience in the large Marshall household. Then there was the small matter of the noise itself. Her sisters were mortified that Lois's screeching penetrated to the outdoors, for friends, neighbours, and potential gentleman callers to hear. They implored their mother to make Lois keep it down, just as they would beg her to "do something" about Lois's noisy singing of the congregational hymns at church. Furthermore, by the time these voice lessons began, Lois's oldest sister, Mary, had brought her husband and baby daughter to share the crowded family home. The baby was a light sleeper. More often than not, Lois's practise sessions had to be abandoned prematurely to avoid waking the baby. It took all of Lois's determination just to meet the practise schedule Kilburn demanded of her.

Almost as soon as they had begun, the lessons came under threat. The Rotarians sponsoring Lois decided to divert their funding to the support of British War Guests, the children being evacuated to safety in Canada for the duration of the war. Miss Hutchinson had to break the news to Lois at school, less than three months into her first term of studies with Kilburn. Now her tears had a different cause. Try as she might to conceal her disappointment, and demonstrate her understanding of the greater needs of the War Guests, Lois's feelings could be read on her face. The prospect of losing her voice lessons was a greater torment to her than any tongue-lashing her new teacher might inflict. Miss Hutchinson rose to the occasion. She took on the cost of Lois's weekly lessons for the following year, and won thereby Lois's lifelong gratitude. When Lois began to need more frequent lessons, Kilburn agreed to provide some of them free of charge. Her lessons continued without interruption.

Today, no one can say with certainty what went on in the studio in those earliest years, when Lois's strong, distinctive voice was being revealed, extended, and strengthened into the instrument she possessed as an adult. In later interviews and reminiscences, both Lois and Weldon agreed that the voice he heard in "Il Bacio" was light, high, and breathy, but agile and flexible, with a natural ability to negotiate scales and decorated passages, characteristic of the coloratura soprano. There was not much strength in the middle range, or register, and virtually nothing at the bottom end, hardly surprising in a female singer of her youth. The comments about the smallness of her voice, however, contrast sharply with her own recollections of feeling free and strong, even in those early years, when singing in private, with her inhibitions forgotten; they contrast with the evidence of the schoolgirl who could project her voice from the muffling confines of the cloakroom to her class at Wellesley Orthopaedic; and they contrast with her sisters' embarrassment about her loud, commanding voice at home and at church. Such evidence suggests that when Lois began her lessons with Kilburn, powerful psychological forces inhibited the freedom of her voice in situations she considered formal or found intimidating. Part of Kilburn's task was to release the natural strength of Lois's voice from the prison of her inhibitions. Bullying his pupil might not seem the ideal way of achieving that goal, but Lois would later acknowledge that she needed someone to keep at her, that the "dictator" and the "ogre" had a place in her musical training.

In his later years as a teacher, when Kilburn had left the Conservatory and set up a private studio, he insisted on a relaxed, full, open, and natural sound, the antithesis of what he referred to disparagingly as the "thin, pinched, Conservatory sound" of the self-conscious and tentative singer. His son Paul, himself a professional musician, would remember that he told his more mature students, "To sing well you need an open throat and a tight arse — and be careful not to confuse the two." Beyond this graphic advice, however, he had difficulty explaining precisely how the desired sound could be achieved.

In fact, he didn't want his students to become self-conscious about the act of singing, of "producing" the voice. An important part of the process was to work until the physical part of singing — the stance of the body, the muscular adjustments to the breathing apparatus and throat, the placement of the mouth and tongue — became completely automatic for the singer. Voice production, in Kilburn's approach, had to be second nature. If he could hear the singer thinking about any of the merely physical factors of voice production, the sound for him became artificial and he could not hear the music. He was so sensitive to these matters that he frequently stopped a student dead on the first note, convinced that nothing good could come from such a carefully contrived beginning.

Kilburn taught an ideal of sound, not a step-by-step method for achieving it. Learning from him could be a frustrating experience. Given his approach and his temperament, part of Lois's eventual success in the studio must be attributed to her own determination to decipher his intent, and to much trial and error on her part. Together, teacher and student embarked on a mutual voyage of discovery and exploration, rather than the simple acquisition of established technical knowledge. As a result, Lois learned how to produce a magnificent sound, without being able to analyse how she did it. In later years, when Weldon wanted to talk voice-production with his cronies, she would leave the room. At the end of her performing career, she confided to Greta Kraus, the harpsichordist and pianist with whom she had a brief but glorious partnership in her final recitals, that she didn't really have a technique, that she never learned how to sing. That statement may have characterized her early training accurately, without in any way diminishing Kilburn's importance to her vocal education.

Despite such an unpromising start, within the first year or so of their working together, Kilburn decided to give Lois a chance at performance. Irene McLellan, a young and very gifted piano pupil of Kilburn's, was giving a recital. Kilburn invited Lois to perform a short set to round out the program. He assigned her a group of English songs to prepare, and with this purpose in view, lessons began to go a little better. Still, Kilburn was nervous, and slept badly the night before the recital, not quite knowing what to expect from his high-strung new pupil.

For both teacher and pupil, that modest student recital in the Recital Hall of the Toronto Conservatory of Music, on June 20, 1941, gave the first unambiguous indication of Lois's real promise as a performer. Accompanied by Kilburn, Lois sang a group of five songs in the middle of Irene McLellan's piano program: "Pastorale," "My Lovely Celia," and "Shepherd thy Demeanour Vary" (Elizabethan songs arranged by Jane Wilson), "The Blackbird's Song" (Cyril Scott), and "The Little Damosel" (Novello). In a new blue dress, a gift from her aunt, Lois was brimming with excitement at performing what she considered to be her first real concert. The audience's welcoming applause buoyed her spirits and Kilburn's sensitive accompaniment gave her all the support and

The program for Lois's first recital at the Toronto Conservatory, sharing the bill with pianist Irene McLellan, June 20, 1941.

Credit: From the collection of Irene McLellan.

confidence she needed. She forgot the restrictions and humiliations of the studio and let loose with a real performance. The audience's warm response confirmed her conviction that she had sung well. But most important of all, her teacher, the person she had been trying so hard to please, heard for the first time what his pupil was capable of. He could hardly believe his ears, and told her so, immediately after the recital. The Lois he heard on the concert platform was completely different from the Lois he had worked with in the studio. Kilburn was astounded. As he put it later, "It was as though a gusher of oil were freed." And for the second night in a row, Kilburn slept badly, this time, as his son Paul remembered more than sixty years later, because of his excitement at the realization of how much talent he had on his hands.

With Lois's confidence awakened, and Kilburn's ears opened to her musical intelligence and what he called her "turbulent musical personality," work could begin in earnest. Lois began learning basic repertoire, which for Kilburn consisted of a steady diet of Bach, Mozart, Handel, and Purcell, composers he believed were fundamental to the training of any musician, whether singer or instrumentalist. These composers, in Kilburn's view, taught one how to respect the values of the printed score and how to make a clean, clear musical line. It was an old-fashioned pedagogy, founded on classical values of absolute respect for the composer's intentions, to which Lois responded naturally and easily. She loved the elegance of the style, from which she learned to think of the human voice as a pure musical instrument capable of creating a sense of architecture in the phrasing of the score. And now, as allies rather than as opponents, she and Kilburn worked together to moderate the febrile intensity and rapt aura of concentration in Lois's platform personality (doubtless remnants of her shyness as well as indicators of her fierce determination). This passionate commitment actually created a barrier between Lois and her audience, even between Lois and her music. At the end of her career, in an interview with Thomas Hathaway, she had the perspective to recognize the damage done by this youthful intensity. "I was drawn so tightly that I didn't know how to relax. Everything was a matter of life and death. I didn't know how to make a phrase or make a thought start here and go there. It was all charged with I don't know what."

As Lois began her serious study of music, the war years brought huge changes in her family life. Her father's death in 1940 put additional financial strain on the family. Her brother Fred found work in a munitions factory during the early years of the war, and by 1942 had abandoned his musical aspirations and moved to the United States, where he joined the merchant marine. As a merchant mariner, he participated in the enormously dangerous Murmansk runs, sailing in convoys above the Arctic Circle, north of Scandinavia, to the Russian port of Murmansk on the Barents Sea, in order to supply the Soviet Union. He survived this perilous work, then met and married a young American woman, a talented musician who had studied with the great Spanish pianist José Iturbi. Soon after his marriage, Fred enlisted in the American army. Again, he survived service, but his wartime experiences left their mark. He was never able to face the stress of a performance career. Fred settled in the

United States and from then on his contact with his family seems to have been minimal. Lois acknowledged his importance in her own musical development, and would try to visit him when she was on tour in his part of the country, but Rhoda would later play down his influence. She seemed to think his presence in the family had been too sporadic for his musical influence to be significant. Fred died in Massachusetts, in 1987.

Lois matured from a schoolgirl into a young woman in a family made up almost entirely of women, with her widowed mother scrambling to provide for her brood of daughters. Florence did not go out to work after her husband died. Fred's paycheques helped to keep the household going, but at the cost of his removal from the family. Once Fred was serving in the army, his young American wife, June, lived with the Marshall clan in Toronto until the end of the war. The older sisters got jobs (Mary and Rhoda at Eaton's, like their father), bringing their pay home to Florence, and Mary and her husband shared the rent while they lived in the family home. Money was tight and commodities were scarce. The family moved about frequently in the constant search for housing that would accommodate their numbers and still fit into their restricted budget.

A house filled with eligible young women was bound to become a hub of social activity. For Lois, much of that activity revolved around music. By her own account in her draft memoir, she was already too focused on her studies to think much about boyfriends, even once her sisters started dating, but young men came calling nevertheless. She remembered two in particular, family friends, who were not in the service and who came over regularly, bearing stacks of their favourite 78 r.p.m. recordings of classical music. They would commandeer the record player in the living room for the evening, leaving Florence Marshall to retreat to the kitchen. "No great music lover, she was probably wishing that we would all get tired and the guests would leave and we could all go to bed," Lois later commented. Whenever a record had to be turned over, or the needle on the old gramophone sharpened, Lois and her friends seized the opportunity to debate fiercely the merits of the particular recording under scrutiny. Lois was hooked. She was living music at every opportunity.

One of her favourite recordings at this time was the 1935 pressing, on four separate 78s, of the last act of Puccini's *La Bohème*, conducted by Sir Thomas Beecham with a strong cast of British and Commonwealth singers — Heddle Nash (Rodolfo), Lisa Perli (born Dora Labbette, Mimi), and John Brownlee (originally from Australia, Marcello). Act Four, in which Mimi returns to her lover, the poet Rodolfo, only to die in his frigid Parisian garret, occupied seven of the eight sides of the set; the final side was filled with a 1936 take of Mimi's farewell to Rodolfo from Act Three, sung by Perli and also conducted by Beecham. Beecham, a legend in British music, was to have a very direct influence on Lois's career, but long before she encountered him in person this experience of his music on records had a profound effect on her musical taste.

This fragment of *La Bohème*, though not nearly as well-known as Beecham's later recording of the complete opera, with Jussi Björling and Victoria de los Angeles, is preferred by some connoisseurs to the more famous version. One can hear in it many of the musical qualities Lois spoke of and exemplified throughout her career. Here are the clean, unadorned lines (very few of the singers employ *portamento*, or the sliding from one note to another for stylistic effect), the respect for ensemble, both vocal and instrumental, the meticulous enunciation of text, and the absolute precision of tuning, especially striking when the music modulates from one key to another, all of which would become hallmarks of Lois's musicality. More strikingly, the performers convey an intimate, thoughtful, and directly personal approach to the music and its drama, another quality that can easily be heard in Lois's work. Most striking of all, in Lisa Perli's phrasing and attack there are fleeting moments of uncanny resemblance to Lois's own distinctive sound. Kilburn later spoke of Lois's instinctive ear for mimicry. He told Carl Morey, in a 1983 interview, that she would sometimes imitate her favourite singer of the moment without even realizing she was doing so. (Rhoda also recalled that she was an unconscious mimic, who would pick up the accent of tradesmen and delivery people as though she were mocking them, but actually without knowing she was doing it, to Rhoda's mortification.) Whether she consciously imitated Beecham's singers or not, their example burned itself into her impressionable imagination during those evenings round the record player.

Lois's favourite soprano in those days was Tiana Lemnitz, renowned for her silvery tone and the ethereal beauty and security of her sustained, high *pianissimo* singing. Lois might have known her as the Pamina on Beecham's famous recording of Mozart's *The Magic Flute*, made in Berlin with a cast of German singers just before the war. As she wrote in her memoir, she certainly knew and loved Lemnitz's recording of the "Willow Song and Ave Maria" from Verdi's *Otello*. Lemnitz was one of the artists who remained active in Germany, a star of the Berlin Opera, throughout the war. For some, the collaboration with the authorities of the Third Reich, which such survival must have entailed, contaminated the purity of her artistry. Lois remained unaware of such considerations, or unconcerned by them.

What she admired, she unconsciously absorbed. As she saturated her imagination with the sound of artists like Lemnitz and Perli, Lois connected to the vocal styles of another era, to a pre-war, northern European way of singing that has been lost. That pre-war sound seems foreign and old-fashioned to listeners now. Even for educated music lovers, tastes tend to be formed by present experience, by listening to what is available. The heavy-hitters in the music business — the major recording companies and broadcasters — promote the most recent of singers almost exclusively, for obvious economic reasons. Over time, singing styles, both the sound of voices themselves and the standards of musicality and musicianship, undergo a constant, gradual yet dramatic process of change. Even the artistry of a Joan Sutherland or a Victoria de los Angeles, relatively recently departed from the musical scene, will now sound strikingly different, perhaps a little out of date, compared to that of a Renée Fleming or an Anna Netrebko, artists currently dominating the international vocal world.

Lois was no stylistic throwback, but she steered her own course with this noble tradition of the recent past as her reference point. Lemnitz had a special way with German Lieder. Nineteenth-century German composers like Robert Schumann and Johannes Brahms, following the example of Franz Schubert, had developed the German Lied, or art song,

into a distinctive form that emphasized as never before the equal importance of the vocal line and the piano accompaniment in animating the
texts of German Romantic poetry. A special breed of singer developed
in response to this repertoire, able to suggest the dramatic range of the
poetry within the confines of the chamber music settings these composers preferred. In contrast to the way Lieder singing developed after the
war, Tiana Lemnitz is a narrator rather than an impersonator. She creates the drama in these songs, not by mimicking sound effects appropriate to the dramatic situation (vocal suggestions of tearful sighs, joyous
laughter, and the like), but by recounting the situation with a degree of
detachment, like a storyteller. Musical values of pitch, duration, attack,
and vocal colouring support the dramatic narration of the song, but are
never lost to total immersion in mimetic effects. The distinction is a
fundamental one, much easier to hear than to describe. And it can be
heard in the way that the German baritone Dietrich Fischer-Dieskau
revolutionized the performance of German Lieder in the 1950s and
1960s, making it a much more psychological and personally tormented
exploration of the music. From his example there has been no looking
back. As her own Lieder singing developed, Lois was certainly aware of
current trends, and took from the new tradition those things that could
make her own performance expressive and involving, but she remained
fundamentally true to the older tradition, ever the narrator, never the
impersonator. To illustrate with a comparison, hers was the art of classical theatre not of method acting, of an Olivier not a Brando.

As the war progressed, Lois felt the pressure to bring home some money,
not only to cover the additional costs associated with her lessons, but
also to make some small contribution to the family finances. Though
Kilburn had expressly forbidden it (and there was a terrible showdown
when he found out), she began to take on whatever singing engagements came her way. During the early 1940s, Lois could be heard all
around Toronto and the surrounding area, singing at weddings, church
and women's organization functions, service club or business meetings

and dinners, home and school association meetings, military and air force bases, almost anywhere where she could pick up a five or ten dollar fee for her services. (Even the fee was chancy; sometimes the wedding couple remembered to pay her and sometimes they didn't.) As she later recalled, she came to enjoy the rowdy welcome of the soldiers at the military bases, but dreaded the smoke-filled business meetings, where the entertainment she provided was often treated with indifference, as background music at best. Experiences like these helped to develop the healthy skepticism she displayed in private for the self-important and the high and mighty. She refused resolutely to be impressed by people who thought their side of the tracks was somehow superior to hers.

Often, if she had managed to collect a fee for a wedding, Lois would blow some of her earnings immediately on an ice cream sundae for herself and Rhoda or one of her other sisters, before handing the rest over to her mother. Throughout her life, her generosity often got the better of her money sense. She gave impulsive gifts to her family, especially to her mother, seldom sparing a thought for the long-term financial future.

By now, Lois was sure of her life's direction, and it did not include any more school. In June of 1942, she left Wellesley Orthopaedic School after completing grade ten. She was seventeen, a year or two older than most students at that stage of their education. Her start at Wellesley Orthopaedic had been delayed, and much of her education had been interrupted by stays in the hospital and periods of convalescence at home. Her further education would be at the Conservatory, and would be exclusively musical. In the world of professional music, which judged performers based on their performances not on academic credentials, her limited academic background never hampered her. But later, when she had become a Canadian public figure, some self-consciousness on the subject manifested itself. Her frequent, half-joking references to herself in press and interviews as "not an intellectual" and "just a singer," reflect her sense of herself as someone with highly specialized gifts and an intensely-focused, practical training, in contrast to the larger intellectual scope assumed to be the province of those with a list of degrees following their names. This down-to-earth attitude placed her in the company of her colleague, Maureen Forrester, who also abandoned an academic education in favour of singing early in her life and never pretended to extraordinary intellectual accomplishments. It set her apart from another colleague with whom she worked often, Glenn Gould, whose presentation of himself as an intellectual, through his CBC radio documentaries and his essays on music, seemed to intimidate Lois, as it did many others.

In 1943, relying on her high school typing skills, she embarked on a brief and undistinguished career with the family employer, Eaton's Department Store. She started out as a typist in the home decorating offices at the College Street location, the branch of Eaton's that catered to Toronto's most affluent citizens. In her memoir, Lois recalled the disaster of her experience there. The job required typing proficiency and care and accuracy with decimal points, which ultimately defeated her. A few days after she had wrestled unsuccessfully with the weekly pay sheet, and all the workers' pay packets had had to be adjusted because of her mistakes, she was transferred to the Queen Street store, to a position handling complaints in the mail order division. Because her supervisor there lived for letters from her husband, who was overseas in the war, she was generally too distracted to give Lois much real supervision. Lois frequently improvised her responses to the complaints, trying always to modify the form letters with a friendly personal touch, but her heart was not really in it. She used to take long lunch hours, when she might book practise time in one of the studios in the Heintzman Building just a few blocks away on Yonge Street, listen to music in their record department, or wander into the matinee at the nearby Loew's movie theatre to take her mind off things. Rhoda told the story that when she finally approached the Mail Order Department to ask if she might drop down to working part-time, the manager asked what she thought she had been doing so far.

There were some advantages to working at Eaton's, however. One summer Lois and Rhoda went to the Eaton's camp for girls, at a lakeside property the company owned outside of Toronto. Lois was the star of the camp. She sang at the Sunday church service and organized an elaborate entertainment for the whole camp, complete with improvised costumes on an Arabian Nights theme. But better than any camp theatricals, as an employee Lois could join the Eaton Operatic Society.

The Eaton Operatic Society originated in 1919 as a choir of the employees of the T. Eaton Company. In 1925, T.J. Crawford, the organist at St. Paul's Anglican Church on Bloor Street and a musician of considerable experience in England and Scotland, took over as conductor. He transformed the group into a light opera society, specializing in the works of Gilbert and Sullivan, and was still at the helm in 1945, when Lois auditioned for the chorus. The selection for that year was *Princess Ida*, one of the less well-known Gilbert and Sullivan operettas, being given its first Canadian performance. The libretto, based on Tennyson's poem, "The Princess," concerned the futile efforts of Princess Ida to ban all men from her exclusively ladies' academy, and the successful campaign by three men to invade the academy's precincts and win the hands of various of its members, including the princess herself. It contained the usual range of stock G & S parts, from imperious princess through scheming contralto to patter-singing buffoon.

Lois recalled the entire experience with evident pleasure in her memoir. Rehearsals were already underway by the time she joined the chorus, and lead parts had long since been assigned, but she was invited to understudy the role of Princess Ida. The company practised after hours in the store's fifth floor cafeteria, still redolent of the day's specials and the fug of hundreds of shoppers who had paused there for a meal or a cup of coffee. The full company rehearsed together, chorus and principals alike, and Lois, sponge-like, absorbed the entire score and all of the blocking from her vantage point in the chorus. Like a plot twist in a Hollywood musical, the day came when the soprano, Heloise Macklem, an experienced musician who had formerly been a harpist with the Toronto Symphony Orchestra, had to miss a rehearsal because of a bad cold and Lois got her chance to step in. And, true to the Hollywood tradition, Lois breezed through the Princess's big scene as though she had been rehearsing it for weeks. Hardly surprising, since she had been rehearsing it for weeks, on her own. Lois impressed her colleagues so much that they arranged for her to sing the title role in two of the scheduled performances, one evening and one matinee, in Eaton Auditorium. Lois was elated. Heloise Macklem's reaction has not been recorded.

Princess Ida is one of Gilbert and Sullivan's magisterial sopranos. The perky, soubrette soprano role falls to another character in the libretto. As such, most of the princess's staging can be fairly processional and static, and need not have called attention to Lois's limp. The finale to Act II, however, calls on Princess Ida to run to a small bridge at the rear of the stage, lose her balance, and fall into the stream below. There is no record of how Lois handled the requirements of this scene, or whether any adjustments had to be made to accommodate her disability. At this time, Dame Bridget D'Oyly Carte, daughter of Gilbert and Sullivan's theatrical partner Sir Richard D'Oyly Carte, still held the copyright on all the G & S operettas. Through this legal authority, she exercised control over all amateur stagings of their works, and required conformity to the original versions of the D'Oyly Carte Company, including general faithfulness to their blocking and choreography. Individual producers had only the most limited ability to deviate from the templates supplied. Despite such restrictions, Lois's later recollection was that she had no trouble with any aspect of the role, including the stage business. The joy of singing in a fully staged production, with theatrical lighting and costumes, supported by a full orchestra, engrossed her completely.

The 1945 *Princess Ida* was a smash hit. Additional performances had to be added to the run, one in Massey Hall, which was sold out for the occasion. All of Lois's sisters turned out for her, vainly trying to control their proud mother, who informed every stranger in the audience that the soprano of the evening was *her* daughter. But we will never know whether Lois's personal success played any part in the production's popularity. Opening night, and therefore the sole review in the Toronto papers, went to Heloise Macklem. Review or no review, Lois knew she had performed well. Kilburn attended one of her performances, and was still talking about it five years later, when Isabel LeBourdais interviewed him for her feature on Lois in the *Canadian Home Journal*. *Princess Ida* confirmed Lois's dreams and her resolve. The stage was her element, and a career as a performer was the only career for her.

Throughout the mid forties, sandwiched between her increasing schedule of singing engagements and her obligations at Eaton's, Lois's lessons continued. Now that she was getting some stage exposure, her stage
presence mattered more and more. Lois still had the habit, though she
staunchly refused to acknowledge it, of closing her eyes while she sang
and withdrawing into a private world that excluded the audience. To her
very last performing days, there remained moments of such withdrawal
in her platform presence, moments so personal and intimate as to cause
her spectators to feel excluded. It was her way of achieving the intense
concentration on the music she had courted since her childhood performances for doctors and visitors at the Hospital for Sick Children. As
Kilburn later recounted to Isabel LeBourdais, he had to resort to trickery
to get Lois to acknowledge her bad habits and change her ways. During
one lesson, when Lois was communing, trancelike, with the glories of
something simple like a major scale, Kilburn stealthily brought his own
face to within inches of hers. When she opened her eyes, she jumped
out of her skin. More important, she had to acknowledge that her eyes
had, indeed, been closed. In order to discourage Lois from standing
awkwardly and moving about the platform distractingly while she sang,
Kilburn recruited her friends to make tactful suggestions to her after performances, since she would accept no such advice from him. If Kilburn
could be demanding and devious, Lois could be headstrong and lazy. On
occasion, Kilburn prevailed on his piano student, Irene McLellan, who
lived near Lois, to make sure Lois did her practising. Irene would have
to sacrifice her own practise time to bring Lois over to her own house, sit
her down and put her through her paces. Lois sometimes forgot a lesson,
or even two. Once, upon her reappearance after one of these unscheduled
absences, Kilburn turned the tables, and refused to teach her.

But through these years, despite temperamental outbursts and interruptions, Kilburn and Lois continued the exploration and development
of her remarkable instrument. Instead of concentrating on the coloratura range and flexibility that came naturally to her, Kilburn urged her to
develop the middle and lower registers of her voice. Lois had established
her versatility when she carried the alto line single-handedly during
the family Christmas carol sessions. For a time, Kilburn placed her in

the alto section of his choir at St. Alban's, to improve her sight-reading ability. Once Lois learned how to produce low notes, which Kilburn described, again to Isabel LeBourdais, as arriving "with a boom," she "worked them to death" (Kilburn's phrase again).

For most singers, the voice falls into different ranges, or registers, and the physical sensation of producing sound varies considerably from one register to the next. Moving across the division points can be awkward and unsettling for the singer. Like most singing teachers, Kilburn emphasized the need to even out the transitions from one register to the next, so that the singer could move easily and flexibly through the full natural range of her voice. He differed from many teachers, however, as he explained later to Carl Morey, in that he believed Lois could extend her range downwards without compromising the high coloratura quality of her sound at the top end. He did not subscribe to the theory that a singer developed one extreme of her range at the risk of damaging the other. In Lois's case, it was a slow and painstaking process, but worth it because of the extraordinary scope of the voice, both in range and in tonal colouring, that was gradually being revealed.

Lois's lessons with Kilburn took place at a time when the Conservatory itself was undergoing radical changes and developing new programs of study that would be crucial to her advanced training. In 1942, Sir Ernest MacMillan resigned as Principal, though he continued in the entirely separate post of Dean of the Faculty of Music at the University of Toronto. MacMillan was succeeded at the Conservatory first by Norman Wilks and then, in 1944, when Wilks died after only two years in the post, by Ettore Mazzoleni. In 1946, under Mazzoleni, the Conservatory inaugurated both a Senior School (to train gifted musicians at the post-secondary level) and an Opera School. Both of these new ventures were headed by Arnold Walter, who had left Europe in 1937 and come to Toronto, initially as a music teacher at Upper Canada College. He soon became one of the principal forces in post-secondary music education in the city. In 1947, with the official permission of

King George VI, the Toronto Conservatory of Music became the Royal Conservatory of Music of Toronto. The Conservatory had recently managed to solve some of its most pressing financial problems, and the two new programs were well supported with scholarship funds. With "royal" status and secure funding, it was the beginning of a period of great confidence for the institution and extraordinary opportunity for its students. These changes in organization and in personnel opened some new doors for Lois just at the time she most needed them. But unthinking prejudice about her disability kept one of them firmly locked against her.

In 1946, Lois won one of the Conservatory scholarships in singing. She shared it with the young Mary Morrison, newly arrived from Winnipeg, who became one of Canada's best-known sopranos, renowned especially for her championing of new music, and in later years a distinguished teacher of voice. Each of them received $250, not enough for living expenses, but enough to make their studies possible. The Conservatory reserved the right to assign its scholarship winners to their teachers, so it was likely in 1946–47, after she first won a scholarship, that Lois had her first experience with a teacher other than Kilburn. Ernesto Vinci, born Ernst Moritz Wreszynski in Berlin in 1898, had trained and practised as a medical doctor in Germany and Italy, but had also studied music in both countries. He sang extensively in Milan before immigrating to New York in 1938. In the same year, he moved to Halifax to become director of the vocal department at the Halifax Conservatory. In 1945, he came to Toronto as the senior member of the Voice faculty at the Royal Conservatory, where he taught until his retirement in 1979. Why Lois and Kilburn agreed to this disruption of their six-year student-teacher relationship is not definitely known. Kilburn may have believed, as he indicated in interview with Isabel LeBourdais, that a change in teacher would help Lois's development. He may also have been under some pressure, as his sons Nicholas and Paul recalled, from piano pedagogue Robert Schmitz, whose summer institutes Kilburn regularly studied at, to stop spreading himself so thin and concentrate on his instrument. In the end, Kilburn's views on the subject probably didn't carry much weight. Kilburn was not a member of the Voice faculty. The Conservatory might have balked at the idea of assigning its prize vocal student to a maverick from the Piano division.

As Lois later confided to a few friends, she felt that her year with Vinci had been of little use to her. She never even mentioned him when giving public accounts of her vocal training. Her contemporaries, commenting in retrospect, were divided on the subject of his influence. Irene McLellan, whose piano recital had given Lois her first real concert exposure, studied voice with Vinci as well as piano with Kilburn. As an outside observer, she thought that, at a crucial stage in Lois's development, Vinci "gave her the boost over the hump, because being a medical doctor there wasn't anything he didn't know about how the voice should work.... For voice placement and carrying the emotion in the voice Vinci was amazing, he really was."

As a performer, Lois certainly knew a thing or two about "carrying the emotion in the voice," but she would later acknowledge a teacher other than Vinci as her greatest influence in that respect. Mary Morrison, who worked with Vinci at the same time and admired him very much, described him as a congenial mentor, who encouraged students to develop and strengthen their natural abilities, but not as a formidable pedagogue with a clearly-defined vocal technique to impose on them. A demanding student, as Lois surely was, might well feel that such a relaxed approach had little to offer. In truth, it seems that no one at the Conservatory had a foolproof technique to impart, and that voice students had to take from teachers what worked best for each of them, and discard the rest. Vinci, one of the dominant forces in voice instruction at the Conservatory at the time, quietly got written out of Lois's official history.

By the fall of 1947, Lois, at the age of twenty-one, felt confident enough to commit herself to the full-time study of music. She quit her job at Eaton's, returned to Kilburn, and entered the Royal Conservatory's Senior School. For the 1947–48 admission cycle the Conservatory had, for the first time, dropped its previous requirement that applicants to the Senior School must present "a standard four-year high-school course or a satisfactory equivalent" as part of their admission qualifications. With admission to the program now based solely on examination, Lois's lack of a high school diploma no longer stood in her way. The Senior School program involved intensive voice lessons and coaching, as well as general musical subjects like theory, history, form and analysis, and language study. The more academic subjects were not Lois's strong suit. She was a classic case of the talented and single-minded performer, having her general musical education rounded out under duress by the requirements of the program she had entered. In any case, in 1948, when she won the André Dorfman Scholarship in Voice, no one seemed inclined to argue with a winning combination. This time the Conservatory made no attempt to assign her away from Kilburn to a member of the Voice faculty.

The new Opera School and the performance opportunities in opera that its creation made possible caused enormous excitement in Toronto's musical world, particularly among the young singers who flocked to it. The Senior School syllabus listed "Opera School" as an available option in every year of the program, clearly establishing the expectation that the best qualified students of the Senior School would be members of the Opera School as well. Admission to the Opera School, however, was a separate process, requiring permission of one's singing teacher and an entrance examination. Lois had hoped to join the Opera School as well as the Senior School. It came as a bitter disappointment when Dr. Walter told her, during an interview in his office, that with her disability there could be no question of a career in opera, and that she should therefore concentrate on concert and oratorio work. All the independence and self-reliance fostered by Jean Hampson and the Wellesley Orthopaedic School rose up in protest. To come up against such an obstacle to her deeply-cherished goal caught her up short.

> This was a painful blow. Like any young singer I had dreams of singing in opera. It seemed to me then the most important aspect of singing. As to my disability, it was certainly real enough, but I had not thought of it as a serious detriment to my career. To be honest, I had not thought about it very much ever. Certainly never at home, and out in the world only sometimes, when I was struck by an awareness that people were uncomfortable

with me. In general though I was able to do almost anything and able also to make adjustments or find a ready
solution when things proved difficult. Perhaps then it
is not hard to understand the disappointment and distress I felt at this cool appraisal of my future. One thing
was quite clear. I would not be admitted into the Opera
School, but I would not believe that I would never sing
in an opera.

Despite this resolve, being denied admission to the Opera School
put Lois at a serious disadvantage. In order to tackle opera in the future,
she would have to compete against young singers, her contemporaries,
who had had training in operatic acting and stage movement, and the
stage experience open to members of the Opera School. If she could not
receive such training now, at the student level, then her chances of breaking into opera professionally in the future became more remote. She did
not, however, protest Walter's decision. Though she resented the judgement, she applied herself in the areas that were open to her through the
Senior School.

By now, Lois's natural gifts had caught the attention of people
who were in a position to advance her career. One of them was the
Conservatory's principal, Ettore Mazzoleni, another European trans-
planted to Canada before the war. Like Arnold Walter, he taught music at
Upper Canada College before carving out a career in professional music
in Canada. A conductor as well as a music educator, Mazzoleni eventually became head of the Conservatory's Opera School and a driving force
behind its Opera Festival, forerunner of the Canadian Opera Company.
In 1947, before any of these developments, however, Mazzoleni chose
Lois as the soprano soloist in a concert of baroque Christmas music
scheduled for December 10 in the Conservatory Concert Hall and for
broadcast on the CBC on December 17. Lois was asked to perform the
Christmas Cantata by Alessandro Scarlatti, a work just sixteen minutes
long in which recitatives alternate with arias on the subject of the nativ-
ity, accompanied by strings and harpsichord. Mazzoleni conducted a
small chamber orchestra, and Greta Kraus played the harpsichord. Kraus,

another formidable European musical émigrée, had trained as a pianist in Vienna, but had fallen in love with the harpsichord, and committed herself to that instrument when it was still a relative rarity, not the staple of baroque performances that it is today.

Given this opportunity, Lois and Kilburn redoubled their efforts. They now had daily coaching sessions, including Sundays, when Kilburn customarily taught one or two students at his home, inviting them to share the Kilburn family Sunday lunch as part of the routine. Together they subjected the score to intensive study. It was not uncommon for them to spend an entire session on one short recitative. As Lois later recalled:

> This work had really very little to do with notes and rhythms. They were quickly learned. It was a search- ing for me to find within my spirit, my soul and intel- lect, the essence of what I was singing about. Once I achieved this vital element, the sound would be right and true, and that sound would be imparted to the responsive listener.

Work of this nature, not only intensive but personal and intimate as well, brought student and teacher, newly reunited after Lois's year with Vinci, closer than ever before.

The recording of this concert in the CBC archives testifies to Lois's extraordinary achievement on that December afternoon. The perform- ance predates many of the scholarly discoveries and revisions to per- formance practice made familiar to today's audiences by the early music revival of the later twentieth century. Thus the tempi chosen by Marshall and Mazzoleni are significantly slower than would be employed today. Their pace lends the music a serious, contemplative air that tempers the mood of Christmas festivity with Lois's characteristic nobility and musical *gravitas*. All the work that she and Kilburn had devoted to extending her range is in evidence. Even at twenty-two, Lois commands two fully developed vocal personalities — a firm, well supported lower register and a brilliant, free-floating high one. In moments of emo- tional climax, when she shucks off the last few vestiges of her student tentativeness, she announces unmistakably the drama and excitement, the "turbulent musical personality" that Kilburn had recognized in her, even as a teenager.

Her listeners knew they were hearing history in the making. In an interview with Carl Morey in 1983, Greta Kraus remembered especially the rehearsal experience.

> She came to the house, and I see her still leaning on the piano, close to my harpsichord, and starting to sing. And it was unbelievable. Perfect. I was absolutely stunned. It was so different from anything I had ever heard. The intensity, the musicality, the sincerity — a young girl. It was out of this world.

According to Kraus, the orchestral players reacted in the same way. "She sang for the first time and the whole orchestra was speechless. Nobody had ever heard anything quite like it." To Lois's surprise, the concert, just a regular entry in the Conservatory's series called "Wednesday Five O'Clocks," attracted the attention of the music critic for the *Globe and Mail*, Colin Sabiston. It pleased Lois that he had taken notice of the concert at all. His hyperbolical praise in this, her first full newspaper review, excited her even more.

> All the ordinary words descriptive of vocal excellence seem inadequate to describe the complete otherworldliness of Miss Marshall's singing. One became so transported that even the outer edges of consciousness were lost to this world, its affairs and even its memories. It was the completeness of this spell, the totality of absorption in a single event, that brought a sensation almost like fear. Had one been transferred to a place where nothing existed but an extreme intensity of beauty? Believe me, such an experience, if it last for but a moment, can be terrifying in the next succeeding moment, when one becomes only gradually conscious

of surrounding applause, then of the lump in one's
throat, and finally, still sort of half lost, of the necessity
of finding one's wraps somewhere in an environment
that still feels unreal.

Even in an age of flowery prose, this was unqualified praise, greater
than anything a beginning performer could hope for. Augustus Bridle,
whose elliptical style gave an eccentric ring to all of his music criticisms
at the *Toronto Star*, reported cryptically and inaccurately, but favourably
nonetheless. "Mazzoleni, who conducted the chamber orchestra at the
'Con' last week, thinks he'll never forget the lyric joy of Lois Marshall
singing a sonatina by Scarlatti...."

The Canadian composer, John Beckwith, at the time the arts editor
for the University of Toronto's student paper, the *Varsity*, provided a
more straightforward and technical assessment.

> Miss Marshall's is one of the freshest, fullest, and pur-
> est soprano voices I have heard in some time. Miss
> Marshall sings with such perfect intonation that one
> would almost think she was producing her tone by
> pressing a system of keys as in a flute. She seems to
> move from one extreme of her register to another with
> effortless ease. Her voice is unusually large and beauti-
> fully suited to the pastoral quality of the Scarlatti work.

As to the mood of the concert, in contrast to Sabiston's exalted sad-
ness, Beckwith contented himself with a more seasonal comment. " ...
I left the hall with a pleasant Christmassy tingle running through me.
Such is the power of good music."

Rose MacDonald, writing in the *Toronto Telegram*, greeted Lois's
talent with uncanny prescience. "It would seem that this young singer,
who belongs to Toronto, by the way, would find in oratorio singing a
field peculiarly hers, and for which not too many are so gifted."

Lois did not need to wait for the reviews. After the applause and
the congratulations, she walked out of the Conservatory Concert Hall

into a quiet fall of snow, highlighted in the pools of light cast by the streetlamps on College Street. Weldon Kilburn and a group of friends accompanied her, savouring the post-concert euphoria. Then, in the privacy afforded by the winter gloom, Kilburn reached out and took her hand. Lois had been around the Conservatory long enough to know of Kilburn's reputation with many of his female students. At nearly twenty-three, however, she had never had a serious boyfriend in her life, and idealized Kilburn for his musical knowledge and sensitivity. Kilburn, for his part, had the ready capacity to fall in love with the ideal performance, such as the one Lois had just given, and then, by extension, with the student herself. It was a heady combination of circumstances. With his little gesture, Kilburn sealed the sense of intimacy and hard work that had led to the shared achievement of that night. He also declared the fact that he felt something more than just a teacher's professional interest in his star pupil.

CHAPTER THREE

1947 to 1950 —
Bach, Handel, and Sir Ernest MacMillan

Lois's years in the Conservatory's Senior School (1947–50) marked an extraordinarily intense phase of her development. She was working with Weldon every other day, sometimes more often, thus strengthening the close bonds that were forming as a result of their work on the Scarlatti *Christmas Cantata*. But at the same time, Weldon encouraged her to broaden her musical horizons. After the unsuccessful interlude with Vinci, Weldon introduced her to the only teacher besides Weldon himself whose influence Lois acknowledged and honoured to the end of her days. Contact with the Austrian singer and pedagogue, Emmy Heim, exposed Lois to a wealth of personal and artistic culture far beyond anything she had encountered to that point in her life. Such a heavy dose of European sophistication could easily have intimidated a down-to-earth Toronto homebody, but in Lois's case it served to strengthen her confidence in her innate musicality and her own special gifts. The larger-than-life Madam Heim, as her students referred to her, inspired Lois's love and admiration, despite her flamboyant displays of worldly experience and artistic sensibility.

Following a performing career in Europe, Emmy Heim (1885–1954) came to Canada after the Second World War, eventually settling in Toronto, where she coached Lieder and song repertoire at the Royal Conservatory of Music. Weldon knew of her through her Toronto recitals and through his work as studio accompanist for her classes. In 1948, with her close friend, Sir Ernest MacMillan, at the piano, Heim recorded three folk songs at an informal soirée in the MacMillan home, which the CBC broadcast in 1955, along with an interview conducted by Ronald Hambleton just a few weeks before her death. This recorded material provides a vivid glimpse of her musical ideas and her teaching personality.

Madam Heim disdained conventional boundaries. In Vienna, she sang the major alto repertoire as soloist with the *Wiener Singakademie* and in concert she billed herself variously as an alto or a mezzo, though current reference material refers to her as a soprano. She seems to have been one of those singers to whom vocal designation meant little, and who sang in whatever range opportunity and inclination dictated. She also taught across the divisions of classical and popular music. She was mainly a coach of Lieder and art songs, but loved folk songs as well. During one of her sojourns in England, she taught Martha Schlamme, who developed an international career in folk song, cabaret, and world music. Heim applied her rigorous standards to many types of music, which she saw as a vehicle for the expression of the individual musical personality rather than a rigidly organized system in which each singer must cultivate a specific *Fach*, or specialty. As a performer, Lois drew frequent inspiration from Heim's musical independence and integrity. When the time came for Lois herself to make the difficult transition from soprano to alto, in order to prolong her singing career, she had the example of Emmy Heim's independent spirit to guide her.

However, Heim's cultured personality had far more to do with her impact as a teacher than anything as arbitrary as her vocal register, since she had no technique to impart. Her connections to Austrian culture, on the other hand, constituted a rich resource for her pedagogy. As a young woman in Vienna, through her brief marriage to the writer Emil Rheinhardt, Heim's circle of acquaintance included famous authors like Rainer Maria Rilke, Hugo von Hofmannsthal, and Thomas Mann, and the painter Oskar Kokoschka, who did a lithograph portrait of her in 1916. She considered the artists Paul Klee and Wassily Kandinsky to be significant influences on her personal education, and worked directly with the leaders of the second Viennese School of composers, Arnold Schoenberg and his pupils Eduard Steuermann, Anton von Webern, and

Left: *Emmy Heim, sketched in 1952 by her student, Joanne Ivey Mazzoleni.*
Mazzoleni emphasized her left hand, because Heim thought it was her only good feature.

Credit: Joanne Ivey Mazzoleni.

Right: *Towards the end of her life, Lois herself portrayed Heim in a different light.*

Credit: Lois Marshall.

From the collection of Cindy Townsend.

Alban Berg. In April 1915, she gave the first performance of Schoenberg's song, "Verlassen" (No. 4 of his *Eight Songs for Voice and Piano*, Opus 6). In her CBC radio interview with Ronald Hambleton, she reminisced about being coached by Webern, and about singing one of Schoenberg's *Gurrelieder*, at the composer's request, at the mess dinner before his regiment departed for the front during the First World War. In Heim's imagination, these connections to twentieth-century Viennese music actually enabled her to appropriate the nineteenth-century tradition of German music and culture. When she sang for Rilke, she believed herself in mystic communion with the greats of musical and literary history:

> I wanted to thank Rilke with the best thing I had, with
> my singing. "Please, Schubert," I probably said, "please
> stand near me. Please, Hugo Wolf, let me do justice to

your music." Those were my prayers. "Goethe, Moerike, Eichendorff, can I feel the melody of your language? Can I feel it as Schubert, Schumann, Wolf did, when they enhanced it with their music?"

In her teaching, Heim could thus invoke the spirits of the immortal poets and composers as though they were personal friends. Nothing in Lois's upbringing or her lessons with Weldon had prepared her for such psychic name-dropping.

That Lois did not feel intimidated by these displays of cultivation and presumed intimacy with the greats is testimony to Heim's warmth and motherly personality. "I'm not teaching my children only how to sing, I'm teaching them how to dig for more wealth in their own souls," she told Hambleton, her "children" being her students. The Canadian baritone Jan Simons, who studied with Heim at around the same time, recalled that she had been unable to coach him in Mahler's *Kindertotenlieder* (*Songs on the Death of Children*) because she herself had lost two children to childhood diseases, and could not face the emotional involvement of these songs, even in the studio. Musically, she wore her heart on her sleeve, and had no compunction about acknowledging music's emotional power. In fact, she regarded it as the singer's responsibility to transmit this power from the score to her hearers. In Lois, who remembered being transported when she first heard a Schubert Symphony as a little girl, Heim's human, involved approach to singing found an apt pupil.

Moreover, Emmy Heim, this figure of continental European experience and authority, actually took the mickey out of Weldon Kilburn and defended Lois against the niggling he still subjected her to. When Lois first sang Schumann's song, "Widmung" ("Dedication"), for Heim, Weldon tried to dampen her enthusiasm for the performance by pointing out that Lois had failed to dot an eighth note in a particular passage, thus altering the rhythm as the score notated it. "Be quiet!" Heim responded. "I'm not interested in that right now," and then took Lois aside for private encouragement, finally paying her the supreme compliment of saying that she was a "real Lieder singer."

Lois regarded Emmy Heim as "the greatest and most inspiring artist I ever knew." To receive such unqualified approval, from Heim of all people, was crucial to the development of Lois's belief in herself as an artist, not just an aspiring student. She needed such encouragement as an antidote to the minute criticism Weldon still dispensed as her teacher and coach. Heim's approval spoke to the important essentials. Whatever her technical limitations might have been at that point, Lois already had the vital elements of musical honesty and integrity within her, qualities without which she could not hope to be the kind of musician she wanted to be.

Emmy Heim taught by inspiring her students with an ideal, not by giving detailed technical instruction. "If you feel a smile, please sing it. If you feel a shiver in your body in singing 'Gretchen am Spinnrad,' please don't think of dark voice production, but say it, say it with all your trembling soul." This highly emotional rhetoric shows that Heim taught an expressive and dramatic approach to interpreting the text of a song. It was an old-fashioned and somewhat florid style, nothing like the austere psychological realism that would dominate the more modern approach to Lieder singing later in the century, but a useful contrast to the utter purity and detachment of Lois's other early idol, Tiana Lemnitz. Thus, Lois began to put together from disparate sources the elements of her own Lieder style, a style narrative rather than mimetic, but powerfully declamatory nonetheless: a bardic style — simple, noble, and sincere.

By her own admission, Emmy Heim's voice had never been remarkable for its natural beauty. "I have no voice, but I know syntax, I know words," Irene McLellan recalls her saying. This knowledge of syntax held the secret to her interpretive powers, a secret which she passed on to Lois. A singer's command of language depends on accurate pronunciation of individual words, but even more on a feel for syntax, for the communicative shape of the phrase and the sentence. Syntactical structure dictates musical effect. That is, from the shape of the syntactical phrase comes the shape of the musical phrase, and from this sense of phrasing come the meaning and the musicality of the song itself. Paradoxically, Lois never achieved fluency in speaking any of the foreign languages in which she sang. To the end of her performing days, she routinely worked up detailed translations of every item in her repertoire as part of her preparation. According to Jan Simons, full linguistic fluency is not essential. "I don't think that's necessary, if you have a good ear." Lois certainly had a good ear, that uncanny ear for mimicry that frequently embarrassed her sister, and it enabled her to sing in foreign languages with fluent inflection, by feeling, not by rote. She recognized the importance of syntax, not just pronunciation, of the phrase and not just of the words. Without necessarily being able to speak the language, she could sing it. Heim could have given her no greater gift, no greater insight into the essentials of communicating through music.

Acutely sensitive to visual stimuli herself, Heim also taught synaesthesia, or the mingling of the senses, where a stimulus to one of the senses can produce a response in a different sense. "We need six senses. This kind of teaching is absolutely necessary for a Lieder singer. I used to say to my pupils, 'Sniff, please sniff the perfume of this song.'" Eccentric as these ideas must have seemed at the time, she was not alone in them; both the artist Wassily Kandinsky and the composer Alexander Scriabin subscribed to similar theories. Synaesthesia as a neurological phenomenon now excites considerable scientific curiosity, documented in some of the case studies of Oliver Sacks.

Even stranger than her theories of synaesthesia, Heim believed that the singer could be possessed by the spirit of the composer at the height of creative inspiration and transmit that spirit to the audience. "I can even conjure up Schubert's kind and shy face, though he wasn't shy at all when he sat at the piano and made music. It is indescribable. But that spirit of his must enter the singer's mind. You must be eager to understand and to give it to your waiting audience." Beneath all the psychic flummery, Heim's access to the composer's intent was assisted by her context, by her confidence in her national, cultural heritage, by her direct contact with the great composers of her day. Lois, who had no such context to draw upon, had to do it by instinct.

Of course there was no way of verifying that the composer's intentions had been reached, let alone transmitted. But the idea that some reference point could exist within her, drawing on her own innate musicality, encouraged Lois to develop the artistic independence and self-confidence that separate the mature artist from the student. As a Canadian artist,

Lois naturally felt at a disadvantage compared to her European contemporaries, who seemed to have been born into the musical culture that she had to labour to acquire. Lois's discipleship with Emmy Heim served to highlight this discrepancy. As Jan Simons remembered, Heim could be authoritarian in matters of taste and musical judgement. "Because of her European background, I think that you had very little flexibility as to your own interpretation. She felt it had to be done in a certain way." Subjecting herself to Emmy's authority, Lois learned the songs of Mozart, Beethoven, Schubert, Schumann, Brahms, Hugo Wolf, Mahler, Schoenberg, and Alban Berg, as well as the Benjamin Britten realizations of English folk songs; much of the repertoire that became the core of her professional recital repertoire. But what she treasured most was an ideal, of art and of humanity, which she absorbed from Emmy Heim and frequently called upon during her performances in order to find the strength and energy to give as fully of herself as the music required. If, as Lois later said, she never really learned how to sing, she compensated by learning how to be fully engaged in her singing. That quality of total engagement in her art, that discovery of "more wealth within her own soul," which Emmy Heim taught her, never forsook her.

At the same time that Lois was working intensively with Weldon and entering into the mysteries propounded by Madam Heim, she also came under the influence of Sir Ernest MacMillan, who would shape fundamentally the nature of her musicianship and the course of her career. Though she absorbed musical ideas from many of the great musicians with whom she had contact throughout her career, these three — Weldon Kilburn, Emmy Heim, and Sir Ernest MacMillan — had the most lasting, the most profound, influence on her.

Sir Ernest had been aware of Lois from the time of her first lessons at the Conservatory, but during her Senior School years he really began to take notice of her gifts. After the attention she attracted with performances like the Scarlatti *Christmas Cantata* in late 1947, he offered her a debut with the Toronto Symphony Orchestra, of which he was the conductor. He scheduled her to appear in a TSO student concert on February 10, 1948. She would perform an aria from Mozart's opera, *Il Re Pastore*, with Ettore Mazzoleni, who had conducted her in the Scarlatti, leading the orchestra. But it was not to be. Just before this important debut, Lois came down with laryngitis and had to cancel. Louise Roy, a gifted soprano from St. Boniface, Manitoba, who was studying and building her career in Toronto at this time, substituted for her, singing with the orchestra "Divinités du Styx" from Gluck's opera *Alceste*, and a group of folk songs, accompanied by Weldon Kilburn at the piano. Lois took her disappointment hard, listening at home, in tears, to a broadcast of her substitute, accompanied by her own teacher.

But before she had fully recovered from her laryngitis, she got another chance. On very short notice, Sir Ernest told Weldon that he would be interested in auditioning Lois for the soprano solos in his upcoming performances of Bach's *St. Matthew Passion* at Convocation Hall at the University of Toronto. These Easter performances of Bach's masterwork were an annual fixture on the Toronto musical scene. Sir Ernest's veneration of the score and almost religious approach to its performance had become legendary since he introduced the complete work to Toronto audiences, conducting from memory, on March 27, 1923. He presented it during every Easter season for the next thirty-five years, using Toronto's established choral organization, the Mendelssohn Choir, developing a group of soloists, and building a huge and faithful audience. For a relative unknown like Lois, the opportunity to audition for this major event constituted an invitation to approach the holy of holies. Laryngitis or not, she had preparations to make, and only three or four days to make them.

Lois, who had never learned the *St. Matthew Passion*, who had never even heard it, borrowed a score from the Conservatory library and Weldon cleared his schedule to devote himself as much as possible to her preparation. He began, not by giving her a crash course in the recitatives and arias Sir Ernest would be expecting to hear, as any other vocal coach might do, but by reading with her through the entire score, which runs to more than three hours in performance. Weldon played, sang, and talked his way through the *St. Matthew* in one marathon session, by the end of which Lois had a clear conception of the entire work that would never leave her. Then he sent her home for the weekend to learn the soprano arias and recitatives on her own, cautioning her to sing as little as possible, in order to save her voice. The following Monday, after a full rehearsal with Weldon, Lois went to Sir Ernest's studio for the audition with her entire part memorized. Sir Ernest heard everything, not just a representative sample. At the end of the audition, he casually asked Lois the question she had been hoping to avoid, "How long have you been singing these arias, my dear?"

Unwilling to admit just how last-minute her preparations had been, she mumbled evasively, "A very short time indeed."

"You sound as though you have been singing them for years," replied the great man, and, contrary to his usual practice, gave her the engagement on the spot. On March 23 and 24, 1948, while still a student in the Senior School, Lois would have name billing in one of the major events of Toronto's musical season. Weldon redoubled his coaching efforts in the month or so remaining before the performances.

Thus began Lois's long and fruitful professional relationship with Sir Ernest MacMillan. She became his favourite soprano. Years later, while on tour in Australia, she took time out to write him a letter during Easter week.

> I can never go through this week without the strongest yearning to sing in, or hear the *St. Matthew*. For so many years this was what I waited for, I always began to think of it still again weeks in advance of our performances. There has never been a single work which has meant so much to me. You will never know what you gave me during those years.

MacMillan's musicianship and reverential attitude to Bach's music coloured Lois's own interpretations as she performed Bach, with MacMillan and around the world. For her, MacMillan's interpretations combined integrity and passion; they realized both the spiritual significance and the emotional drama inherent in Bach's music.

MacMillan adhered firmly to Victorian performance practice, with huge forces deployed in old-fashioned oratorio style. For the 1948 *St.*

Matthew, the Mendelssohn Choir mustered 210 members, a huge and unwieldy instrument compared to the smaller, more streamlined and vocally flexible forces that recent Bach scholarship has taught us is truer to the performance practices of Bach's time. MacMillan favoured broad *ritard*s at the end of the dramatic choruses, instead of keeping them up to tempo and running them briskly into the following section, and frequently took *ritard*s at the ends of recitatives as well, all typical of the Victorian approach to Bach. Even in MacMillan's day, his conducting of Bach's music had its detractors, who nicknamed him "Lord Largo." The approach that Lois found so deeply moving some critics found to be restrained, reserved, even fossilized, his tempi notoriously slow, the overall mood merely pious, rather than genuinely devotional. Sir Ernest's style of Bach has since been challenged by modern musicological scholarship and the move to historically authentic performance practice, which seeks to perform Bach with period instruments and the types of forces he himself would originally have employed. These historically-based standards are familiar to today's listeners from the work of groups like Toronto's Tafelmusik and Andrew Parrott's Taverner Consort in England. With performances and recordings of the major Bach choral repertoire using a single singer on each vocal part, Parrott and the American conductor Joshua Rifkin have shifted assumptions about Bach performance to the opposite extreme from the Victorian one of mammoth forces, expansive tempi, and murky sonorities more influenced by Elgar and Mendelssohn than Bach.

Without question, Lois's Bach, because it was so heavily influenced by Sir Ernest's aesthetic, fell squarely within the old school. Her conservative approach (she never ornamented a phrase of baroque music in her life, unless it was specified in the score) finds little favour according to the evolving standards of twenty-first century musicology. But innate musicianship counts for something. A fair assessment of her considerable achievements in singing Bach requires a sympathetic understanding of the tradition from which she came, and attentiveness to the fundamental musical values that underlie her Bach. In listening to her recordings today, one needs to hear beyond the obvious differences to recognize her fundamental values of eloquent phrasing, communicative diction, and emotional involvement in the music.

For Lois, the 1948 performances presented an additional challenge. Sir Ernest wanted the Evangelist, who provides the narrative of the Gospel story, and the Christus, who sings Christ's direct speech, to stand separately from the rest of the soloists, who offer reflective commentary. Given the layout of Convocation Hall, which is the University of Toronto's space for public ceremonial, not designed as a standard concert hall at all, this meant that the Evangelist and Christus occupied what little space was available at the front of the stage, near the conductor's podium, while the remaining soloists had to stand in the choir, at some remove from the conductor, behind the orchestra and hemmed in by the 210 choristers of the Mendelssohn. Lois, who had needed lots of space around her when singing ever since she was a child, found the setup unbearably confining. Fortunately, her audience noticed nothing of her distress.

The *Globe and Mail* critic, Colin Sabiston, recognized a great career in its early stages. He saved the best of his review of the 1948 *St. Matthew Passion* for Lois.

> Lois Marshall, even younger in years and experience, seems to have a limitless store of artistic surprises. Singing entirely without a score, she sang the arias Break In Grief, Thou Loving Heart, in part 1 and For Love My Saviour Now Is Dying in part 2, with such simple greatness that their poignancy was about all the emotions of musical auditors could bear. In addition to a voice of exquisite quality and clarity, she sings with a kind of spiritual urge that is completely compelling.
>
> Already she has what may be called one of the most "communicative voices" of our time; and a few years easily could confirm her position as one of the greatest of all sopranos. With all her emotional intensity, she yet sings with perfect control and ease, as though song were her only appropriate form of communication, and as though all of its requirements were basic among her talents.

On these last two points, the communicative urgency of Lois's voice and her apparently innate ability to touch an audience through it, Sabiston's comments were prescient. Lois stood on the threshold of a career that would be founded on her power to communicate in live performance, exploiting the chemistry between singer and audience in the immediacy of the concert hall. Sabiston recognized the natural gifts which equipped her so admirably for this intensely individual pursuit of her art.

Like her brother Fred, Lois began picking up regular experience in church choirs. By late 1948 or early 1949, she had left St. Alban's, where Weldon had placed her in the alto section to develop her sight-reading and her lower register, to become the paid soprano soloist at Bloor Street United Church. The organist and choirmaster there, Frederick C. Silvester was, in the close-knit world of Toronto music, also registrar of examinations (and then registrar) at the Conservatory, as well as the assistant conductor and coach of the Mendelssohn Choir. In those roles, Silvester had ample opportunity to observe Lois's rising star, and the wit to snag her for his church choir before she soared beyond his reach. With typical loyalty, Lois sang regularly in his choir until 1953, through the busiest years of her career's launch.

In Frederick Silvester, five years older than Weldon Kilburn, eight years younger than Sir Ernest MacMillan, Lois found another musical mentor of the type she seemed most comfortable with — an older man and an old-school musician, familiar with church music and the British tradition. Silvester had emigrated from his native Manchester to western Canada, then moved on to Toronto, from Saskatoon, to study, like Weldon, with Healey Willan at the Conservatory. In 1931, just three years after Kilburn became "the youngest cathedral organist in captivity," Silvester obtained a major Toronto post as organist and choirmaster at the Church of the Messiah, moving to Bloor Street United in 1938, where he remained until his death. If similar age, background and training counted for anything, it was no wonder Lois felt comfortable with

"Freddie," or "Freddles" as she came to call him, comfortable with his no-nonsense directness and sense of humour, and with his extended family.

On weekends when there was a Sunday evening concert as well as a morning service at Bloor Street United, Lois spent her entire Sunday with the Silvesters. She warmed up at home then arrived at church early for a private rehearsal session. As further warm-up, she liked to run through the bass arias from *Messiah*. Silvester might take her through the tenor and alto arias as well, before she tackled the soprano ones. Such strenuous warm-ups were typical for Lois throughout her career. She had to work her voice a great deal before she felt confident that it would respond readily to the demands of a full performance. Yehudi Wyner, who accompanied Lois much later in her life, said that "Lois prepared for her concerts with more singing than I've ever heard from any singer."

Stuart Hamilton, her pianist on her farewell tour, noted the same strenuous approach to vocal preparation. "She would sing three or three and a half, four hours solid, and as hard as she could sing, before a performance."

After the morning service at Bloor Street United, Lois usually went with Silvester to his home in north Toronto, where she joined his family — wife, daughters, and mother-in-law — for Sunday lunch. Then an afternoon nap and a cup of tea, before they returned to church for the evening performance. And often, to round out the evening, there might be a party at the Silvester home, where Lois met and made friends with members of Toronto's church music establishment, including Sir Ernest (himself an accomplished organist) and Lady MacMillan; the organist and choral conductor John Hodgins and his wife Mary; and the organist Charles Peaker (Hodgins' teacher and another expatriate Englishman who had immigrated to Toronto via Saskatoon) and his wife, Marie. In the summer, the Silvesters invited Lois to their cottage outside Huntsville for vacations. Lois treasured the affection as much as she did the musical atmosphere. Gradually, she acquired a musical family. From paternal figures like MacMillan and Silvester, she finally experienced the approval she had never received from her own father. When Frederick Silvester died in 1966, Lois, accompanied by Charles Peaker, sang at his memorial service at Bloor Street United.

Despite a youth dominated by regular attendance at Roman Catholic, Anglican, and then United churches, as an adult Lois adopted a spiritual but vigorously skeptical attitude towards questions of faith. One of her favourite tag lines, "I thank whatever gods may be," which she used both in writing and in speech, gave a clue to the distance she had travelled from the literal faith of her childhood days. Her early professional commitments outside of her home church helped to ease the transition from the devout Catholicism her mother had expected of her as a child to the agnostic position she favoured as an adult. But whatever her personal religious views might have been, at that time she was still seen as a Roman Catholic invading Bloor Street United, one of the bastions of Protestant Toronto, and in 1949 such things still mattered. Her presence in the choir initially raised a few eyebrows in the congregation, especially as she seemed to court unseemly attention by her habit of singing without a score. The intense concentration of her platform manner probably struck some as a bid for attention too. But she really overstepped the bounds one summer night when she unthinkingly tucked a white flower in her hair before entering the chancel for the evening performance. This evidently smacked too much of Papist ornament. A distressed member of the congregation asked Silvester to speak to his wayward soloist about such unseemliness, but Silvester squashed the objection with his typical brusqueness. "For all I care, if she sings like that, she can wear carrots in her navel!"

Silvester's ambitious musical program at Bloor Street United went well beyond the provision of service music and anthems on Sunday mornings. With his choir and the quartet of paid soloists (some of them, like Mary Palmateer, Arthur Bartlett, and Eric Tredwell, soloists in Sir Ernest's Bach and Handel performances), Silvester regularly presented Sunday evening concerts of the major oratorio and sacred choral repertoire, substituting organ transcriptions for the full orchestral scores. Under Silvester's direction, Lois first learned major works like Bach's *Christmas Oratorio* and *St. John Passion*, Handel's *Samson* and *Judas Maccabaeus*, Mendelssohn's *Elijah* and the Brahms *Requiem*. She got paid to lead the soprano section, as well as sing the solos, so a performance of any of these works, which Silvester presented complete, not in abridged formats, meant that Lois had to sing the soprano line in all choral materials, and then try to remain fresh-voiced for the solos as well. It was hard work, but it gave Lois an intimate knowledge of complete scores, consistent with Weldon's approach to her musical preparation. She learned the major oratorio and sacred repertoire in its full context, not just her own solos with the necessary cues. And she learned them in a church setting, not for the concert hall. Thus she experienced the full drama of these sacred works, and continued to approach them with a fervency and sincerity that belied her personal agnosticism. In later years, concert promoters would marvel at the extent of Lois's experience in this area of repertoire, much of it based on her work with Silvester at Bloor Street United.

Along with her studies at the Senior School of the Conservatory and her regular work at Bloor Street United, Lois took on whatever other engagements came her way. She continued, of course, with the weddings, service club meetings, and business luncheons that had provided pin money for her during the war. More significantly for her musical and professional development, she began to participate in run-outs from Toronto to smaller communities, organized by the Department of Education of Ontario as part of its general educational mandate. A small, portable group of young musicians — perhaps two singers, a violinist, and a pianist — would arrive in town, set up, often in the high school auditorium or gymnasium, and perform for an audience of school students and townspeople. Such touring was physically strenuous, especially for Lois with her physical disability. Schools and public buildings of the day had not been designed with barrier-free access in mind, so Lois had the physical exertion of stairs and inconveniently located bathrooms to add to the normal rigours of travel and adaptation to unfamiliar concert venues. Nevertheless, she thrived on the work. It provided the frequent performance experience, under a wide variety of conditions, essential to the development of an artist. More practically, it tested the young artist's commitment to the unglamorous life of the working professional musician.

In her second year of the Senior School, Lois caught the attention of Nicholas Goldschmidt, and through him, in her final year, got a taste of the operatic experience that had thus far eluded her. Exuberant, irrepressible, and impossibly energetic, by 1948 Nicholas Goldschmidt was well on his way to becoming the driving force in Canadian music and music promotion, which he continued to be until his death at the age of ninety-five, in 2004. He was born in 1908 in Moravia, now part of the Czech Republic but then still under Habsburg rule, received his musical education in Vienna and, during the thirties, served his theatrical apprenticeship as conductor, chorus master, and coach in the German-speaking regional theatres of Bohemia, also now part of the Czech Republic. In 1937, alert to the signs of gathering conflict in Europe, he immigrated to the United States, where, after knocking about in a variety of musical jobs, he was eventually recommended, almost by chance, to Arnold Walter, who was looking for a music director for his new Opera School in Toronto, the program to which Lois had been denied entrance. Goldschmidt learned about her through his great friend, Emmy Heim, and used her as one of the soprano soloists in his CBC radio broadcast (April 28, 1948) of Mozart's *Mass in C Minor*, billed as the work's first Canadian performance. From that first encounter, he valued the person as well as the musician. "Her personality was an example of the greatest artist and a supremely modest personality."

Then, in 1949, Goldschmidt cast Lois in the lead role of Donna Anna in his CBC concert performance of Mozart's opera, *Don Giovanni*. These were the palmy days of live opera on CBC radio, when singers like Mary Morrison, Marguerite Gignac, Elizabeth Benson Guy, Jan Rubes, Edmund Hockridge, and James Shields formed the nucleus of the CBC Opera Company, performing regular broadcasts of the standard repertoire. These performances were transmitted live, not from pre-recorded tape, and generated a sense of immediacy and participation for listeners across the country. Many of the same operas were then mounted, with mostly the same casts (although without Lois Marshall) in the Opera Festival performances (precursors of the Canadian Opera Company) at the Royal Alexandra Theatre in Toronto.

Don Giovanni was performed and broadcast live on two separate occasions (April 20, 1949 and January 11, 1950), both times with Lois as Donna Anna. The surviving tape of the 1950 performance reveals Lois's ability to create a powerful sense of drama, despite the limitations of the concert performance and the broadcast medium. Her recitatives, especially the extended description of her father's murder that precedes the aria, "Or sai chi l'onore," are models of vocal acting, at times plaintive and tenuous, at others wild and impassioned, but always completely controlled and fully supported vocally. Her skills as an ensemble singer, absolutely crucial in *Don Giovanni*'s many glorious ensembles, are impeccable. Lois and Elizabeth Benson Guy, the stunning Donna Elvira in this production, work co-operatively to achieve extraordinary blend of tone and unanimity of musical purpose. It is a remarkable performance on any terms, but especially for a singer of twenty-four, with no previous experience of a lead role in a full-length opera.

Lois's Donna Anna obviously impressed Goldschmidt. In March of 1950 he was well into rehearsals for his next broadcast, a performance of Beethoven's *Fidelio*, when he encountered a serious problem. He had cast Louise Roy, the soprano who had substituted for Lois when laryngitis forced her to cancel her TSO debut, in the punishing role of Leonora.

> Louise had a fabulous voice, and was a wonderful musician, and we were all thrilled … Well, as we got closer to the performance, when we rehearsed at the piano, one day Louise was wonderful, the next day — everything gone. So I said well perhaps she is nervous, or whatever. Next time she was superb and thrilling. That was about two weeks before the performance. Then we had an ensemble rehearsal. Everything gone. Well I tell you, I became very, very apprehensive.

Goldschmidt had a heart to heart talk with Roy, and discovered that a chronic health problem was affecting the consistency of her performance. Reluctantly, they agreed that it would be too much of a risk for her to go on in a live broadcast. With very little lead time, Goldschmidt needed a new principal soprano for a role which includes one of the most difficult arias in the repertoire, the notoriously challenging "Abscheulicher, wo eilst du hin?" What was he to do?

> I went through the hall at the Conservatory, and there was Lois Marshall, sitting, studying a score, Bach or something. I said, "Oh Lois, tell me, have you ever sung the great aria from *Fidelio*, 'Abscheulicher, wo eilst du hin?'"
>
> She said, "No, but of course it's a terrific piece."
>
> I said, "Do you think you could look at it and let me know if you could do it? We have a performance in about ten days of *Fidelio* for the CBC."
>
> "Oh, well I'll look at it. I'll come tomorrow."
>
> I said, "Tomorrow?"
>
> She said, "Sure." She came to me the next day and it was incredible. And she took on the role within five days, for the first orchestra rehearsal.

With stunning *sang-froid* and her usual capacity for quick study, Lois had saved the day.

According to the announcer's preamble on the CBC tape, the 1950 broadcast was the Canadian premiere of *Fidelio*, an indication of the length of time it took for opera to establish a presence in Canadian musical life. While admittedly not the most popular of operas, *Fidelio*, a major work by one of the great composers, had its first performance in 1805, one hundred forty-five years earlier. For the CBC broadcast, it was performed in English, with the spoken dialogue provided by actors, not the singers assigned to the parts themselves. The noticeable disjunction between speaking and singing voices detracts from the overall consistency of the drama. Lois does herself credit, although she does not rise here to the heights she achieved in the *Don Giovanni* performances. The opening section of her "Abscheulicher," more workmanlike than affecting, fails to rouse the emotions to a very high pitch. Despite this unpromising beginning, she tackles the aria's impossibly difficult conclusion in fine style. Introduced by horn solos in the orchestra, this section of the aria shifts to a more tempestuous mode, with a passage of difficult vocal arpeggios and treacherous leaps from the high soprano to the low mezzo range. Lois sails through the passage, which defeats many more experienced sopranos, with confidence and bravura, displaying a glorious upper register and powerful chest tones at the lower end of her voice. Elsewhere, there are a few moments of vocal strain, hardly surprising in a singer who learned the role on such short notice, but in the great duet between Florestan and Leonora all signs of strain vanish, and Lois's voice is supple and clear throughout. She never got the opportunity to perform the complete role of Leonora again, although "Abscheulicher" remained in her concert repertoire until the mid sixties.

Even though Lois was beginning to make a name for herself, her growing reputation remained mostly confined to the relatively small world of the Toronto musical scene of Conservatory, church, and concert hall. She needed to establish some national popularity, and the CBC radio competition, "Singing Stars of Tomorrow," offered the perfect opportunity. Through March and April 1950, just when she was busiest with her final days in the Senior School, with *Fidelio*, and with other major performing commitments, Lois took on the added pressure of competing in one of the best-known Canadian vocal contests of the day.

More than just a talent contest, "Singing Stars" fostered pride in Canada's emerging vocal talent through its extensive program of auditions and radio recitals, and its hugely-anticipated final awards show. Every year, forty or more young singers, chosen by audition from across Canada, appeared in a series of twenty-three national radio broadcasts. The winners of these rounds then competed in the semifinals, with the finalists performing on a climactic CBC broadcast from Massey Hall in Toronto, culminating in the announcement of the results and the presentation of the grand prize of $1,000. For twenty-six weeks of the year this radio show generated excitement and sustained interest in the best new singing talent of the day in households across the country.

The show was sponsored by York Knitting Mills, whose president and vice president, J.D. Woods and Hugh Lawson, had the foresight and interest to commit their company from the program's inception in 1943. "Singing Stars" restricted itself to female singers until 1947, when, with the war finally over, the competition expanded to include men. In 1950, sponsorship shifted to Canadian Industries Limited (CIL), who kept the program on the air until 1956. Rex Battle, who conducted the popular Promenade Concerts at Varsity Arena every summer, led the orchestra for "Singing Stars." Winners of the program could thus count on an appearance at the Proms in addition to their cash prize. The show was produced by John Adaskin, a champion of Canadian composition and Canadian performers, who also created "Opportunity Knocks," the other popular CBC radio competition of the day.

"Opportunity Knocks" was a little more downscale than "Singing Stars." It adopted a variety show format, used audience participation in the judging (like "Canadian Idol"), included instrumentalists as well as vocalists, and extended its range to embrace popular as well as classical music. Never one to turn her nose up at popular venues if they gave her a performance opportunity, Lois had appeared on "Opportunity Knocks" at Toronto's Fairlawn movie theatre the year previously, in 1949, singing Puccini's "One Fine Day" on an eclectic program that also included Peggy Kane with the pop standard "Bei Mir Bist Du Schoen" and Angelo Burlgano performing "Come Back to Sorrento." She seems to have trounced the competition on that round, but made it only as far as runner-up on "Opportunity Knocks" for 1949.

No matter. "Singing Stars of Tomorrow" offered bigger cash prizes and a more consistent standard of competition. Lois set her sights accordingly, and refused to be discouraged. It wasn't her first attempt. She had competed twice before, in 1948 and in 1949, when she had lost out to her ever-present competition, Louise Roy. Formidable competition in 1950 came from Doreen Hulme, a Toronto singer with extensive professional experience, who would go on to a long career in England as principal soloist in the BBC's Light Music Department. Lois's own schedule around the time of the finals was exhausting, with the CBC *Fidelio*, *St. John Passion* at Bloor Street United, *St. Matthew Passion* at

Convocation Hall, a variety show at Maple Leaf Gardens (for the Easter Seal campaign), and Sir Ernest's ambitious Bach Festival (three major Bach works on three consecutive nights), all in the month running up to the "Singing Stars" finals on April 23, 1950. She must have been tired, but she couldn't have been any better warmed up. The panel of judges from Toronto, Winnipeg, Vancouver, and Montreal (Healey Willan served as the Toronto juror) declared her the winner in the women's division. A Montreal-born tenor, Abramo Carfagnini, who had begun vocal studies after his discharge from the Royal Canadian Air Force, won the men's division. After three consecutive tries, the $1,000 prize and the appearance at the Promenade Concerts were finally Lois's.

Far more important than the prize money was the national popularity of "Singing Stars of Tomorrow," which meant the kind of publicity and exposure that Lois had never had before. To the end of her

The announcement of the winners of the 1950 "Singing Stars" of Tomorrow contest, from the stage of Toronto's Massey Hall.

From the collection of Cindy Townsend.
Credit: Canada Pictures, Toronto.

performing days, she encountered Canadians who recalled her winning performance on "Singing Stars," could remember her competition repertoire, and told her how they had rooted for her every step of the way. But most important for building a career, the win on "Singing Stars" opened the door to engagements in regional concert series across the country, most of which were still dominated by American booking agents who promoted American artists. As an indicator of the program's influence, one of the first queries Lois received for an out-of-province engagement, from Liverpool, Nova Scotia, came to her just one month after her win, addressed simply: "Miss Lois Marshall, c/o Singing Stars of Tomorrow."

On June 29, 1950, Lois and Abramo Carfagnini made their Promenade Concert debuts at Varsity Arena. For her part of the program, Lois sang operatic arias by Verdi, Weber, and Debussy, with the Romance from Sigmund Romberg's *The Desert Song* thrown in as her gesture towards pops concert crossover. Two weeks later, on July 10, she performed as Canada's representative at "North American Night," in Washington, DC, part of the festival celebrating the city's sesquicentennial. Eric McLean, the music critic for the *Montreal Daily Star*, who would later review Lois very favourably in her Montreal appearances, was puzzled about the advance publicity material he received in connection with this Washington event. He wrote to Paul Hume, his counterpart on the *Washington Post*, with a query.

> … I'm writing you to ask you who Miss Lois Marshall is. She is billed in the enclosed release as "the leading Canadian soprano". She may very well be all this release claims, but I've been unable to find any record of her work in this district…. Without wishing to offend, the programs have struck me as strangely inadequate for an anniversary of the national capital. I strongly suspect, too, that Miss Marshall might be the Canadian counterpart of Miss Truman.

Even with her recent success in "Singing Stars," Lois had not yet come to McLean's attention. He feared that Canada was being represented by an inferior artist, like President Truman's daughter, Margaret, whose career owed more to her family name than to her musicianship. McLean's query speaks volumes about the chasm in understanding and awareness that separated the musical scenes of Toronto and Montreal in 1950, despite the attempts of the CBC to bridge the gap. Some civic rivalry may have motivated his enquiry as well. By 1950 Montreal had its own rising star to promote, contralto Maureen Forrester, who had entered "Singing Stars" in 1950, but, in the vagaries of music competitions, had failed to place.

Back on her home turf, Lois, prodded by Weldon, earned one more honour to mark the conclusion of her student days and launch her professional career. In her final year in the Senior School, Weldon had a frank conversation with his pupil. "She was being very, very lazy about theoretical subjects, counterpoint, harmony, and I told her that I thought, if she'd only get down to business and do some work on those, she had a good chance of winning the Eaton Scholarship. She said to me Arnold Walter, who of course at that time was head of the school, would never give it to her." The Eaton Graduating Scholarship, the Conservatory's highest distinction at the time, recognized the outstanding graduate of the Senior School. Perhaps Lois's defeatist attitude stemmed from Walter's refusal to allow her to enter the Opera School, or from some of the tearful interviews she had had with him over the years, as he chided her for her lapses in attendance or failure to apply herself to her studies. But Weldon the taskmaster prevailed, and Lois, along with all the performing commitments of her graduating year, got back to the books. In early June, Toronto papers carried the news that Lois had crowned her victory in "Singing Stars" by winning the Eaton Graduating Scholarship. This award brought more than just prestige. The $1,000 prize was to be used to finance a solo recital debut at Eaton Auditorium in the fall of that year.

Eaton Auditorium, a 1,014 seat recital hall on the seventh floor of Eaton's College Street store, where Lois had begun her brief career in business, was a jewel of Art Deco design, the prestige recital venue in the city for all the great visiting artists of the day. Over the years it presented singers of international stature like Edward Johnson, Lucrezia Bori, Richard Crooks, Kirsten Flagstad, Lotte Lehmann, Marian Anderson, Bidú Sayão, Jan Peerce, Jussi Björling, and Dame Maggie Teyte. It was also home to the Eaton Operatic Society, with which Lois had performed *Princess Ida* in 1945. After 1977, Eaton Auditorium fell into neglect and disrepair, but has recently been restored and found new life as the Carlu Centre.

On October 12, 1950, a large and enthusiastic audience welcomed Lois and Weldon to Eaton Auditorium. Setting the precedent she would follow through much of her career, she sang a varied and strenuous program: "Come Visit" by Bach; "Et Incarnatus Est" from the Mass in C Minor by Mozart; "So Shall the Lute and Harp Awake" by Handel; three Schubert songs ("Gretchen am Spinnrade," "Im Haine," and "Seligkeit"); "Abscheulicher, wo eilst du hin?" repeated from her CBC *Fidelio* performance; four song settings of poems by e e cummings, specially commissioned for the recital from Canadian composer John Beckwith; four of the Benjamin Britten arrangements of English folk songs; and, to round out the recital, "Casta diva," the *bel canto* showpiece from Bellini's opera *Norma*. Her friends and supporters celebrated the occasion with a deluge of flowers. At the conclusion of the concert, Weldon had to help Lois lift the basket of roses and several huge bouquets across the footlights.

The reviews were thoughtful and encouraging. Hugh Thomson, in the *Star*, commented on her overall musicianship and discipline, then noted the tonal variety and dramatic intensity of her performance, qualities which her earlier work in oratorio and sacred music had not allowed her to display to such advantage.

> Those expecting a concert from a soprano with a chronically velvet quality in the "music-to-doze-by" style were in for a surprise. Lois showed … she could caress lyrical lines with the best of them. But she also showed she was a musician of considerable temperament, with a ringing dramatic style. She didn't mind an edge on her tone expressing intense emotion.…

The *Globe and Mail* sent Leo Smith, an experienced musician and teacher, who, after his retirement from professional music, occupied the music desk at that paper for several years. Like Thomson, he drew attention to the range and variety of Lois's vocal instrument, but made a more personal observation in that connection.

> Miss Marshall's voice is classified as a soprano. It has, however, some of the characteristics of the mezzo. There is no disproportion between upper and lower octave. Her technical dexterity is remarkable, and she can produce a beautiful quality. She can sing, too, with abandon, and always with fine artistic feeling.
>
> While experience is not associated with youth, yet last night I had the impression that life's journey had not been devoid of ordeal, but something had been gained in the struggle.

Already, Smith recognized in Lois an artist of maturity and interpretive power.

Neither critic referred overtly to her disability. If Smith's discreet comment about ordeal and struggle was intended as an indirect acknowledgement, he at least framed it as a comment on the effect her disability had had on her artistry. Besides, as a former teacher at the Conservatory and member of the Faculty of Music at the University of Toronto, Smith likely knew of Lois from her student days. His comment might have been based on any number of observations of her progress through the Senior School, not necessarily on her disability.

Smith admired her Beethoven, but thought her Bellini "not quite so successful, evidently … chosen to show she had studied the problems of Italian vocal art." In assessing these operatic credentials, he spoke from his experience of five years in the cello section of the orchestra at the Royal Opera House, Covent Garden. In the Beckwith, of which he had been unable to understand a single English word, he was highly critical of her diction. On the whole it was a positive but temperate review, and therefore more useful than some of the hyperbole Lois had received as a student. The shift in tone was noticeable. No longer the promising young student, from now on Lois would find her every performance fair game for critical comment.

If the demands of the professional were greater, so were some of the perks. Toronto in 1950 may not have been the most cosmopolitan of cities, but it could rise to certain occasions with its own brand of hometown style. After her Promenade Concert debut in July, Lois, still wearing the pale blue evening gown in which she had performed and carrying the bouquet she had received, went out with friends to celebrate. After she and her party had been seated, the restaurant musicians, alert to the presence of a celebrity in their midst, struck up "Alice Blue Gown."

CHAPTER FOUR

1950 to 1953 —
With Toscanini at Carnegie Hall

Even for "Alice Blue Gown," the celebrity of a win on "Singing Stars" and the hoopla of her graduation accomplishments would have a limited lifespan. They had to be exploited immediately if they were to be of any use as a stepping stone to an enduring career. Lois lost no time in capitalizing on these early successes, and from her graduation in 1950 to 1953, she worked single-mindedly and with an apparently unshakeable self-confidence to establish herself as more than just an overnight sensation. She chose the difficult route of trying to break into the essentially closed shop of the Canadian concert circuit. Decamping to Europe, as Jon Vickers and James Milligan did at around the same time, was not for her. If Lois's choice to stay in Canada during those formative years of her career initially denied her a certain international glamour, it nevertheless ensured her place in the affections and loyalty of her Canadian audience. And while concentrating on developing her domestic audience, she also remained alert to any important international opportunities that came her way. During her years as an itinerant Canadian concert artist, Lois got two such lucky breaks. In both cases, of course, she made her own luck, with the guts to step from relative obscurity into the glare of international attention on very short notice, and the hard work and preparation necessary to succeed. Her reward, in March of 1953, placed Lois onstage at Carnegie Hall for a performance of major historical significance that took her career over an important threshold to the next stage of its development.

By September 1950, with the assistance of the Concert and Placement Bureau of the Conservatory, she had already booked a tour of western Canada for the following January, with stops, for both solo recitals and orchestral appearances, in Regina, Calgary, Edmonton, Vancouver, and Victoria. She promptly followed those up with a Canadian maritime tour in November 1951, and a second western tour in January 1952. Although such touring is relatively common now, in Lois's day it was no easy matter for an emerging Canadian artist to get domestic tours of this nature. In the absence of a national strategy for promoting Canadian artists, American promoters controlled access to most of the Canadian market.

In the early 1950s, Community Concert Associations had a virtual stranglehold on concert tour bookings to medium-sized Canadian centres. The Community Concert movement had originated in the United States, where it practically and efficiently organized musical enthusiasts into local associations. These associations pre-sold concert series in their own communities and co-operated with associations in other towns to offer group bookings, organized in a logical sequence, to individual artists. Such group bookings cut down on artists' travel costs, provided them with attractive multiple bookings, and thus made available to medium-sized centres, visiting performers of a quality they could not otherwise afford, or hope to attract. The movement's success soon caught the attention of Columbia Artists Management, the huge New York-based booking agency, which created a subsidiary company, Community Concerts, Inc., to work with local associations in promoting its artists for national tours. Canadian Associations began in 1930. Though the goals in Canada remained the same, and the organization did bring famous international artists to Canadian towns, the link to a large American concert promoter skewed the choice. In Canada, as in the U.S., Columbia's roster of artists received the heaviest promotion for Community Concerts bookings. Because very few Canadian artists made it onto Columbia's books, very few Canadian artists appeared in Community Concerts in Canada. The extent of the booking agencies' control can be judged from the 1955 official complaint by the United States government, under anti-trust legislation, against Columbia Artists and its nearest competitor, National Concerts and Artists Corporation. The complaint alleged that these two booking agencies had, through the Community Concerts organizations they controlled, divided the American territory between them and compelled their local concert organizations to book only the artists they represented, thereby limiting choice and excluding independent artists from potential engagements. The courts upheld the complaint, and ruled against Columbia Artists and National Concerts and Artists Corporation. In the same year, Community Concerts of Canada, Ltd., a subsidiary of the American parent company, was formed. Until that judgement the Canadian Community Concerts circuit was an exclusive club, to which Canadian artists, by and large, need not apply.

The Concert and Placement Bureau of the Conservatory played David to this American Goliath, and helped its senior students and graduates to buck the trend. Under the direction of Anna McCoy, who headed it from its inception in 1946 until 1952 when Ezra Schabas took it over, the Bureau found the chinks in Community Concerts' armour. As Schabas described it, the Concert and Placement Bureau booked Conservatory students first for small local engagements. Many of Lois's dinner meeting and business club gigs of the late forties probably came through the Bureau, as did her appearances at the Canadian National Exhibition and her student recitals at the Art Gallery of Ontario. Then, in the name of cultural nationalism, the Bureau approached small centres not yet organized by Community Concerts, but with an appetite for good music nonetheless. Gradually, it began to find engagements for the aspiring musicians, like Lois, passing through the Conservatory's halls.

The Conservatory's motives in establishing the Bureau were not solely altruistic. As its work prospered, the Bureau began charging a 10 percent commission on its fees to accustom young professionals to the realities of their chosen careers, but also, as Schabas points out, to help fund the salary of the Bureau's director. The Conservatory had its own interests to promote. With a nationwide system of examination centres, boards of examiners, and music examinations for which it charged a fee, the Conservatory stood to solidify its reputation as a national standard-bearer in music education by promoting its graduates to a national audience. The bulk of the Conservatory's large network of examination centres was in Ontario, but it also spread westward to British Columbia.

An artist of Lois's calibre and popularity, prominently billed as the Conservatory's top graduate, could only increase the Conservatory's prestige as a national music educator and attract more young students as paying customers.

As she built her Canadian audience, Lois also defined her musical personality. In these early solo recitals, she established the broad outlines of the repertoire she would favour throughout her career: early English songs (with a strong preference for Purcell); German Lieder, including the songs of Mahler, who had not yet gained the general popularity he enjoys today; arias by Bach, Handel, and Mozart; occasionally some French art songs; one or two operatic arias for effect (she liked dramatic Verdi selections, like "Pace, pace mio dio" from *Il Trovatore*, or romantic Puccini, but included coloratura dazzlers like "Una voce poco fà" from Rossini's *The Barber of Seville*, the "Jewel Song" from Gounod's *Faust*, and, on occasion, Adele's "Laughing Song" from Strauss's *Die Fledermaus*); Manuel de Falla's "Seven Popular Spanish Songs," for which she gained a considerable reputation; sometimes a group of songs by contemporary Canadian and American composers; and always, a selection of British folk songs, often in the traditional arrangements by Marjorie Kennedy-Fraser but also in the (then) avant-garde treatments by Benjamin Britten. Most recitals included a solo piano selection by Weldon, who travelled as her accompanist. Together, they adhered to the standard principles of programming for the time — show off the singer's versatility and range, vary the mood during the course of the evening, cover a variety of historical periods and styles, and make sure to include a guaranteed showstopper or two. Programs devoted to a single theme, period, or composer had not yet gained the popularity they have today, and the closest that classical artists came to crossover was with folk songs in concert hall arrangements or perhaps a sentimental ballad. For orchestral concerts, Lois enjoyed performing her operatic selections with full orchestral accompaniment. During this early period of her career, she also made a specialty of the Mozart motet for solo soprano and orchestra, *Exsultate, Jubilate*, with its extreme vocal demands of wide range and the rapid-fire coloratura precision of its concluding "Alleluia." And she began the steady succession of engagements with orchestras and choral societies across the country as soprano soloist in the standard oratorio repertoire, performing the works of Bach, Handel, Haydn, and Mendelssohn. Vocally, none of this posed a problem for Lois, who even in the early stages of her career sang fearlessly in public over a range of two and a half octaves, from the A below middle C of Brahms' *Vier Ernste Gesänge* to an E-flat above high C in the Queen of the Night's arias from Mozart's *The Magic Flute*.

Clearly, Lois was a traditionalist, a conservative artist more at home in the standard repertoire than at the cutting edge of experimental contemporary composition. (Her friend and colleague, Mary Morrison, would be the one to carve out a career for herself as a champion of new music.) But if she was a conservative in her tastes, she was nevertheless a reckless adventurer in the demands she regularly placed on her artistry, her stamina, and her vocal resources. In these early days of her career, Lois performed with abandon, like a high wire artist without a safety net. Her programs, which would have taxed the abilities of any two of her contemporaries, dazzled audiences and left them cheering. For starters, she had something few sopranos had or dared to use — a strong, sexy, lower register, which she exploited shamelessly for its dramatic effect and sheer shock value. With it came a range of passion and sensuality that no one expected from a well-mannered concert soprano. Lois delighted in playing against type, and did it most frequently by including the Falla songs on her programs, which she performed with a gutsy contralto sound and a raw passion that hinted at, but never quite allowed, a dangerous loss of control. When the same program included the meditative tranquility of Bach and the stratospheric pyrotechnics of the Mozart "Alleluia," the emotional range, for both singer and audience, stretched almost to the breaking point.

A singer's vocal stamina is directly affected by the emotional pressures she places on it during performance. Lois never hesitated to push herself towards the precipice in that respect. Nor would she ever cheat by hiding behind technical display in order to lessen the emotional strain of performance. Weldon had worked with Lois as a student to harness the visible emotion of her stage presence, but never to eliminate it. Her audiences on these early tours responded, not only to a singer of technical versatility and accomplishment, but to an artist of emotional honesty and integrity. Singers have compared this aspect of their art to stripping themselves naked before an audience. Lois, who guarded her privacy fiercely and shunned the spotlight when she was offstage, never shied away from the public vulnerability and exposure which her artistic honesty required of her onstage.

Lois, with Weldon at the piano, in a 1948 student recital in the Concert Hall of the Royal Conservatory at College and University Avenue. Note the rapt and awkward intensity of her youthful platform manner.

Credit: Courtesy of University of Toronto Archives and Records Management Service.

An account of her appearance at the Moncton High School Auditorium in November 1951 provides a glimpse of this Lois in performance, and of her audience's response. Under the heading, "Young Soprano Charming in Stirring Performance," the reviewer notes:

> The singer had a habit of holding her arms firmly in front of her, giving the impression of a sort of restrained emotional intensity, in some selections more than in others. She also had a habit of closing her eyes and tilting her head skyward, especially in passages of great feeling. To the audience, her strong, clear voice seemed to take on added stature through this mannerism.

When she appeared on a Vancouver Symphony Pops Concert in January 1951, with Nicholas Goldschmidt conducting (Mozart's *Exsultate, Jubilate* followed by "Abscheulicher! Wo eilst du hin?" from *Fidelio*), the audience applauded her so long and so enthusiastically that it threw off the timing of the broadcast portion of the concert. A few years later, in 1956, Roy Maley, critic for the *Winnipeg Tribune* and loyal Marshall supporter, wrote: "Miss Marshall showed astonishing bravura and capacity to make the most florid vocal ornamentation of emotional significance." And, in a personal letter to Lois written in 1970, recalling Puccini's "Sola, perduta, abbandonata," which she had performed from the very outset of her career, Maley said simply, "I repeat *ad infinitum* this was the most soul-searing performance of an aria I ever 'endured.'"

All this touring came at the expense of the rigours of cross-country travel in the early fifties. A writer for the *Brandon Daily Sun* provides a glimpse of the travelling Lois most concert audiences never knew. "That same winter we saw her on a westbound train, probably between Swift Current and Medicine Hat. The day coach was chilly. She sat, a small, rigid figure, bundled in coat and overboots, radiating misery."

But at home, in between tours, she didn't exactly take it easy. Lois combined those early years of touring with a steady string of Toronto engagements, both large and small: church and radio work (she was still doing weddings at Bloor Street United and at Holy Name as late as 1953); benefit appearances; more of the dreaded dinner and service club engagements; performances of Handel's *Messiah* with Sir Ernest, the Toronto Symphony Orchestra, and the Mendelssohn Choir; more *St. Matthew Passion*s; and in November 1951, a trip to Detroit, as guest artist with the Toronto Symphony Orchestra, where she performed "Pastorale for Voice and Orchestra," Sir Ernest's, and Lois's, gesture towards contemporary composition. Hardly cutting-edge, even in its own day, "Pastorale," by Herbert Elwell, a Cleveland musician and music critic, was a setting of words from the "Song of Songs." John Beckwith, reviewing Lois's last performance of the work in 1962, lampooned its feeble attempt at exoticism by invoking the name of Canada's most vit-riolic critic of stuffiness and sexual repression: "The mixture of near-east-ern voluptuousness (once removed) with Anglo-Saxon fustian would require an Irving Layton to do it justice." But in 1951 it had novelty, if nothing else, to recommend it, and a grateful Herbert Elwell presented Lois with an inscribed copy of the score after the performance in Detroit. Lois did well to build her stamina with all this variety of work. The first months of 1952 would challenge it to the utmost.

In February 1952, the dream that Lois had cherished since *Princess Ida* finally came true, after a fashion. She got her chance to appear in a fully staged opera. The third annual Opera Festival, featuring the Royal Conservatory Opera Company, programmed Mozart's *The Magic Flute* in its repertory at Toronto's Royal Alexandra Theatre. These Opera Festivals, an offshoot of the Conservatory's Opera School, were the brainchild of Nicholas Goldschmidt, music director, and Herman Geiger-Torel, stage director. The Canadian Opera Company eventually emerged from them. With tie-ins to CBC broadcasts, touring, and, occasionally, appearances at Toronto Symphony Orchestra subscription concerts, the productions of the Festivals generated huge excitement. Their participants, all the aspiring operatic stars of the Conservatory Opera School, were breaking ground for a new and promising venture in the arts. Having been denied access to the Opera School itself, Lois now took to the stage in a spectacular but thankless role, arguably the most glorified walk-on in opera.

Aside from participating in the closing ensemble, the Queen of the Night makes only two brief appearances in *The Magic Flute*. But on those occasions, without warm-up or preparation, she launches into two of the most fiendish arias in the repertoire, endurance tests of coloratura singing that call for a series of high Fs, probably the highest note a soprano is asked to produce in public. She comes on (or, more frequently, is revealed), does her bit, and disappears. The rest of her evening she spends waiting around backstage. This combination of boredom and flat out terrifying singing has made the role one of the least sought-after among operatic stars. Goldschmidt and Geiger-Torel were aware of Lois's coloratura abilities — and her limp. Because the part could be staged with a minimum of movement, they offered her

Queen of the Night. As far as operatic roles were concerned it looked like that or nothing, so Lois took it.

She had distinguished colleagues. Mary Morrison sang Pamina, Joanne Ivey the Third Spirit, Donald Garrard the Priest, and in the chorus were Bernard Turgeon, Patricia Rideout, and James Milligan. Milligan, after an auspicious Bayreuth debut, was headed for international stardom when he died suddenly of a heart attack in 1961, only thirty-three years old. All of them achieved prominence as professionals on the Canadian and international music scenes in the years to come. Their names give some indication of the quality and energy percolating through the Opera School at the time. For her three years in the Senior School, Lois had been a bystander to the operatic opportunities that these singers enjoyed. Now she finally got to be a part of it.

She seems to have had a mixed success. Joanne Ivey recalled that the production took the opera's many scene changes literally, and seemed to spend more time shifting sets than singing Mozart. Photographs

Lois in costume as the Queen of the Night, in the Opera Festival production of Mozart's The Magic Flute *at Toronto's Royal Alexandra Theatre, February 1952.*

Credit: Ken Bell/ GetStock.com, courtesy of Mary Lea Bell.

show a sombre Lois in an elaborate headdress and heavy necklace, with a robe that dwarfs her small frame and makes her look more like a tarted up church chorister than the embodiment of evil. Pearl McCarthy, reviewing for the *Globe and Mail*, liked the production on the whole, and said that "Lois Marshall achieved heroic brilliance as the Queen of the Night, although with slightly strained quality of voice now and again." Hugh Thomson, in the *Star*, was more positive, but hardly any more detailed. "Lois Marshall was Queen of the Night with its music of Italian coloratura and one prescribed high F. And what a hit she made!" (Did Thomson file his review at intermission? The second-act aria contains four more high Fs.) The reviewers and the public did not realize that the part had been transposed down a tone for Lois, so that she sang high E flats instead of the prescribed high Fs. Mary Morrison, from her vantage point as Pamina, recognized Lois's performance as "a great, great occasion," even with this accommodation. "I think we were all very much aware of having this person up there, wailing away in those damned arias, and it made the rest of us very aware of what we had to live up to." Even for her professional colleagues, Lois set the standard.

She seldom talked about her experience with the Queen of the Night. In 1957 she told Day Thorpe, critic for the *Washington Sunday Star*, that she didn't want to sing the role again, because she didn't think her high F was dependable. She later turned down an offer to perform the role at the Glyndebourne Festival in England. The Queen of the Night led to no other Canadian operatic roles. By that time, of course, Lois had none of the stage training given to her peers at the Opera School, so she was starting at a disadvantage, but it was likely her mobility impairment that discouraged opera directors from casting her. Such hesitancy showed a startling lack of imagination. In 1942, Marjorie Lawrence, one of the Metropolitan Opera's Wagnerian sopranos (she created a sensation in her youth by leaping astride Brünnhilde's horse and actually riding it into Siegfried's flaming funeral pyre in *Götterdämmerung*) made a highly-publicized comeback after polio in a production of *Tannhäuser*, staged so that she could perform sitting down. Her story became the basis of the sentimental 1955 movie of her life, *Interrupted Melody*. Lois didn't need accommodation on that scale; Canadian opera producers simply missed the boat.

Lois, on the other hand, did not. After back-to-back performances of *The Magic Flute*, on February 22 and 23, she went to Winnipeg for her debut with the Winnipeg Symphony on February 28. Patricia Snell, with whom she shared the role, took over as Queen of the Night. In Winnipeg she performed a demanding program, perhaps even a vocally foolhardy one, because of the extremes of dramatic and coloratura singing it required: Mozart's *Exsultate, Jubilate* and a string of operatic arias — "Dich theure Halle" (Wagner), "Pace, pace, mio dio" (Verdi), and "Leise, leise" (Weber). They loved her so much in Winnipeg that they promptly booked a return engagement for the following October. All of this activity, however, paled in comparison to another project she was undertaking at the same time. Even as she was travelling back and forth between Toronto and Winnipeg, Lois was deep in preparations for the competition sponsored by the Walter W. Naumburg Foundation in New York, the most important opportunity of her career to date.

Walter Naumburg had created this competition, still administered today by the foundation that bears his name, in 1926. The prize, intended to promote artists on the verge of a major career, was a fully-sponsored New York recital debut at Town Hall, then one of the most prestigious concert venues in the city. Lois might not have ventured into these international waters, had it not been for personal encouragement from a major international musical celebrity, Edward Johnson. Born in Guelph, Johnson had sung in Europe (as Edoardo Di Giovanni) and the United States, most notably at the Metropolitan Opera House, where he was one of its most popular tenors from 1922 to 1935. On his retirement from singing in that year, he took over the management of the Metropolitan Opera Company for the next fifteen. He had been appointed Chairman of the Board of the Toronto Conservatory in 1947. When he retired completely from the Met in 1950, he returned to Canada and involved himself actively in the work of the Conservatory and the concerns of its students. The Edward Johnson Building of the University of Toronto's Faculty of Music is named in his honour. With his background as one of the most powerful musical administrators in North America, Johnson knew how important the Naumburg Award could be to an artist like Lois. He also believed it had a particular advantage for her; the Naumburg was not restricted to singers. (The violinist Betty-Jean Hagen was the only other Canadian to have won the competition to this point.) Unlike strictly vocal competitions, it stressed concert and recital repertoire rather than opera. However much Lois may have resented being reminded of such considerations, Johnson's logic was clear: the jurors of the Naumburg would be less likely to view her disability as an impediment to her future career choice than the jurors of a strictly operatic competition. On Johnson's recommendation, and with Weldon's support, Lois entered the competition.

Its requirements were gruelling. She had to prepare and submit two complete recital programs, some forty different numbers in all. If she made it beyond the first round, in which she could make her own choices from the list, she had to be ready to sing any of her prepared repertoire on demand. The Naumburg took place in New York, a city Lois had never visited, and the field was daunting. George Kidd, the music columnist for the *Toronto Telegram* and a faithful supporter of Lois's career, quoted Anna Molyneaux, the business manager of the Naumburg Foundation, on the level of competition in Lois's year. "There were 125 competitors this year. They played almost every instrument. There were 44 vocalists and they were all good, but Miss Marshall looked like a sure winner from the beginning. Of 17 finalists she was first." To get to the finals, she had to commit to the suspense of three rounds of competition before the final announcement. And to preserve standards, the jury reserved the right to withhold the award, if, in its judgement, none of the competitors proved worthy. "Singing Stars" began to look like a Sunday school picnic by comparison.

In between her busy round of regular engagements, Lois subjected herself to a gruelling regimen of preparations. Not content to recycle her existing repertoire, she included a substantial selection of new pieces. That meant extra work to achieve command of the nuances of feeling and interpretation that normally build gradually through repeated performances. "Weldon and I lived, breathed, ate and slept with that mountain of songs. He found time every day to rehearse with me." Their personal relationship deepened with the intensity and intimacy of this collaboration. As she put it herself many years later: "He was an inspiration and a tower of strength. Whatever desolation came about in our later lives, nothing can obliterate the times we shared in those incredible early days when everything was new and exciting."

In March 1952, they made their way to New York for the competition. As Lois recalled, "It was our first ever time there and it was not love at first sight. We were shocked by the blatant rudeness. We had never encountered anything like it. We often became irritated when we were barked at for not having correct change ready, and failure to call your deli order in rapid-fire staccato could result in having hot coffee poured over your head." But gradually they got used to it, and got down to business. The competition format, in Town Hall, was impersonal and intimidating. Competitors drew lots for their order of performing, waited outside the hall until called upon, and then left without knowing any results. For the first round, Lois and Weldon hadn't booked a studio for warm-up. Lois thought she was off her form and that she sang badly. After their turn they didn't loiter, but went directly to their hotel and waited until Weldon could make the telephone call to the Foundation to find out the results. Lois was despondent, sure that she had been eliminated.

But she was wrong. She had passed the first elimination round, and was on her way to the semifinals on March 20. This time, Lois and Weldon booked a studio in the Steinway Building on West 57th Street and did a thorough warm-up. Lois felt in top form and, although she still avoided hearing any of the competition, she felt quite confident of the results. When Weldon phoned and got the good news that Lois had survived to the finals, they finally allowed themselves to hope that she might actually win.

The first two rounds had been judged by singers or professionals closely connected with vocal music. The seventeen finalists would be judged by an interdisciplinary panel — keyboard, strings, wind, and voice. The news that Edward Johnson would be one of the jurors did little to put Lois's mind at ease, and his behaviour during her performance was downright distressing. After every number, Johnson sauntered down the aisle to the Town Hall stage, beckoned to Lois, and, when she bent down towards him, urged her, *sotto voce*, "Don't be nervous. Just relax!" Lois, who had thought she was doing fine, began to doubt the impression she was making. But with Weldon's reassurance she stopped trying to second-guess Johnson's behaviour and she and Weldon returned to their hotel. Once again, they waited fretfully to make the phone call. Finally, when Weldon went to his room to place the call, Lois, unable to stand the pressure, bolted and went for a walk. Only a dumbfounded cleaner, tidying Lois's room, was on hand to welcome Weldon when he burst in without knocking, shouting, "Darling, we've won!"

"We've won. Put out the banners, Lois," read her telegram home, announcing that she had won the vocal division of the three-part competition. However, everything was dark when she arrived at Toronto's

Lois en route to New York for her Town Hall debut, December 1952.

*Credit: Image by Paul Rockett (1952), courtesy of Elliott Contemporary, Toronto.
From the collection of Cindy Townsend.*

Malton airport in the middle of the night. "I wanted to go right over and give her a big hug," her mother told the newspapers. "I could hardly wait to see her, but, of course, I knew she was too tired, so I waited." The celebrations had to come later, although Lois did make a point of phoning her brother, Fred, in Boston, with the good news. Not that there was much time for celebration. Lois may have had to cancel the *St. Matthew Passion* she had been scheduled to do in Kitchener with Jon Vickers and James Milligan on April 1, but she was heading for Hamilton to do *Elijah* in a few days, and the Toronto *St. Matthew* was coming up in just over a week. Her New York victory made the front pages of all the Toronto papers, and was soon carried by virtually every paper in the country, but the demands of the professional singer did not go on hold.

Winning the Naumburg gave Lois a chance at an international career, but no guarantee of one. Everything depended on the New York debut provided by the award, and the all-important critical notices Lois would receive for it. After a summer of local engagements and her second western tour in the fall, Lois and Weldon headed back to New York, and to Town Hall, for Lois's official New York debut — Tuesday December 2, 1952, at three o'clock in the afternoon. A snowy day, as it turned out, and hardly a time to guarantee an audience of any kind. June Callwood gave a graphic backstage account of the event in a feature article she prepared for *Maclean's Magazine*. Even though two thousand free tickets had been distributed by the Naumburg Foundation:

> ... there was no chance at all of getting a good audience. "She's got two strikes against her," [Mrs. Anna Molyneaux, motherly manager of the Naumburg Foundation,] explained, whispering so that Lois, leaning exhaustedly against the stage piano, could not hear. "She's Canadian and she isn't known. The house will be awful."

Walter Naumburg remarked to his wife just before the concert started: "You know, there'll be no one here at all.

"Why?" she asked.

"Well, she's Canadian and it's snowing."

Weldon helps Lois disembark from the flight in New York.

Credit: Image by Paul Rockett (1952), courtesy of Elliott Contemporary, Toronto.
From the collection of Cindy Townsend.

But Mrs. Molyneaux and the Naumburg organization knew this debut wasn't about audience, it was about critics, and it would have been foolhardy to compete for the critics' attention in the evening, given the full slate of recitals and concerts by established artists requiring their services. Their strategy worked. Critics from the *New York Times*, the *New York Herald Tribune*, and the journal *Musical America*, along with scouts from Columbia Artists Management had been lined up. The strenuous efforts at papering the house had yielded an audience of between

In a New York hotel room, Weldon gives Lois some last-minute coaching before the recital.

Credit: Image by Paul Rockett (1952), courtesy of Elliott Contemporary, Toronto.
From the collection of Cindy Townsend.

350 and 500 souls (estimates varied), leaving only about 1,200 empty seats in the house. As stipulated by the Naumburg Foundation, Lois herself received the total box office receipts — thirty-seven dollars and fifty cents. No matter. On this occasion, Lois sang for her future and, as always, for her art.

Her program began and ended with fairly standard, sedate repertoire choices: a group of Elizabethan and early English songs, followed by three of Schubert's Lieder to open, three songs by Samuel Barber to close and to fulfill the Naumburg stipulation that an American composer be included. But what happened just before and after the intermission must have blown the roof off the hall.

She concluded her first half with two demanding, contrasting arias from Mozart's *Mass in C Minor*, "Laudamus te" and "Et incarnatus est," the second of which she had used in her Eaton Auditorium debut. Peggy Glanville-Hicks, the Australian-born composer and eminent music critic for the *New York Herald Tribune*, greeted them ecstatically. The Mozart arias, she said, "Were the final proof — if any were needed — that there is simply nothing this singer cannot do with ease, with insight and with the eloquence of the great artist." But more proof was forthcoming. Lois opened the second half of her program with Puccini's heroic "In questa reggia," the steely-voiced aria in which Princess Turandot declaims, at the upper extremities of her register, the grisly story behind the test of the three riddles she has interposed between herself and any prospective suitor. Glanville-Hicks said that here, her dramatic gift "blossomed and glowed to hugeness … and the continuous flow of indescribably lovely and accurate tone carried this melodic music to the heights that only a great voice can carry it." Lois then plunged into contralto depths with her party trick, Falla's "Seven Popular Spanish Songs." According to the critic for *Musical America*, "the emotional fire and vocal sensuousness she brought to these songs were stunning."

Like his colleagues, John Briggs, writing for the *New York Times*, appreciated the vocal acrobatics, but singled out for special praise the control and technique Lois exhibited when singing more intimately. "A scale, so simple-appearing on paper, in practice seems to be very difficult to execute, and it was a delight to hear Miss Marshall perform the opening phrase of 'have you seen but a whyte lillie grow?' [which concludes on a simple ascending scale] with absolute evenness and without distorting the vowel." The vocal pedagogue in Weldon Kilburn must have glowed to read that praise.

Lois glowed too, even though the major reviews were not without their criticisms. Glanville-Hicks failed to fall under Lois's spell in the Falla songs because, prophetically, she found fault with Weldon's accompaniment, and *Musical America* struck a generally more reserved tone than the other two. But the reviews were unquestionably positive and provided Lois with hyperbolic extracts she could use in her publicity, and use honestly, for years to come. "One of the most superb singers this reviewer [Glanville-Hicks] has ever heard."

Her technique was like that of "Emmy Destinn and other artists of the 'Golden Age,'" wrote Briggs, comparing her favourably to some of the greatest singers of the past.

Even *Musical America* said her voice was "a surprise and delight to the ears." Only two comments really rankled. The one about Weldon's playing would have upset Lois, who, throughout her life, believed that the critics' focus on his technical shortcomings blinded them to the significance of his artistic contribution to their genuinely collaborative achievement. And why did John Briggs have to preface his praise with this comment, however well-meant?

> What made a distinguished recital even more remarkable was the fact that Miss Marshall's achievements as a singer have come about after she had been partly crippled by polio.
>
> The fact that Miss Marshall moves on the stage with difficulty may hamper her in opera. This is not true in recital, however; her splendid voice and the uncommon skill with which she uses it are all she needs.

To minimize the disparity between their gaits, she and Weldon had practised carefully to synchronize the timing of all their entrances and exits, but apparently it hadn't worked. For readers of Briggs' influential review, knowledge of her disability would now precede her as she developed new audiences. It galled Lois that something she considered inessential to her art should be given such prominence. And the assumption about her unsuitability for opera rubbed salt into an old wound — though not enough to stifle her celebration. Lois enjoyed the flowers in her dressing room and the cables of good wishes from home, from her friends Sir Ernest and Lady MacMillan, from her beloved Emmy Heim, and even from her cat, Noni. That night, she dressed up in a blue gown and went out on the town, to have a bang-up dinner at a restaurant and hear the great Edith Piaf in cabaret.

Lois's New York triumph (it was not too strong a word) unleashed another torrent of publicity in Toronto and the Canadian press, publicity tinged with a charming brand of hometown pride. The *Toronto Telegram* published a full page spread on the day of the recital, featuring domestic photos of Lois's mother helping her daughter pack, and of Lois's four-year-old nephew kissing his aunt goodbye, as well as Lois's comment that her busy career was cutting into her time for favourite activities, such as bowling. On her return, the Toronto Board of Education honoured "the most illustrious graduate of Toronto's school for crippled children" with flowers, a gift, and the creation of two bursaries, the Lois Marshall Bursaries, to help other children at the school. Lois's aversion to the critics' and publicists' attempts to highlight her disability did nothing to interfere with her acknowledgement of the school that had been so important in her development. She smiled broadly for the press photo with Elsie Hutchinson, her old music teacher, and must have been especially touched when Jean Hampson, the physiotherapist and teacher who had done so much to strengthen Lois's fierce childhood sense of independence, rose to speak. Now that Lois had made a name for herself, she was pleased to lend it to the cause of children with disabilities. Later in her career she expressed regret that she wasn't asked to do so more frequently. In April 1953, she and Weldon appeared in recital jointly with the young Mario Bernardi, performing as a solo pianist before his illustrious career as a conductor, in a concert sponsored by the Canadian Physiotherapy Association to raise funds for the battle against polio. In May 1953, the Council of Women of Toronto organized a gala recital at Eaton Auditorium, in which Lois repeated her Town Hall program for the fans at home. Seldom have the Canadian press and Canadian public delighted more visibly in the success of one of their own.

Lois wasn't in the habit of sticking around to network and make connections. She left New York immediately after the Naumburg recital, before the scouts from the booking agencies could find her and pin her down to a contract. So it wasn't until a few days after her return from New York, when she was in Ottawa preparing for *Messiah* with the Ottawa Choral Union, that Columbia Artists Management

Lois and Weldon examine her first contract from Columbia Artists Management, with Arthur Judson and William Judd looking on.

Credit: Image by Paul Rockett (1952), courtesy of Elliott Contemporary, Toronto.
From the collection of Cindy Townsend.

tracked her down. Lois sang her *Messiah*s in Ottawa and in Toronto, then flew to New York, where, in mid-December, she signed a three-year contract with Columbia, from June 1, 1953 to May 31, 1956. Her initial fee was $1,000 per performance ($750 for Community Concerts engagements). Even after her commission to the agency (10 to 20 percent, depending on the nature of the engagement), this was a huge leap in earning capacity for Lois. During the 1952–53 season she was getting just $250 to $375 per concert. That season, through the Concert and Placement Bureau of the Royal Conservatory, she had earned a total of $6,675, twice as much as her closest competitors, James Milligan and Jon Vickers. Columbia would remain her managers until 1973.

Signing with Columbia gave Lois insider access to the all-important Community Concerts circuit, which, if managed wisely, could be the bread and butter of a professional career. But it could also be a dead end if Columbia used you as cannon fodder in the hinterlands and never gave you a chance at major engagements. Lois was spared that fate because of the prejudice of the time against her disability. In her *Maclean's* article, June Callwood called a spade a spade.

> Her marvellous voice had already been scouted thoroughly but her heavy limp ... had sent agents away without offering her a contract.
>
> However heartless this may seem their decision was made on a sound business basis. New artists signed by such a colossus as Columbia Artists Management Inc. are sent to small towns who have signed up for a community concert series. Such communities have slender budgets and can afford only the lower-priced performers on Columbia's lists, the unknowns. Columbia is convinced that these relatively unsophisticated audiences rarely appreciate the fine difference between a good singer and a great one — it was felt they would be untouched by Lois Marshall's magnificent voice and dismayed by her limp.

The Town Hall recital, however, changed all that. June Callwood's article picks up the story again.

> The scouts from Columbia Artists Management Inc. decided the night of the concert to reconsider their stand. Her voice had been even more impressive in New York than it had been in Toronto and William Judd, a Columbia vice-president who hadn't seen Lois before,

observed that her limp hadn't been as distracting as he had expected.

Arthur Judson, honorary president of Columbia Artists Management, a founder and stockholder of CBS radio network and a former manager of both the New York Philharmonic and the Philadelphia Orchestra during the Stokowski regime, decided to take on Lois' career himself. Nothing greater could have happened to Lois, because Judson's recommendation on an artist is accepted without question anywhere in the world. Countless fine musicians of international fame have pined in vain for his sponsorship.

To circumvent the problem posed by Lois' disability Judson decided to reverse the success formula of his organization and start Lois at the top, with guest appearances with the major symphony orchestras and choral groups and radio and television appearances. When her reputation was firmly grounded she could safely tour the sticks without confusing her audiences.

So, Lois actually got the kind of attention and promotion her musical abilities deserved for all the wrong reasons. Without Callwood's contemporary account, this important testimony to the kind of barriers Lois faced would have disappeared completely from the record. So great were Lois's sensitivities on the subject, however, that she reacted against Callwood's important article. Her frosty response moderated in the 1990s, when Lois became one of the *National Treasures* profiled in Callwood's influential series for Vision TV.

Immediately after her Town Hall debut, Lois did a run-out to Edmonton between Christmas and New Year's (Mozart, Verdi, and Puccini arias with the Edmonton Symphony), where the local papers published a post-performance picture of her without Weldon, but with Weldon's mother, Hilda Kilburn, who lived in Edmonton. Two days later she was back in Toronto for another *Messiah*, and by the end of January she and Weldon had embarked on a two week whistle stop tour of the Maritimes. Their schedule entailed early-morning departures ("Leave Charlottetown January 28, 5:30 a.m." read the itinerary provided by the Royal Conservatory Concert and Placement Bureau), frequent plane changes, travel by snowmobile in Newfoundland, between Stephenville and Cornerbrook, and provision for an alternate concert date in Cornerbrook, in case the snowmobile didn't work out. They did concerts in Charlottetown, Sydney, Cornerbrook, St. John's (two concerts there), Moncton (having passed through it twice already, but just to make connections), and Saint John. Given winter conditions in the Maritimes, the travel logistics alone were exhausting.

On the evening of February 5, 1953, Lois was scheduled to sing a concert in Moncton, then fly to Saint John, New Brunswick, the next day, where she had a three day break before her final concert of the tour. A few minutes before the Moncton recital, Lois received a phone call from Nora Shea, Arthur Judson's secretary. True to his plans for launching Lois at the top, Judson had arranged for her to audition for Arturo Toscanini, who was looking for a soprano soloist for his upcoming benefit concert, radio broadcast, and recording of Beethoven's *Missa Solemnis* at Carnegie Hall. The great Italian maestro, almost eighty-six years old at the time, was legendary for his direct links to the world of late nineteenth-century Italian opera, his temperament, and his demanding musical standards. He was also, by that time, a household name in North America, thanks to his frequent radio broadcasts with the NBC Symphony Orchestra. Beethoven's *Missa* was legendary as one of the monuments of Western classical music, and notorious for the impossible difficulty of its soprano part, which Beethoven composed apparently without reference to the capabilities of the human voice. For a young singer like Lois, even with Town Hall behind her, it was a double whammy — a reputedly difficult conductor and an unquestionably difficult work. And Toscanini wanted to hear her, in New York, on the 10th. She would have to cancel the Saint John recital to make it in time.

It took a lot to faze Lois and Weldon. Immediately after this bombshell had dropped, Lois went on in Moncton, unperturbed. Then, with remarkable aplomb, she and Weldon informed Columbia that they couldn't make the proposed audition date, and asked for a postponement so they could fulfill their engagement in Saint John as promised. The staff at Columbia gulped and made the arrangements. Lois and Weldon scurried around Saint John, getting their hands on a vocal score of the *Missa*, and set about learning the work. Once again, as with her *St. Matthew* audition, Lois had no prior knowledge of the part. The three day break in her schedule turned into three days of intense preparation.

On February 11, Lois and Weldon presented themselves as requested at the small recital hall in Carnegie Hall, exhausted from the Maritime tour and strung out with anxiety at the prospect of the audition. It was a relief to find the auditorium itself in total darkness, with only a handful of people visible and Toscanini himself undiscernible in the back row, but Lois missed the responsive warmth of an audience, and found the acoustics of the hall dry and difficult to cope with. Toscanini did not ask to hear any of the *Missa*. Instead, he asked for the two contrasting Mozart arias she had sung at her Town Hall debut. After the mezzo-ish "Laudamus te," Lois heard a call of "brava!" from the back row. After the "Et incarnatus est" it was "bravissima!" After that, it was over. Weldon and Lois left the stage. When, after a few minutes, no one came to give them the verdict, they left the theatre, picked up their luggage at their hotel and went to the airport to catch the first flight home. Lois assumed, since no one had come to find them backstage, that the audition had been unsuccessful. She didn't even care very much. She was just happy to be on her way home at last, after the long tour and the gruelling audition experience. On her arrival at home, a cable was waiting for her.

> Congratulations. You are engaged by Arturo Toscanini to perform in Carnegie Hall performance Beethoven Missa Solemnis, March 28 1953. Also R.C.A. Victor recording to follow. Love, Nora Shea.

Toscanini's broadcasts were heard throughout the United States and Canada, their audience estimated in the millions; R.C.A. Victor was a major recording company; the historical significance of both the performance and the recording (it turned out to be Toscanini's last performance of the work and, for many years, the only recording of it by him available to the public) guaranteed that it would remain in the catalogues virtually indefinitely; the "Brava! Bravissima!" story, which Columbia's press office seized on immediately, would sell Lois to concert promoters and symphony orchestra managers large and small. Even though, at eighty-six, Toscanini's powers were waning, the value of his *imprimatur* simply could not be overestimated. The Toscanini engagement offered Lois the opportunity of a lifetime. She responded, as usual, by working like hell.

Between the audition and the performance of the *Missa*, Lois had various local engagements to fulfill, including two *St. Matthew Passion*s, one at Bloor Street United, the other at Massey Hall, with Sir Ernest and the Mendelssohn Choir, as well as a recital in Barrie, Ontario. She honoured all of these engagements, instead of cancelling to concentrate on preparations for her big break. In whatever time remained, she and Weldon studied the Beethoven score. Years later, Weldon still took pride in the fact that Toscanini had made no major corrections, asked for no major changes to the interpretation he and Lois worked out on their own. Their self-assurance in this regard was remarkable. Any other professional, given this kind of challenge, would have sought out expert guidance from a battery of coaches with extensive experience of the work and of Toscanini's approach to it. Lois and Weldon just did it on their own, confident that hard work, musical intelligence, and meticulous attention to the score would carry them through. They were like a mom-and-pop operation, calmly conducting business as usual, unintimidated by the exalted professional circumstances in which they suddenly found themselves. Lois, as was her habit, committed her part to memory.

Perhaps Lois had a death wish or, more charitably, her sense of loyalty outweighed her common sense. Toscanini's first full orchestral rehearsal began on Thursday, March 26, at 1:30 p.m. sharp on the Carnegie Hall stage. Strict professional protocol dictated that all musicians, chorus, orchestra, and soloists had to be in their places, composed and ready for the downbeat at the appointed time. Lois nevertheless chose to keep her commitment to Sir Ernest and sing the *St. Matthew* in Toronto on the preceding evening, Wednesday, the 25th. No resting up to be fresh for a first impression for Lois, and little provision for travel delays either. On Thursday morning, she was up at 5:30 to get to the airport for her flight. Low ceiling kept Lois and Weldon grounded until 9:15. Then heavy traffic at La Guardia kept them stacked for an hour, waiting to land. Officials at NBC, frantic about the delays, arranged for a police escort to meet her car at the airport and accompany it directly to Carnegie Hall, sirens blaring to clear a path through the red lights on the way. Lois, surely a little flustered from all this nervous excitement and the physical exertion of walking as quickly as possible, made it to her seat with one minute to spare.

Earlier in the month, during the preliminary rehearsals for the solo quartet, Lois had taken Toscanini aback by appearing without a score. The maestro, who conducted the performance from memory himself, questioned her at first, but after hearing her rehearse decreed that at the next rehearsal all the soloists would have their parts memorized. Lois, by far the junior member of the quartet, had demonstrated yet again the unflappable self-confidence that characterized so much of her early career. Regardless of the unfamiliar surroundings, the high-stakes circumstances, and the nervous tension, her commitment to the music carried her through.

Toscanini refused to allow the many celebrity trappings of the event to overshadow his high musical purpose. A charity gala, the evening raised over $50,000 for the "Artists Veterans Hospitals Programs of Hospitalized Veterans Music Service." Crowds of well-wishers thronged the stage door before the concert, waiting for Toscanini's arrival, some still hoping in vain for last-minute tickets. When he appeared, an admirer pressed a bouquet of flowers on his son and personal manager, "for the maestro." As he took the podium, the capacity audience erupted in a prolonged ovation, as if anticipating the self-denial the concert itself would impose on them. Toscanini had requested that no applause interrupt the five-movement, hour and fifteen minute work. The overwhelming concluding applause was acknowledged by all the assembled forces together, since, in deference to the work itself over any individual performer in it, there were no solo bows.

The reviews rightly acknowledged the ensemble nature of the achievement, but a few singled out Lois's contribution for special notice.

> In a performance that even Toscanini has rarely equalled for fire and devotion, there was no single standout. But Marshall's soprano, as the highest solo voice, could be heard floating magnificently above even the massed ensemble.... In the more subdued section of Beethoven's Mass, her tone was pure and well-rounded, her florid passages had a liquid sound and her phrasing a natural warmth that her colleagues, for all their greater experience, never quite matched.

Today, the closest one can come to this performance is the recording, made in Carnegie Hall in three sessions following the concert, on March 30 and 31, and April 2. On the strength of that recording, and the radiant performance of Nan Merriman, the mezzo-soprano, one might take exception with *Time*'s last judgement, but the praise of Marshall's contribution is not overstated. The strong, emphatic phrasing of her declamation of the three-note opening phrase of the *Kyrie* matches the entire Robert Shaw Chorale for dramatic effect. But her performance in the *Benedictus*, inspiring for the audience and punishing for the soprano, is an even greater wonder. In her 1983 interview with Carl Morey, Lois relived the experience:

> Terrifying. Really terrifying. Every time I had to do that I prayed to whatever gods may be to get me through it. I was never sure whether I would make it. It was so difficult. The *tessitura* really is incredible. It's taxing. It never comes down. It just keeps building in intensity and you keep going up and up.

During a break in that arduous recording session, when everyone else had left the stage, Lois kept her place on the platform, as she often did during breaks, to avoid unnecessary stairs and to save her energy for the next session. In the silence of the hall, a technician called from the control booth and asked if the Maestro would like to hear a playback of the last take. He nodded agreement. At first, as the music began to fill the hall, he sat listening intently, his head bowed in his arms, oblivious to Lois's presence. Then, she recalled, "little by little he started to move his arms and his head and then he slowly got up and stepped up on the podium and then he faced what should have been the choir and started conducting madly, as though everyone was there, in place, and the performance was happening." How far Lois's gift had taken her. Not so many years ago, in the noisy, crowded house on Ellerbeck Street, she used to listen to the broadcasts of the Metropolitan Opera and the NBC Symphony, introduced by the magical phrase, "direct from New York City." Now, silent and transfixed, a soloist herself on the stage of Carnegie Hall, she shared with this giant among musicians, this symbol of Europe's glorious musical past, the intensity of his private encounter with the genius of Beethoven.

CHAPTER FIVE

1953 to 1957 —
Beecham's Protégée

I f any lingering doubt remained whether Lois was embarked on a major career in professional music, the Toscanini engagement of 1953 dispelled it completely. The publicity value of Toscanini's name, ably exploited by the marketing skills of Columbia Artists Management, filled her calendar to overflowing for the next few years. All this activity came at a price, however, and the price was touring. Not for Lois the more stable life of the opera singer, who could enjoy relatively protracted stays in one centre, playing a variety of roles at a single opera house, or who might, in Europe, sign a contract for one or more seasons at a regional house that could even allow her to establish a residence and put down roots. Lois became the itinerant concert singer and recitalist, based in Toronto but living on the road. Her longest stay in any one place might be a week, for rehearsals and a run of two or three performances with a symphony orchestra as part of its subscription series. On the recital circuit it was likely to be a day or two at the most, performing in one concert hall, high school auditorium, or local arena after another, living in hotel rooms and spending most of her time on trains and planes, packing as many appearances as possible into a tour of one part of the continent or another. Such conditions governed the day-to-day pattern of her life for the remainder of her long career. In these early years the conditions of touring, though disruptive, afforded her opportunities for personal fulfillment as well. While they were on tour, she and Weldon had more freedom than in Toronto to enjoy their romantic and sexual relationship in private.

It is impossible to chronicle precisely the progress of Weldon's attentions to Lois, or of her responses to him, after those first tentative advances he made to her in 1947, following her December concert at the Toronto Conservatory. Gradually, however, the teacher and coach transformed into the collaborator, then the guiding spirit, and finally the lover of his star pupil. Concert organizers at their recitals outside of Toronto observed them giggling and holding hands like teenagers in love, indifferent to the gap of nearly nineteen years in their ages. In Toronto, however, they needed to be more circumspect. As long as Lois studied with Weldon at the Conservatory, any acknowledgement of a sexual relationship between student and teacher would have been dynamite, a major public relations catastrophe for the venerable Con. Furthermore, it was during this period of her career that the apocryphal story of Lois beginning her lessons with Weldon at age twelve started to gain currency, aided by Lois's cavalier attitude towards accuracy in matters of dates. In fact, she was fourteen, turning fifteen when she began her studies, and according to her own testimony, Weldon made no advances to her until 1947, when she was twenty-one years old. But the two stories, one of a student-teacher relationship beginning at age twelve, the other of a romantic entanglement between the same two people, would have merged sensationally in the public imagination. Even after Lois graduated and reached adulthood, Weldon still remained a married man with four sons, the oldest of them only seven years younger than Lois herself, not the kind of love interest the Columbia Artists' publicity machine could use in public-interest stories. So the relationship between Weldon and Lois remained publicly unacknowledged, even as it became an open secret in Toronto musical circles.

The press exercised extraordinary discretion, referring to Weldon as Lois's teacher and close friend, but rarely even hinting at a more intimate relationship between them. For the progress of Lois's career, it was just as well. In the early 1950s women in public life, especially in the arts and entertainment, could be held to absurdly rigid standards of conduct and morality. Lois's public image was wholesome and sweet, thanks in part to early publicity promoting the courageous young girl who triumphed over polio. Who could predict what effect the acknowledgement of an affair with an older, married man might have on her bookings? Ingrid Bergman's affair with the Italian director, Roberto Rosselini, had caused scandal of such magnitude that she left North America for six years, not returning to work in Hollywood until 1956. The world of the concert artist was far less exposed than the movie star's, but it would have been unwise to test the public's level of tolerance on the issue. And there was the matter of Marion Kilburn's privacy to be considered as well. Weldon had not separated from his wife, had not moved out of the family home, and, on the surface, continued his domestic life without visible disruption.

Lois's own strong sense of personal privacy could be traced back to the unwanted attention her disability had attracted since her early childhood. The circumstances of her affair with Weldon further strengthened the desire to protect her private life from public scrutiny. But she knew that she had to provide some information about herself to keep her name before the public and generate interest that would lead to further bookings. Her career depended on good press coverage, and so she became adept at giving the bland interview, enthusiastically discussing matters of wardrobe, favourite foods, tastes in popular music, and the like, while completely glossing over the details of her private life. She even carried on a public correspondence with George Kidd, the music critic for the *Toronto Telegram*, in which she described for publication, in somewhat breathless tones, her personal experiences on foreign tours. She signed these effusions, "Love and kisses to everyone back home," and then, in a bold, youthful scrawl, "Bestest, Lois." But although she openly acknowledged Weldon in such materials, one had to read between the lines to know the full significance of his presence in her life. From her youth, then, Lois established the habit of maintaining silence about the most private issues in her personal life, and her experience as a young woman in love only deepened that secrecy. She may have confided in her sisters, but even her closest friends in later years received few revelations of this intimate kind. Whether by conscious decision or simply through force of circumstance, Lois found herself leading, not just a public life, but a double one as well. The public might see her as The Woman of the Year, but never as The Other Woman.

By 1952, Lois had moved out of her mother's home on 151 Bingham Avenue, where Florence had moved from the Millbrook Crescent house immediately after David's death. Lois now shared an apartment with her older sister Jean on Williamson Road in the Beach area, near Kew Gardens. Although she remained very close to her mother, she was embarked on the adventure of independent living, no longer forced to account for her daily comings and goings. Her career, meanwhile, gave her her first real financial independence. At last, she could support herself and indulge at will the impulsive generosity that had characterized her from her adolescence. But now, instead of splurging on the occasional ice cream sundae, she gave more lavishly — a surprise vacation for her mother, toys for her nephews and nieces, expensive clothes for her sisters. Success failed to teach her financial prudence and her itinerant way of life offered no encouragements to domestic economy. Like her mother, but without the financial restrictions her mother had had to endure, Lois enjoyed the luxuries and indulgences of life.

When she had the time, that is. For the most part, the three years following her appearance with Toscanini, her first three years under Columbia Artists management, immersed her in a high-pressure round of engagements that stretched and extended her professional capabilities: new cities, new colleagues, new and challenging repertoire. Between April 1953 and May 1956, Lois made major orchestral debuts in Boston, Chicago, Cincinnati, Los Angeles (the Hollywood Bowl), Montreal, Minneapolis, and San Francisco; she appeared at important summer festivals in Ann Arbor, Michigan; Berea, Ohio (the Baldwin-Wallace Bach Festival); North Carolina (the Brevard Festival); Stratford, Ontario; and Tanglewood (the Berkshire Summer Festival). She worked for the first time in her career with conductors Alfredo Antonini (a New York Christmas radio broadcast), Eduard van Beinum (the Los Angeles Philharmonic Orchestra at the Hollywood Bowl), Antal Doráti (the Minneapolis Symphony Orchestra), Thor Johnson (the Cincinnati May Festival and the Philadelphia Orchestra at Ann Arbor), Otto Klemperer (l'Orchestre Symphonique de Montréal), Josef Krips (the Cincinnati May Festival and l'Orchestre Symphonique de Montréal), Nicolai Malko (the Grant Park Symphony Orchestra, Chicago), Charles Munch (the Boston Symphony), Boyd Neel (at Stratford), Fritz

Reiner (the Chicago Symphony Orchestra), Leopold Stokowski (at Carnegie Hall), Heinz Unger (the York Concert Society), and Geoffrey Waddington (Canadian League of Composers). She added to her repertoire: *Carmina Burana* (Carl Orff); *The Book With Seven Seals* (Franz Schmidt); *Shéhérazade* (Ravel); *Two Mystical Songs of John Donne for High Voice and Orchestra* (composed for her by Godfrey Ridout); Beethoven's Symphony No. 9; *Four Songs of Contemplation* (Alexander Brott); Act III of *Die Meistersinger* (Wagner); Mozart's *Requiem* and his lesser-known *Davidde Penitente*; and Arnold Schoenberg's *Gurrelieder*. While undertaking all of that, she and Weldon continued to introduce her recital programs to Canadian towns and small cities, including Chatham, Fredericton, Hamilton, Kapuskasing, Kingston, Kirkland Lake, Kitchener, London, Oakville, Owen Sound, Ottawa, Peterborough, Regina, St. Catharines, Sault Ste. Marie, Smiths Falls, Sainte-Anne-de-Bellevue, Sherbrooke, and Welland; and, on Columbia's Community Concerts circuit, to a similar range of mid-sized centres in the United States.

Lois's old friend and mentor, Sir Ernest MacMillan, introduced her to Montreal when he guest-conducted l'Orchestre Symphonique de Montréal at one of its summer popular concerts at the Mountain Chalet in Mount Royal Park in 1953. Six months later, in December of the same year, Lois returned on her own, as soprano soloist in Beethoven's Ninth under the baton of the legendary Otto Klemperer. The alto soloist for that engagement was an up-and-coming singer just five years younger than Lois, the pride of Montreal, Maureen Forrester. It was the first of over 150 times these two giants of Canadian music would share the stage, and one can picture them at those performances: young, coming into their prime, perhaps a little nervous, and probably sizing up the out-of-province competition. It was also, as far as the records show, the first of relatively few encounters for Lois with the Beethoven Ninth. She found it "thorny," and later characterized its vocal writing as "very difficult, more than it should have been." After wrestling with it a few times, she made her feelings official in no uncertain terms. An undated but early listing of Lois's repertoire from Columbia Artists discouraged any future enquiries about the Beethoven with the bold notation, "NO NINTH SYMPHONY."

Maureen Forrester was not the only one sizing her up in Montreal. Eric McLean, the critic who had questioned Lois's suitability as Canada's representative at Washington's sesquicentennial celebrations in 1950, accorded her an extensive and carefully-considered assessment when she made her Montreal recital debut under the Community Concerts banner. Writing in the *Montreal Star* (May 11, 1954), he pulled no punches. "Miss Marshall's radio performances, particularly the one with Toscanini, had revealed a tendency to go sharp, and in long sustained notes there appeared to be a dangerous wobble." But, assessing the range and variety of accomplishments which her recital program displayed, he now came on side.

> … Miss Marshall gave an exhibition last night that could have been matched by very few sopranos today. The voice is pure and strong throughout its great range. One feature which came as a real surprise was the strength of her middle register — at times it seemed to have almost the dramatic soprano timbre.… Whether by intuition or training, Miss Marshall is a first-rate musician, and revealed interpretive powers which would have guaranteed her a career with only half her vocal powers.

Like a few other critics, McLean sounded an early warning note about Weldon's limitations as an accompanist. "Weldon Kilburn provided workmanlike accompaniments though they were too often erratic and overly sentimental, but if Mr. Kilburn has been, as the program proclaims him, Miss Marshall's only teacher, he may be forgiven anything." Emmy Heim seemed to have been temporarily written out of Lois's official biography, and Kilburn the pianist was tolerated out of respect (somewhat grudging on McLean's part, given his comment about "intuition or training") for Kilburn the teacher and mentor.

Reviews in major centres weren't necessarily the only ones that mattered. In Peterborough, Ontario, her 1954 appearance at the Peterborough Collegiate and Vocational School Auditorium was covered by the Canadian man of letters, Robertson Davies, at that time the

editor of the *Peterborough Examiner*. Davies had an informed, sophisti-
cated knowledge of vocal technique and musical taste, and he put both
to use in his lengthy, enthusiastic review in the *Examiner* of March 30,
1954. His comments on the operatic arias in Lois's program offer a fascinating view of Lois's abilities in opera, an aspect of her art that is now
largely forgotten.

> We have heard "Faust" too many times, but we have
> never heard a Marguerite who suggested innocent
> delight as well as Miss Marshall, or a Rosina who was
> arch and playful in so enchanting and humorous a way,
> quite free of grimacing and cheap coquetry. The col-
> oratura elaboration in "Una voce poco fa" was not mere
> lacework hung on the melody, but an organic part of it,
> as Rossini intended. Similarly, she made Violetta's deci-
> sion to embrace a life of wild pleasure really dramatic
> and important, and Tosca's struggle between love and
> art a real struggle, and not a sham....
>
> Young singers should give special heed to the clar-
> ity, free of affectation, with which Miss Marshall sings
> the words of four languages. This means a well placed
> voice; it means careful study of the beauties of language;
> but it also means a love of words and a recognition of
> the importance of words and meaning over mere pretti-
> ness of tone. It means a cultivated understanding, and a
> great deal of disciplined emotion. Technique, in singing,
> is only a means to carry out the singer's understanding
> of the music she sings. Miss Marshall is sometimes bet-
> ter than a great singer; she is a great artist.

Davies wrote from a deep interest in the subject. By 1954, he had
published the novels *Tempest-Tost* and *Leaven of Malice*, which eventually became the first two parts of his Salterton trilogy, and he would
already have been turning his thoughts to the final book in the series. In
A Mixture of Frailties (published in 1958) he draws a detailed portrait of

a small-town Canadian singer named Monica Gall as she pursues an international musical career. Writing just ten years after Lois's big break with Sir Ernest MacMillan in the *St. Matthew Passion* at the University of Toronto's Convocation Hall, Davies gives Monica Gall a strikingly similar professional debut. Monica, the heroine of *A Mixture of Frailties*, gets only the tiniest solo part, but her debut work is the *St. Matthew*. And she performs it, under the personal guidance of an established, titled conductor of the old-school, in an unusual setting — not a church or traditional concert hall, but the Sheldonian Theatre, Oxford University's much older, much more famous answer to Convocation Hall. Though Davies' works of fiction are first and foremost works of the imagination, it is difficult to believe, given the time of writing and his admiration for Lois, that she did not inhabit some corner of his mind as he created the career of Monica Gall.

Many years later, in 1992, Davies and Lois exchanged small gifts and words of admiration about each other's work. Davies' graceful, old-world tribute is one of the few fan letters preserved in Lois's papers in Library and Archives Canada.

Reviews alone cannot tell the full story of the power Lois had to touch her audiences. In March 1956, Lois included Kapuskasing, a remote lumber and paper mill town in northern Ontario, on her tour. Even if the snow was melting, the town's wooden sidewalks would not have been replaced by concrete in time for her arrival. That civic project had barely got underway in 1956. And the town of 5,729 certainly didn't have television, which wouldn't arrive in Kapuskasing until 1957. With radio the sole means of mass communication, residents of Kapuskasing who cared about such things would have followed Lois's career through her frequent appearances on CBC. Her presence brought a whiff of spring and a dash of excitement to the winter-weary audience of that isolated town. She played the Community Club and certainly touched the heart of one of the town's inhabitants. Gray Knapp, a high school music and English teacher in Kapuskasing, had once had a passing acquaintance with Lois in the cafeteria of the Royal Conservatory, when both were students there. In 1956, he came to the Community Club to see the artist she had become, and to re-establish a personal connection to the world she represented. Forty-one years later, when Lois's death was announced, he said simply, "I think I died a little in 1997."

Columbia Artists' estimation of her growing popularity can be gauged from their decision to use her, in 1955, as last-minute replacement for two of their most highly paid international headliners. It always created a delicate problem for management when one of their major stars cancelled, since entire series had often been sold to the local organization on the strength of one big name (and expensive) artist. The replacement for the indisposed star had to be available on short notice, but also had to be able to win over a disgruntled audience expecting to fry somewhat bigger fish. Lois filled the bill in Cedar Rapids, Iowa, delighting audiences who had come to hear the Metropolitan Opera coloratura soprano and recording star Lily Pons, and in Elmira, New York, where the great Chilean pianist Claudio Arrau had been the name attraction.

There were other important firsts during this period. In May 1953, Lois appeared for the first time with Toronto's York Concert Society, conducted by Heinz Unger. The York Concert Society organized annual series of concerts at Eaton Auditorium and Massey Hall in order to provide a podium for Unger, a German conductor who had settled in Toronto and made his living primarily through guest conducting engagements, in Canada and around the world. Unger championed the works of Mahler and Richard Strauss, at a time when Mahler still needed a champion in Toronto musical circles. A review of Unger's performance of Mahler's Symphony No. 9 by Udo Kasemets in the *Toronto Star* (January 24, 1963) spoke of "Mahler's anxiety-laden, long-winded musical speeches," and characterized his treatment of ideas and forms as "heavy-handed and unskilled." Undaunted by such critical hostility, Lois became Unger's ally in educating Toronto's audiences to Mahler. She sang a few of the songs from *Des Knaben Wunderhorn* with Unger in 1953, and the soprano solo in the Symphony No. 4 in 1957, and was scheduled to sing in Unger's performance of the Symphony No. 2 (the "Resurrection") in 1958, but had to cancel the latter because of a last-minute attack of laryngitis. (Later in her career, there would be another last-minute cancellation and even more dramatic vocal difficulties, in part as a result of the repertoire Unger programmed for her.) But her strongest identification with Unger came through Richard Strauss's *Four Last Songs*, which she sang three times under his direction, including performances at Ontario's Stratford Festival and on CBC Television.

In these years, Lois also established the connection with the Stratford, Ontario, Shakespearean Festival that would involve her in some of the most adventurous repertoire of her career. Louis Applebaum, the first Director of Music at Stratford, managed in the very first season to insinuate a few musical performances into the Festival's dramatic offerings, but it took him two years to get its Directors to agree to a full-scale musical program. From that 1955 inaugural music season onwards, Applebaum and then Glenn Gould, who, with violinist Oscar Shumsky and cellist Leonard Rose, succeeded Applebaum as Music Directors in 1961, established music as one of the most exciting components of the Shakespearean Festival. They brought artists of international stature together with the best Canadian musicians, broke traditional programming barriers by mixing classical music with jazz, folk, and world music, experimented with chamber music, opera, operetta, and ballet, championed obscure and avant-garde composers, popularized Handel and Bach, and succeeded, against all odds, in filling Stratford's theatres with audiences hungry for this feast of musical tastes and styles. Before the Broadway musical sailed triumphantly into Stratford, swamping all competition in its wake, music in all its vitality and variety — lively, stimulating, challenging, uplifting — made Stratford a summer mecca for performers and audience alike.

Over the years at Stratford, in addition to her standard repertoire and the *Four Last Songs* with Unger (1957), Lois sang Paul Hindemith's *Das Marienleben* (in 1962, with Gould at the piano), Alban Berg's *Seven Early Songs* (1964), and a complete performance of Handel's oratorio, *Solomon* (1965) — as well as a concert of popular Italian operatic arias and duets with famed Canadian baritone Louis Quilico (1970), which she had to abbreviate because of a throat infection. Lois appeared in recital in the tent theatre in 1953, the very first year of the Festival, but perhaps her most memorable appearance came two years later, on July 9, 1955, when, with Boyd Neel conducting the Hart House Orchestra, she joined the Festival Chorus in a performance of Purcell's *Ode on St. Cecilia's Day*, just part of the program inaugurating the Festival's first official season of Music at Stratford in the new Concert Hall. The Concert Hall was actually a building (known previously as "The Casino") belonging to the Stratford Lawn Bowling Club, overlooking the Avon River, refurbished as a makeshift concert hall and repainted so recently that the smell of paint still hung in the humid summer air as the audience of one thousand filed in. The twenty-five members of the Festival Chorus (later to become the Festival Singers) had been auditioned and recruited a few months earlier by three Toronto singers, the baritone Jan Simons, Gordon Wry (a frequent soloist in Sir Ernest's performances of the *St. Matthew*), and Tom Brown (moonlighting from his job as editor of the *CBC Times*). Together, they had approached a young school teacher and conductor named Elmer Iseler and invited him to come on board as conductor of their group, the first fully professional choir in Canada. This Stratford Festival gig was one of its earliest engagements.

The concert, which opened with *A Song of Welcome*, a specially-commissioned work by Healey Willan, was a great success despite the stifling heat. By the time Lois had finished her solo workout, Bach's demanding Cantata No. 51, "Jauchzet Gott in allen Landen," she was drenched in sweat. The temperature inside the un-airconditioned theatre had reached 104° Fahrenheit. Considerate organizers had brought buckets of ice into the back of the concert hall and directed large fans to blow air across the ice at the audience and performers, but these did more to increase the humidity in the auditorium than to lower the temperature. All the forces soldiered on through the second half, though some audience members decamped to the lawns of the adjacent park, to listen in the cooler evening air, through the opened windows of the hall. In the Purcell *Ode*, Lois and Jan Simons had prudently swapped vocal lines in those portions of their duet which lay too low for Lois, too high for Simons. Otherwise, they might never have made it through the evening.

Meanwhile, unchronicled by the press, Weldon's relationship with Lois was putting strains on his family obligations. The preparations for Lois's second Town Hall recital, in January 1955, highlighted his divided loyalties. Lois required lots of personal attention and a degree of "handling" before a major event like her second New York appearance. Weldon had always provided it. On this occasion, however, he faced a conflict of loyalties. The day before the recital in New York, Weldon's eldest son, Nicholas, was to marry the soprano Ilona Kombrink just outside Philadelphia. The journey from New York to Philadelphia could have been made in under two hours, but would have cut into Lois and Weldon's preparation time for the recital. Forced to choose between his profession and his personal life, between his lover and his family, Weldon chose to stay in New York and missed his son's wedding. While avoiding public proclamations or confrontation, Weldon was nevertheless establishing his priorities.

By her choice of programming, Lois clearly hoped to present herself on this second outing in New York as a mature artist, capable of handling weighty, challenging repertoire. Purcell's noble *Divine Hymns*, Brahms's *Vier Ernste Gesänge* (*Four Serious Songs*), Ravel's song cycle, *Shéhérazade* — all of which she had tried out two months earlier in a recital in Ottawa — any one of these would have challenged the interpretive powers of an artist considerably more mature than the not-quite-thirty Lois. By programming them together in one recital (a group of folk songs was the only concession to more popular tastes), Lois and Weldon threw down the gauntlet before their American critics. The winsome coloratura soprano and charming singer of folk songs wanted respect. Somewhat grudgingly, she got it. The critic for the influential *New York Times* thought she had overextended herself in the Brahms. In the Ravel and Purcell, however, he granted that she had sung with warmth, sensitivity, and musical intelligence. "In a certain type of repertory," sniffed H.C.S. (likely the eminent music critic, Harold C. Schonberg) in his concluding sentence, "Miss Marshall is an entirely convincing artist." On the other hand, *Musical America*, which had been qualified in its praise of her New York debut, threw caution to the wind. In a judgement that echoed the tone of Robertson Davies' comments, the reviewer wrote:

> But most important — and it is the factor that makes
> her a genuine, mature artist — is her power to project

with great immediacy and conviction what she feels about the words and music she is singing; singing seems as natural to her as speech to a great actor.... In Miss Marshall's performances, the Purcell "Hymns" ranged from the blazingly proclamative — like sermons in song — to ineffably lovely....

Musical America had praise for Weldon as well, even if it assessed his accomplishment in terms of Lois's, and in a single, brief sentence. "Weldon Kilburn, Miss Marshall's accompanist and teacher, played with comparable musicianship." The teacher now had to measure up to the standards set by his pupil. The Town Hall audience expressed no reservations. They gave Lois and Weldon a standing ovation, with more than a dozen curtain calls.

No professional career, especially one as hectic and demanding as Lois's, simply marches on from triumph to triumph. Lois experienced her share of setbacks on the way, one of the most humiliating of them her debut with the Chicago Symphony under Fritz Reiner in March 1955. The repertoire was a new work by Samuel Barber, *The Prayers of Kierkegaard*, and Carl Orff's *Carmina Burana*. Orff composed his now enormously popular *Carmina Burana* in 1936, but it had been slow to make its way to North America. At the Cincinnati May Festival in 1954, Lois sang in the second performance of the work on this side of the Atlantic, and under Reiner's direction, participated in its Chicago premiere. The soprano part of this percussively orchestrated set of medieval secular songs includes some lovely *piano* singing in the middle of the soprano range, but also reaches perilously into the stratosphere, where it sits for uncomfortable stretches of time. This is Queen of the Night territory, and calls for similar vocal talents and stamina, which must be carefully conserved through rehearsals and a run of performances if the singer is to go the distance. Accounts of the Chicago performance, though brief, indicate that Lois failed.

As was often the case, Lois's schedule was so tight that she rushed from the plane straight to her first rehearsal. Reiner, a notoriously stern taskmaster, then over-rehearsed the Orff with no regard for Lois's energy or vocal reserves, insisting on a particular pronunciation of the text that made the high *tessitura* impossibly difficult, and so contributed to the problems she encountered in performance. So unyielding was Reiner in his demands that Lois joked privately at the time that all the members of the Chicago Symphony must have been in psychotherapy. In later years, however, she refused to be drawn into public comment about the Reiner experience, and Weldon would say only, "That man, I couldn't stand him." In any case, the end result was disastrous for Lois. After the build up of a promotional piece in the *Chicago Daily News* entitled "Polio Conqueror Sings Tomorrow," three of the music reviewers for the four Chicago dailies maintained a pointed silence about her performance in *Carmina Burana*. They praised Reiner; they admired the chorus; they gave favourable mention to Morley Meredith and Leslie Chabay (the baritone and tenor soloists); one of them even complimented Lois's performance — in the Barber. But Roger Dettmer's damning comment on her contribution to the Orff in the *Chicago American* said it all: "Last evening, in all particulars except Lois Marshall's unlovely soprano labors, the performance was spectacular...."

Not until two years later, in April 1957, when Lois replaced the Canadian tenor Léopold Simoneau on thirty-six hours notice in a recital program in Orchestra Hall, did she redeem her reputation with the Chicago critical press. She performed before a tiny audience, partly because of the cancellation, partly because of the scheduling — a matinee on Easter Sunday afternoon. But all the major newspapers sent reviewers. Roger Dettmer, the only critic on the four dailies to have reviewed Lois's previous appearance, had the grace to recall, and revise, his earlier criticism. "On [that] occasion she was not in the best of voice. Yesterday, however, she most certainly and excitingly was." He admired her daring choice of repertoire (ranging from Purcell's elaborate "The Queen's Epicedium," a seventeenth-century elegy on the death of Queen Mary II, to Puccini's "In questa reggia"). In his view her vocal technique, nearly perfect, though not always effortless, enabled her to sing "invariably excitingly, whether effortfully in slow sustained music lying in the middle voice or, as in [Rossini's] 'Una voce,' with superlative ease." Dettmer here pinpointed a quality in Lois's singing, the occasional sense of effort

required to sustain her vocal production that would become more prominent in the later years of her career. He was not the only listener who
found such "effortful" voice production, on occasion, extremely dramatic
and deeply moving.

In 1956, Lois got the break that eventually introduced her to European
audiences and propelled her career onto the worldwide stage. Sir Thomas
Beecham was one of the most flamboyant and popular British conductors of the twentieth century, famous for his wealthy background (he was
the heir to the Beecham Pills fortune), his wit, and the women in his life.
It was Beecham's 1935 recording of the final act of *La Bohème* that had
moved Lois so deeply when she was a young student. At the time of that
recording, Beecham was estranged from his first wife, in a long-standing
relationship with Lady Cunard, who raised funds for some of his musical ventures, and conducting an affair with the Mimi in his *La Bohème*
recording, Lisa Perli, who had a son by him. The Lady Beecham whom
Lois would meet in 1956 was yet another woman, a pianist named Betty
Humby, whom Beecham had married in 1943 after both he and Humby
had obtained divorces from their uncooperative spouses in Idaho City,
Idaho, outside British jurisdiction. Beecham had a prolific recording
career, and by early 1956 had nearly completed a recording of Handel's
oratorio *Solomon*, with the beloved British singer Elsie Morrison as one
of the two sopranos. He had omitted the other soprano part, claiming
to be unsatisfied with any of the singers at his disposal in Europe at
the time of the recording. (According to Maureen Forrester, Beecham
delighted in leaving major recording projects unfinished in this way,
part of an ongoing vendetta with his recording company.) While on
a North American tour in the first months of 1956, he contacted Lois
and invited her to come to Cleveland to audition for the role in *Solomon*.
Lois squeezed the trip to Cleveland into her touring schedule and won
the recording contract. Then, in March 1956, Beecham came to Toronto
to conduct the Toronto Symphony Orchestra. It is likely on this visit
that he contacted Lois a second time and invited her to audition for

another of his projects, a recording of Mozart's opera *Die Entführung aus dem Serail* (*The Abduction from the Seraglio*). He had been looking, he said, for a soprano for the part of Konstanze, the dramatic heroine, for twenty-five years. Lois had major bookings in San Francisco and Minneapolis at the end of the month, but again, she shoehorned the audition into her schedule.

It took place at a Toronto church, with Weldon providing accompaniment. Lois had been singing one of Konstanze's big arias, "Martern aller Arten," since at least 1948, when she performed it at Massey Hall in the Royal Conservatory's annual closing concert, an audacious choice for a twenty-three year old student. The title translates freely as "Tortures of all sorts," and for all but the most accomplished singers it can be pure torture to sing. Lois didn't know the rest of the opera, however, so she swotted up another of Konstanze's arias and went to the audition with two of the three major solos under her belt, memorized as usual. After taking her through her prepared material, Beecham asked her to sing the third aria as well, brushing over her objections that she had never looked at it. "Never mind. Sing it anyway. We'll then find out what kind of a sight-reader you are." With only one score between them, Lois had to peer awkwardly over Weldon's shoulder while they both sight-read the aria. Beecham offered her the recording contract at the conclusion of the audition.

Then came the real challenge. Sir Thomas asked Lois if she would mind driving him to the King Edward Hotel in downtown Toronto, where he was staying. For the first time in the entire audition process, Lois panicked. She had passed her driving test and received her driver's licence only the day before, and had never driven by herself in central Toronto. But she calmed her nerves and threaded her way carefully through downtown traffic to the King Edward, with her eminent passenger blissfully unaware what a greenhorn he had chosen for a chauffeur.

Getting her driver's licence, such a common event in most people's lives, gave Lois another degree of independence, one which she treasured and protected fiercely almost to the end of her life. She may have been forced to wait so long, until she was thirty-one, to get this ticket to personal mobility because of the pace of development in the car industry. Though automatic transmissions were available in the United States as early as 1940, other features necessary to accommodate someone with Lois's disability, such as power brakes and power steering, didn't become available until the early 1950s. Lois, of course, had to be able to drive safely using only her right leg, but beyond these options, she needed no custom modifications to enable her to operate a car. As she aged, and became more restricted in her ability to walk, she also needed a car large enough for her to be able to stow her wheelchair in the back. One of her last was a gold Cadillac, with the vanity registration plate BACH 85.

With two recording projects for Beecham lined up, Lois took her first trip to Europe in the spring and summer of 1956. Most of May was spent in recording sessions with Sir Thomas. In the case of *Solomon*, it was simply a matter of recording Lois's solo tracks with the orchestra, since the rest of the work had already been recorded in two separate sessions in November and December 1955. Lois was somewhat surprised by Beecham's casual informality. Time did not seem to be an issue, and he was always ready to digress for a joke or an anecdote. However, for the *Abduction* recording sessions the opera's full forces assembled in London's Kingsway Hall — the Royal Philharmonic Orchestra, the Beecham Choral Society, Sir Thomas accompanied by Lady Beecham, and the vocal soloists, Lois, Ilse Hollweg, fellow-Canadian Léopold Simoneau (already acknowledged as one of the supreme Mozart interpreters of his day), Gerhard Unger, and Gottlob Frick. Lois had worked with Simoneau the preceding April, in a Montreal performance of the Mozart *Requiem*, but the rest of the vocal soloists were unknown to her. They had never worked together as an ensemble. They were surprised to discover that Beecham had no piano rehearsals planned for them, as would normally have been the case. He liked to throw his singers directly into full orchestral sessions and see what happened. Then, after listening to playbacks, he began the serious work. The soloists approached Lady Beecham to intercede on their behalf with the maestro for some piano rehearsals, but she replied airily, "Oh, no, you don't need a piano rehearsal. You need only to come down to the rehearsal and listen to the orchestra, and then you'll record and that's all the rehearsal you shall need." (When Lois told this story in later years, she delighted in a wicked parody of Lady Beecham's plummy tones.) And that's all the rehearsal they got. A well-known recording of Beecham in rehearsal, which includes a few takes from the *Abduction* sessions, shows him to be much more concerned with details of orchestral texture than with vocal coaching. In one of his digressions on that recording he laments the need to rehearse at all, suggesting that a performance is much more interesting for the audience when the musicians are struggling with the music; then at least something is happening.

Beecham certainly made something happen for Lois when, on May 26, he presented her in her London debut at the Royal Festival Hall, with the Royal Philharmonic Orchestra. For this major appearance, she sang Mozart's *Exsultate, Jubilate*, by now one of her standard concert pieces, with which she felt completely at ease. It was her only item on the symphonic program, and once she got through it she could take her bows, go back to her hotel, and relax. It had been a strenuous month and she had every right to be tired. Immediately after her performance, standing just offstage at the Royal Festival Hall, waiting with Beecham to go back on and acknowledge the applause of the audience in the cavernous, modern auditorium, Lois could not quite believe the spur of the moment suggestion that Beecham muttered to her. They really needed an encore — would Lois like to do "Martern aller Arten" from the *Abduction*?

"Do you mean uncut?" Lois stuttered.

"Yes, of course," said Beecham cheerfully, as he strode through the door and onto the podium. And so, with no more preparation than that, Lois returned to the stage, summoned up her energy, and launched into one of the acknowledged killers of the soprano repertoire. Even though they had recently recorded the aria, Sir Thomas's little plot took Lois completely by surprise. Not so the players of the RPO, who mysteriously found the music for the unscheduled encore in their music folders, as if on cue.

Suddenly, Lois's London debut was all about that encore, not about her prepared programming. The critics were unanimous in their praise, but divided in their particulars. Because of the well-known difficulties of vocal range posed by "Martern aller Arten," the critic for the *Times*,

unaware of Beecham's little offstage surprise, took the encore to be a
calculated gesture on Lois's part, "a plea, in fact, for judgment as a fundamentally serious artist." Lois's only plea, a silent one at that, had been
to get through the surprise addition to the program without disaster. He
cavilled about Lois's success at spanning the wide vocal range required
by the aria. "[W]here Mozart insists that the soprano not only range
high in her natural atmosphere but also sink to the gloomy depths where
contraltos weave their spells, Miss Marshall could not quite compass that
extreme range with the resonance that came easily to the other registers
of her fine voice." Listening to the same aria, the critic for the *Edinburgh
Scotsman* clearly fell under some spell, whether of the contralto-woven
variety or not. "What is so astonishing is that the break in her voice is
difficult to detect; the lovely, velvety quality of the chest voice seems to
go up and up until she has assumed the head voice without any loss of
the velvety tone."

"I cannot remember," he concluded, "being so in love with a voice at
first sound since I heard Sena Jurinac in 'Cosi fan Tutte.'"

Judging by the account in the *Daily Telegraph*, the audience sided
with the *Scotsman*. "Martern aller Arten," according to the *Telegraph*,
"combined the dramatic and coloratura elements of her voice with a skill
and thrillingness the like of which have not been heard in London for
a long time." The audience gave her "the kind of ovation which is only
reserved for the few."

How can one reconcile the apparently contradictory testimony of
the critics? The only contemporary evidence, aside from their criticisms,
remains the recording of the aria on the complete *Abduction*, made under
studio conditions sometime in the two and a half weeks preceding the
Festival Hall concert. Such evidence, particularly where projection in the
lower register is concerned, must be assessed carefully, since Beecham
was not averse to having a musician approach the recording microphone
directly in order to bring out a particular passage he thought was not
coming through clearly enough, as he does in the "Beecham in Rehearsal"
recording. Moreover, the final version was sometimes spliced together
from several different takes to make the ideal recording. A suspicious fragment of dead air at the five minute, twenty-three second mark of this aria

suggests at least one such splice. With all those cautions in mind, Lois's recorded version of "Martern aller Arten" nevertheless articulates all the lower passages in the aria clearly, and projects them adequately, though not dramatically, above the texture of the orchestra. She punches out her concluding note, a C above middle C lying in the middle, not at the top, of the soprano range, with surprising dramatic force, but on the whole she avoids the exaggerated use of chest tones that characterized her performances of Falla's *Seven Popular Spanish Songs*. She has clearly centred herself in the soprano part of her voice, and dips down into the mezzo range carefully, so as not to disturb the general placement of the aria.

The factor of overriding significance is Beecham's interpretation of the score. Following Sir Thomas's lead, Lois approaches the aria as an ensemble work in which the voice is an equal partner with the orchestra, not as a star vocal turn with background orchestral accompaniment. In the lengthy orchestral introduction, fully two minutes before the soprano makes her first entrance, Beecham strives for a delicate, open orchestral sound, with the individual lines for solo strings and woodwinds clearly articulated as they call to one another. Lois's performance is consistent with the standard set by the orchestra (the Royal Philharmonic in the recording, as at the Festival Hall). She responds and defers to the solo players in those passages in which their voices are as important as hers (some of them precisely those under discussion, where her own voice dips into the mezzo range). To have used the exaggerated chest tones she was capable of might have sabotaged the quality of the rest of her performance, and certainly would have been out of keeping with Beecham's demands for Mozartian clarity and nuance. The critical division of opinion probably points out Lois's sense of the responsibilities of musical ensemble rather than any inherent shortcoming in her vocal powers. Not that anyone was alleging serious shortcomings. Even the *Times* called it "a notable performance," and the *Scotsman*'s comparison to Sena Jurinac placed the newcomer in the company of one of the best-loved European sopranos of the century.

Lois had another recording session scheduled for late July (an oratorio album for HMV with Anthony Bernard conducting the London Symphony Orchestra), so she spent the intervening months in England, where she fulfilled a variety of engagements, including the Harrogate Festival with Sir John Barbirolli and the Hallé Orchestra, and the International Eisteddfod, the mammoth annual festival of song in Wales. She also made an excursion to Hamburg, Germany, where, as an unknown artist, she sang for a small house, and then received a torrent of praise from the critics. Four separate papers reviewed her Hamburg appearance in June 1956. The critic for the *Hamburger Abendblatt* outdid his colleagues only slightly in rhetorical flourishes, when he spoke of the recital as an "overwhelming experience," praised Lois for her "faultless technique and profligate powers of expression," and concluded that "something radiant," something that made one "forget time and place," seemed to emanate from her when she sang. It took one back to the *Globe and Mail*'s Colin Sabiston who, reviewing Lois's 1947 student performance of the Scarlatti *Christmas Cantata*, had become "so transported that even the outer edges of consciousness were lost to this world."

Back home in North America, Lois faced a gruelling fall/winter tour. With all sixty-six of her available dates sold out, she had more recitals than any other vocal artist on Columbia Artists' roster. She sacrificed her planned Christmas break to return to England for the month of December 1956, for performances of *Messiah* in Sheffield and Manchester (both with Barbirolli and the Hallé Orchestra) and at London's Royal Albert Hall. From England, she made a quick side trip to the Netherlands to conquer Amsterdam, a city with a sophisti-cated musical audience and a notoriously demanding critical press. As in Hamburg, the audience was sparse, but Lois held the critics in thrall. "This must not happen again: an almost empty hall and Lois Marshall on the podium," admonished one of the Amsterdam papers after her appearance in the small recital hall of the famed Concertgebouw. The review was headed, "The Miracle."

> We stood, after the official part of the programme, clap-
> ping in small clusters, with tears in our eyes, because
> we wanted to protract this unique experience as long
> as possible. Thus we behave once in a long while in the

small hall, because under the spell of the miracle even the most jaded concertgoer forgets his objectivity and his train home.

Weldon appears not to have accompanied Lois on this European trip. In Britain, all of her performances were with orchestras. In the Netherlands, an accomplished Dutch pianist, George van Renesse, played for her in her concert appearances and on a tape made for broadcast on Dutch radio, which resurfaced after her death and was broadcast on CBC Radio in 1998. Lois loved working with van Renesse, with whom she collaborates happily in this recording. He exercises strong musical initiative throughout, but always allows her the interpretive freedom and room to breathe, which were vital things that she could rely on in all her collaborations with Weldon. In the early English songs and five Mahler songs on the program, the piano shares equally with the voice in the creation of a transparent clarity of texture and loving delicacy of tone. As she did at her second Town Hall recital, Lois also programs the contrasting Brahms *Four Serious Songs*, usually performed by the male voice, and sings them in their original, low keys. The recital concludes with her signature piece from this period, the *Seven Popular Spanish Songs*. Van Renesse's accompaniment in the Falla is spirited and rhythmically exciting. The value of this tape lies not only in its documentation of Lois's vocal powers, but in its almost unique record of her recital work with a pianist other than Weldon at this stage of her career. Lois made four more trips to the Netherlands, where she was always received with love and admiration. She worked with van Renesse again on two of those visits, in 1957 and 1962.

Recording *The Abduction* with Beecham rekindled Lois's burning desire to perform opera, an ambition that had been damped but never extinguished by Arnold Walter's decision to deny her admission to the Opera School. In the three years following her Beecham experience, from 1956 to 1959, Lois made a concerted assault on the operatic bastion, in concert, on television, and, most important of all, onstage. She had individual victories, but in the end she lost the campaign. After this period, she made no significant operatic appearances until the very end of her career.

Unstaged or semi-staged concert performances offered the easiest point of entry to the operatic repertoire Lois longed to perform. She had sung Donna Anna in *Don Giovanni* on CBC radio much earlier in her career, in 1949 and 1950, and had done a concert performance of the same opera in Washington, DC, in January 1956, even before her Beecham experience. In January 1957, she undertook *Don Giovanni* again, in St. Louis, Missouri and added to her repertoire the title role in Puccini's *Tosca* in Wichita, Kansas. Baron Scarpia in the Wichita concert performance was Walter Cassel, a veteran baritone of both the Metropolitan and the New York City Opera companies. The St. Louis *Don Giovanni* was conducted by Vladimir Golschmann, known to Canadians for his recording of the Bach keyboard concerto with Glenn Gould and the Columbia Symphony Orchestra, made the following year. The distinguished American soprano, Phyllis Curtin, sang Donna Elvira in St. Louis. Lois would perform the role of Donna Anna at least one more time in her career, in a concert performance in Cleveland in 1969, with the well-known American tenor Jan Peerce as her Don Ottavio. Surprisingly, she never sang Donna Elvira, the passionate, vulnerable, and betrayed lover of the faithless Don, a role to which she would have been both vocally and temperamentally well-suited.

Lois planned to make her first foray into fully-staged opera in Washington, DC, a city where her star was decidedly on the ascendant. She had appeared there five times in three different programs (Mozart, Beethoven, and the *St. Matthew Passion*) in the first four months of 1957. So when the fledgling Washington Opera Society approached her about appearing in staged operatic performances, her chance finally seemed to have come. In September 1957, the Opera Society announced Lois as their Ariadne in Richard Strauss's *Ariadne auf Naxos* and as Fiordiligi in Mozart's *Così fan tutte*, both for the new year. These were demanding roles, Ariadne a dramatic Straussian part requiring a big voice and huge stamina, Fiordiligi a complex exercise in high comedy that combined coloratura technique with subtle characterization. But somewhere between that September announcement and the opening of *Ariadne* on

February 6, 1958, Lisa della Casa, already a star at the Metropolitan Opera, replaced Lois in the Strauss, without any announcement or explanation. The reason why remains a mystery. Lois had had to withdraw from the first Toronto performance of Mahler's Symphony No. 2 with Heinz Unger on January 22, just two weeks before the opening of *Ariadne*, so it is possible that she bowed out of the production because of her health. But why, then, was she replaced in April in *Così* as well? By then, she was singing regularly once again, but an American soprano, Marguerite Willauer, sang Fiordiligi, not Lois. Again, there was no explanation. The detailed records of the Washington Opera do not go back as far as 1958, and the opening night reviews make no mention of replacements. Whether Lois withdrew from the productions, or whether she was removed from them, simply cannot be determined. Silently, the references to these Washington engagements disappeared from her Columbia Artists publicity materials.

The fall of 1957, just before the projected Washington operas, had been hectic, even by Lois's energetic standards. In late July, during rehearsals for her *Four Last Songs* concert at Stratford, she spoke with Leslie Bell, conductor of the popular Toronto-based all female choir, the Leslie Bell Singers and music columnist for the *Toronto Star*. In this conversation, Lois's schoolgirl enthusiasm won out over any diva-like *hauteur*. "Just think! I have to give 52 concerts in Europe by next December, and there are so many recording sessions that I can't even count them. Could you please tell me how I am going to learn all that music?" Perhaps the hope of learning Ariadne and Fiordiligi as well on such short notice simply had to give way to the pressures of Lois's other work. Her operatic ambitions were thus disappointed, but only temporarily.

In January 1959, Lois sang the role of Ellen Orford in the CBC television production of Benjamin Britten's *Peter Grimes*, one of the most complex and costly productions the CBC had ever undertaken. This was television of the old school of cultural programming, a two-hour transmission of a demanding modern work, broadcast live without intermission. The experience gave Lois enormous pleasure and artistic satisfaction. The technical challenges alone were formidable. The production, broadcast on January 13, 1959, had to be coordinated between two separate

CBC buildings, one on Jarvis Street and the other on Mutual Street in downtown Toronto. It occupied two large TV studios for the action as well as a separate basement soundstage for the orchestra. The conductor, Ettore Mazzoleni, worked with the orchestra from the basement studio, linked only by closed circuit TV to his singers in their remote locations. At no point in the production could any single member of the cast see all its other members. The public questioned the outlay of cash, nearly $150,000, on an opera then considered obscure and avant-garde, but Lois staunchly defended it. "My only regret," she said, "was that the opera could be given only one performance."

An unscripted event, unnoticed by most viewers, provided one of the most poignant moments in the show. In a live transmission, there are no time delays, no ways to edit out mistakes or miscalculations. The CBC's Franz Kraemer, director of the production, later described one small crisis, over almost as soon as it had begun, and Lois's fortitude in the face of it.

> In this scene, played in a pub, when Peter Grimes enters, there's a storm and in order to make it more realistic, we poured water over him just before he entered. So there was real water, and of course it dripped from his leather coat to the floor and made the floor slippery. And so Lois slipped, as you could see if you looked at it carefully. She immediately got up and went on. Didn't bother her at all.

A review of the video tape of the production clearly shows Lois's fall, her quick recovery, and the visible concern of James Whicher and Trudy Carlyle, the cast members nearest her, as they reach forward, without breaking character, to help her up before she is fully down. For someone without a disability, such a fall might be merely disconcerting. For Lois, it could pose a much greater problem in getting herself up and re-establishing her equilibrium. In her later years, falling became such a commonplace occurrence for Lois that it no longer bothered her. Stuart Hamilton, her accompanist during that time, recalled a bad fall she had while on tour, at the Ottawa airport, and her performing in Toronto the following day, despite the bad bruises she had sustained in the fall.

Reviews of the *Peter Grimes* telecast praised Lois, both for her singing and for her dramatic presence. Nathan Cohen, the *Toronto Star*'s acerbic drama critic, reviewed *Peter Grimes* (on January 14, 1959) as a groundbreaking experiment in televised drama.

> Soprano Lois Marshall was outstanding as the quiet young woman who tenaciously, tenderly, and uselessly loves Peter Grimes. What a splendid voice Miss Marshall has, so pure in enunciation (never a quaver), so controlled in phrasing.

In the *Globe and Mail* (on January 15), John Kraglund praised her singing, but singled her out especially for her dramatic effectiveness.

> Of special interest was the TV opera debut of soprano Lois Marshall, whose appearances in lyric theatre have, unfortunately, been virtually non-existent. Her interpretation of the role of Ellen Orford had the ease and conviction of a veteran actress.

Kraglund's lament about Lois's absence from the lyric stage was soon to be challenged. In December 1958, while preparing for *Peter Grimes*, she had received word that she had been engaged to perform the role of Mimi, the tragic heroine of Puccini's popular *La Bohème*, in a fully staged production in Boston. So, on January 29, 1959, a scant two weeks after her televised operatic debut, Lois opened a run of thirteen performances of *La Bohème* in Boston, her first experience with live opera onstage since *The Magic Flute* seven years before. This Boston *La Bohème* brought Lois into contact with one of the most imaginative, determined, and eccentric individuals in the field of opera in North America.

Sarah Caldwell might best be described as elemental, a force of nature. For this enormous woman, huge in body as she was in ambition, nothing in the world mattered as much as opera, certainly not the niceties of personal hygiene or the observance of conventional hours for sleeping or eating. In 1957, Caldwell had dragooned a few friends into helping her to found an opera company in Boston. She brilliantly adapted the Community Concerts model of pre-selling a season to local subscribers in order to raise working capital, then located a small theatre (the former Fine Arts Theater) and renamed it "The Little Opera House," and by 1958 had mounted her inaugural production, Jacques Offenbach's *Voyage to the Moon*. Caldwell was a one-woman band. As she would do throughout her career, she conducted the musicians, directed the stage action, and involved herself in every other aspect of the production as well. The unexpected success of *Voyage to the Moon* attracted the notice of Columbia Artists Management, who arranged to tour it around North America a few years later. (It may have been the Columbia connection that brought Lois to Caldwell's attention, though Lois already had a following in Boston, based on her recitals there and her appearances with the Boston Symphony Orchestra, both in Boston and at Tanglewood.) From this relatively modest beginning, Caldwell established a reputation in Boston for brilliantly innovative and ingenious productions of difficult, often obscure repertoire that attracted the world's great singers to work under her inspired, unpredictable leadership. Donald Gramm, Jon Vickers, Joan Sutherland, and Beverley Sills happily submitted themselves to the Caldwell mystique. On the strength of her Boston achievements, and without ever moderating any of her eccentricities (she conducted from behind a screen to avoid diverting the audience's attention from the music), Caldwell eventually directed operatic productions at New York City Opera, guest conducted the New York Philharmonic for one of its prestigious Pension Fund concerts, and became the first woman ever to conduct at the Metropolitan Opera. In 1976, again from behind a screen, she would conduct the Toronto Symphony Orchestra at Ontario Place, with Lois as guest soloist. Lois's 1959 *La Bohème* opened the first full season of Caldwell's Boston Opera Group.

Ever the director concerned with stage effect, when she first set eyes on Lois Caldwell burst out, without thinking, "You know Lois, this is wonderful. I've always wanted to have a Mimi who was really sick." Lois often told that story on herself, a touch ruefully, and it is testimony to

Caldwell's charisma and essential good nature that Lois never held it against her. More than that, she soon learned to ignore Caldwell's quirks, and the pungent odour she often exuded, and became genuinely fond of her. In Caldwell, despite her tactlessness, Lois recognized an operatic director for whom her disability was no impediment to effective stage action. Lois, it must be remembered, was about to act onstage without any of the theatrical preparation and training most aspiring operatic singers would have had. She needed basic theatrical guidance, not just accommodation for her disability.

> Caldwell was wonderful. We would rehearse together and she would come up onstage and walk through every single movement that she had planned for me, *with* me, and we would decide whether it would work or not. And then she would go out and see how it looked and that's the way we did it. I thought she was absolutely marvellous as a stage director. Not only for me, for everyone.

Weldon, who of course observed the rehearsals and performances, shared Lois's admiration for Caldwell's genius. With a keen eye for effect, Caldwell kept enough movement swirling around Lois to involve her in the action. It looked as though she was as mobile as the rest of the cast, even though her blocking was carefully tailored to her individual abilities. To add to the challenge, Lois had to learn the role of Mimi, which she had not studied before, in two languages. After opening night, she sang Mimi three times a week for four weeks, one week in the original Italian and the next in English translation.

Of the other members of the cast, only the American baritone Donald Gramm, who played Colline, went on to a major operatic career. Harold Rogers, who reviewed the production for the *Christian Science Monitor* (January 20, 1959), thought Caldwell's choice of Lois for Mimi was "a masterstroke of casting," and had the wisdom to comment on the stage direction ("there was nothing dusty about Miss Caldwell's staging") without reference to Lois's disability. The first-rate pickup orchestra included players, past and present, from the Boston Symphony.

In November 1959, Lois returned to Boston to open Sarah Caldwell's second season with three performances in the title role of Puccini's *Tosca*. Despite the briefness of the run, she once again had to perform the role in both English and Italian on different nights. Lois had already sung the role at least once, in the Wichita concert performances of 1957, but the staged version posed particular challenges. The most athletic of them occurs in the opera's finale, when Floria Tosca leaps to her death from the parapet of Rome's Castel Sant'Angelo. Caldwell solved this particular problem by having a double, dressed in identical costume, take the plunge in Lois's place. Harold Rogers, in the *Christian Science Monitor* (November 10, 1959), while once again full of praise for Lois's singing, was less enthusiastic about her acting: "Miss Marshall is not the most convincing of Toscas: as an actress there were times when she didn't rise to the full heights of the drama involved."

In a newspaper interview in the *Winnipeg Tribune* a few weeks after the performances, Weldon concurred with this critical judgement, but then elaborated on Lois's closing performance.

> When I attended the third and final *Tosca* performance, this time sung in Italian, I was startled at Lois's performance. Despite the fact that I am her teacher, I am also her most severe critic. But this final performance was magnificent, both vocally and histrionically.

With her typical determination and tenacity, Lois had finally pried open the door that others had so often said was closed to her. But despite Weldon's praise and the optimistic headline of the story that reported it, success in Boston was not enough to "herald a new career in opera." No matter how much Lois willed it, her career as a concert singer and recitalist was too far advanced, her successes in opera too limited and too far removed from its main centres, for her to remake herself as an opera star.

CHAPTER SIX

1957 to 1960 —
To Russia with Love

By the late 1950s, Lois and Weldon were firmly identified in the public eye as professional partners and constant companions. Weldon accompanied her in virtually all her recitals, including her numerous CBC radio broadcasts, and usually travelled with her as coach and advisor for her orchestral and operatic engagements. They spent months of each year together on the road. Lois, now entering her thirties, wanted to establish a home of her own, one that included Weldon, but he continued to maintain his residence at the home he shared with his wife, Marion, and their family, on Strathallan Boulevard in north Toronto. Here, on the subject of Lois, unnatural silence prevailed.

In the spring of 1955, after Nicholas Kilburn and his young wife, Ilona Kombrink, graduated from the Curtis Institute of Music in Philadelphia, they moved into the Kilburn family home in Toronto for about two years, until they could establish their own apartment. Ilona thus had an intimate view of Weldon's family life during this period. Her recollections are of domestic arrangements in which, despite Weldon's frequent absences on tours, no overt acknowledgement of his relationship with Lois disturbed the conventional surface of normal family life. When he was in Toronto, Weldon was in residence at Strathallan, the head of a large, musical family. His mother, Hilda Kilburn, paid regular visits from her home in Edmonton. During the Christmas holidays, the Kilburn clan enjoyed family fun together, with the whole family joining Hilda in her favourite card game, "Pounce." As late as 1962, a feature story, with photographs, in the *Toronto Star* tactfully glossed over any rift in the family. A prominent photo showed Marion and her children in the family home, while a separate headshot of Weldon accompanied his glowing praise of their musical offspring. Lois never visited the house, nor was her name ever mentioned. It was as though the major part of Weldon's professional life simply did not exist.

Once in Toronto, Ilona and Nicholas quickly set about establishing themselves in their profession. Nicholas, a superb bassoonist, joined the orchestra of the National Ballet of Canada and freelanced in Toronto, playing in the CBC Symphony, in various ensembles, and in regional festival orchestras at the Stratford Festival and further afield at the Peninsula Music Festival in Fish Creek, Wisconsin, where both Lois and Ilona would appear. In 1959, Nicholas joined the Toronto Symphony Orchestra as Principal Bassoon. Ilona, who had coaching sessions with Weldon during her early years in Toronto, found the doors to opera opening readily to her. A statuesque beauty with a ravishing soprano voice, she starred in *Tosca* with the Canadian Opera Company, sang the Countess in *The Marriage of Figaro* at the Stratford Festival, and played leading roles in CBC televised productions of opera. She also carried on a busy concert career in Canada and then in the United States, after her return in the early 1960s. Weldon's second son, Michael, played cello in the Toronto Symphony Orchestra from 1957 to 1964. Another son, Paul, became an accomplished pianist in his own right. Weldon's family members were everywhere in Toronto's world of professional music. Except for Ilona, who never appeared on the same bill with Lois, they might share the stage with Lois and their father (who sometimes accompanied a set of folk songs for her during an orchestral appearance), then return to the family home with Weldon and their mother. Quite apart from the family stress involved, it was a perilously small world in which to conduct a life as complicated as Weldon's.

As a newcomer to this scene, Ilona found herself plunged into a family situation she did not fully understand, and which no one explained to her in advance, a situation she would later describe as "a silent kind of impasse." In musical circles, she heard a few oblique, sympathetic comments — "Little did Ilona know, when she married into *that* household...." She even received veiled warnings about Weldon himself, when he replaced her scheduled accompanist and travelled with her to fulfill an engagement in western Canada. Ilona was a beautiful young woman, after all, and Weldon had a certain reputation. But as far as Ilona was concerned, nothing untoward ever happened. It took many years, long after her marriage to Nicholas had dissolved, before she would piece together the complete picture for herself. Not until 1977, when Lois toured Madison, Wisconsin, where Ilona was teaching voice at the University of Wisconsin, could the two meet as professional colleagues, without all the baggage of a complicated, secretive family situation to weigh down their encounter.

In August 1957, just before departing with Weldon on a five month European tour, Lois signed an offer to purchase a house of her own in Toronto. Her younger sister Pat and her husband were buying a house in a new subdivision near the Scarborough Golf and Country Club, in an area being developed just north of Lawrence Avenue. As Lois's sister Rhoda remembered it, the subdivision then was mostly muddy fields, but Lois quickly made her choice. Her new home was to be built at 32 Golfhaven Road, on land adjoining Pat's property. By then she could easily afford it. A 1957 profile reported that she received the highest concert fee in Canada, and estimated her annual income at a hefty $50,000, before taxes, accompanist's fees, and management commissions. This estimate was probably conservative, given her base fee of $750 to $1,000 per concert and the hectic pace of her schedule. Her house, however, was neither large nor lavish, just a conventional bungalow with an attached carport, very similar to every other house in the subdivision. Close proximity to her sister was one of its major attractions. Lois's immediate departure for Europe left no time for her to supervise its construction, so Pat acted on her behalf. Throughout her trip, letters flew back and forth between Pat and Lois with progress reports.

Probably as early as 1958 (and certainly no later than 1960), Weldon finally left his family and moved into Lois's house on Golfhaven, although for some years he maintained an apartment on Church Street as his official address and teaching studio. The move, though pleasing to Lois, could not eliminate the tensions inherent in their difficult situation. Weldon's sons felt their mother's hurt at this public rupture of the marriage. Lois, they believed, was putting pressure on Weldon to get a divorce and marry her. Weldon's own feelings in the matter remain unclear. Paul Kilburn believed that his father temporized by telling Lois that Marion would not give him a divorce; Nicholas remembered his mother saying that she would give Weldon a divorce, as long as he could pay for it. Since Weldon had no financial resources for an expensive settlement, stalemate ensued.

As soon as Lois moved into the house on Golfhaven she furnished one room as a music room, with two pianos, an upright and a grand (ordered over the phone from Eaton's), folding chairs, and music stands. Over the years that room was home to much music-making, some of it planned and formal, but much of it of the impromptu variety, at the many boisterous parties Lois loved to throw. When the spirits moved them, she and her friends might belt out a few choruses from *Messiah*, and were not too proud to tape-record the results for playbacks and hilarious post-mortems.

Lois's attempts during the late 1950s to break into the world of opera had done nothing to slow down her recital career, which moved confidently forward throughout that period. The international stardom that eluded her in opera came to her on the concert stage. Those years took her around the world, on the road for months at a time, back to Europe for important engagements and recording sessions, and on to exotic new destinations.

Her most prestigious engagements on the August 1957 tour were at the Edinburgh International Festival. Founded by Rudolf Bing in 1947, before he became the General Manager of the Metropolitan Opera in New York, the Edinburgh Festival had, by the end of its first decade, established itself as one of the major European summer festivals. In contrast to the Salzburg Festival, which specialized in opera — especially the operas of Mozart — Edinburgh, with its more eclectic mandate, showcased the best in orchestral concerts and solo recitals. By 1957, it was one of the most coveted engagements a young singer could list on her resumé.

As part of the 1957 Festival lineup, Lois sang the Brahms *Requiem* (with German baritone Heinz Rehfuss, the Hallé Orchestra and Sir John Barbirolli) and Strauss's *Four Last Songs* (with Eugen Jochum and the Bavarian Radio Symphony). She and Weldon appeared in solo recital at Edinburgh's Freemason's Hall on August 27, performing a program of Schumann, Mahler, Purcell, Debussy, and Britten. Since the Festival prided itself on presenting only the best in international music, Lois and Weldon found themselves participating in a star-studded series. The other vocal recitals that year were given by the French baritone Pierre Bernac, accompanied by the eminent French composer Francis Poulenc, by the international superstars Victoria de los Angeles and Dietrich Fischer-Dieskau (both accompanied by Gerald Moore, far and away Europe's best-known accompanist), and by two European artists well-known to connoisseurs, the baritone Heinz Rehfuss and the tenor Anton Dermota.

Weldon's third son, Paul, by now a young man of twenty-one, accompanied Lois and Weldon to Edinburgh and turned pages for his father onstage during the recital at Freemason's Hall. For Paul, that concert demonstrated yet again the electric atmosphere which his father and Lois could generate uniquely in live performance. Studio recording sessions simply could not duplicate the conditions under which their expressive art thrived and reached its full potential, could not capture their best performances. That night in Freemason's Hall, their onstage chemistry worked as powerfully as ever on the musically sophisticated Festival audience. Gerald Moore was the first person through the dressing room doors to congratulate Lois and Weldon after the recital.

Lois and Gerald Moore had a connection going back almost ten years. Moore, born in England, had lived and studied music in Toronto for part of his youth, during the First World War. He had been a choirboy and, at age sixteen, the organist and choirmaster at St. Thomas's Anglican Church on Huron Street. On his return to England, he continued his career as an accompanist for vocal and instrumental soloists and, before the term "collaborative pianist" had been coined, achieved name recognition as a collaborator equal in stature to the musical greats with whom he appeared. His brother, Trevor Moore, remained in Toronto, where he eventually became a Chair of the Toronto Symphony Orchestra Board. This family connection drew Gerald Moore back to Toronto. In 1948, he had given a set of master classes at the Conservatory summer school, and Lois had been one of the students selected to work with him and his piano students. In 1949, at the end of his second summer school stint in Toronto, Lois had performed in concert with Moore at the keyboard. Moore recalled the experience vividly in his memoirs. "As soon as she sang I was staggered by the beauty of her voice, by her knowledge and grasp of Schubert's songs. When she sang, the time flew by, she inspired the lot of us."

In October 1957, Lois moved on from England to the Netherlands for an eighteen-concert tour that included both solo recitals and appearances with orchestras, among them the world renowned Concertgebouw. And this time, in contrast to her first visit there in 1956, she played to sold-out houses. Thus began a love affair between Lois and the Dutch public that brought her back to the Netherlands at least three more times. Sitting in the audience at one of Lois's recitals in The Hague, in the elegant recital hall called Diligentia, was a young student of voice named Elly Ameling, who would go on to become an international Lieder singer and exponent of Bach, much loved for the warmth and sincerity of her interpretations.

> I remember Lois sang [Schumann's] *Frauenliebe und Leben*. And right from the first tone, she imprinted something of "soul" quality in my young girl's mind. I think those are very important experiences, that you get in the beginning of your life, first as a child and then certainly as a young student. She had that warm, embracing personality when she sang, and when her soul shone out of her. I'll never forget that. I think it has helped build me up.

Back in London, Lois sang for the first time under the baton of Sir Malcolm Sargent, in a performance of Elgar's *The Apostles* at London's venerable Royal Albert Hall. Sargent, one of the prominent English conductors of the day, had already become a champion of Lois's friend and classmate, James Milligan, during his meteoric, all-too-brief European career. Three days after *The Apostles*, Gerald Moore accompanied Lois for her London recital debut at the Royal Festival Hall on November 10, 1957. Perhaps Weldon had returned to Toronto early, or perhaps the London promoters decided that for this important engagement Lois needed a collaborating musician better known to British audiences. The noted British clarinettist, Jack Brymer, appeared on the program as well, in "The Shepherd on the Rock," Schubert's charming trio for voice, piano, and clarinet. By the end of December, after a brief trip to Germany where she performed and recorded the Bach *B Minor Mass* (again with Eugen Jochum), Lois returned home to Canada.

Despite a few Toronto engagements, Lois had little time to enjoy her new home on Golfhaven Road. In the new year she headed to western Canada, on a Community Concerts recital tour, and by late July 1958 she was in Vancouver again, to appear with a galaxy of stars at the inaugural Vancouver International Festival, the brainchild of the unstoppable Niki Goldschmidt. Not content to rest on the laurels of his Toronto achievements, Goldschmidt had shifted his sights to Vancouver, where he dreamed of a world-renowned international festival, lotus land's answer to Edinburgh or Salzburg, and set about realizing his dream on the grandest possible scale. In the inaugural season, the centrepiece was a production of Mozart's *Don Giovanni*, with Joan Sutherland, the reigning international diva of the day, making her North American debut as Donna Anna. Niki conducted.

But Goldschmidt loyally promoted Canadian stars at the Festival as well, including Léopold Simoneau, Maureen Forrester (under the baton of Bruno Walter), Glenn Gould, and, of course, Lois. At the Festival she performed Bach with the CBC Chamber Orchestra, did a solo recital with Weldon, and appeared in the premiere performance of *Judith*, a cantata by a young Canadian composer, Paul McIntyre, which had won the $1,000 Festival Prize for new Canadian composition. McIntyre had been a student at the Conservatory during Lois's time there. William Steinberg, conductor of the Pittsburgh Symphony and later of the Boston Symphony, conducted, and Leo Ciceri, the Canadian actor who would soon become a regular member of the acting company at the Stratford Festival, narrated.

But the most memorable performance from the VIF was unquestionably Lois's appearance, in a stellar quartet of vocalists, in Verdi's *Requiem*, with Steinberg conducting the Festival Chorus and Orchestra. Lois shared the stage with Maureen Forrester, Jon Vickers, and George London (an honorary Canadian in the group, by virtue of his birth in Montreal). Vickers squeezed Vancouver into a demanding summer schedule that included his debut at the Bayreuth Festival. They performed the work twice, on August 2 and 3, 1958, in Vancouver's ornate old Orpheum Theatre.

The more Lois's career took her into oratorio, German Lieder, and the works of Bach, the harder it became to remember her as a singer capable of the dramatic intensity and the vocal weight required by a work like the *Requiem*. Yet Lois had sung this taxing, operatic version of a requiem mass eight years earlier, in Toronto, and would do so again in 1964, in Winnipeg. In 1978, at the end of her career, when she was singing as an alto, she even took the mezzo role in the solo quartet at a performance in Thunder Bay, Ontario, with Maria Pellegrini in the soprano part. Although the Vancouver Verdi was broadcast by the CBC, no tape of that radio performance has come to light. Judging by the evidence of surviving tapes and recordings of Lois performing other Italian operatic repertoire, however, our conception of her as strictly a recitalist, working on a smaller scale, fails to do justice to the power and dramatic range of which she was capable, especially in her youth. In a 1956 video, in the unlikely surroundings of Jackie Rae's popular TV variety show, Lois makes spine-chilling drama of "Sola, perduta, abbandonata" from Puccini's *Manon Lescaut*, bringing the aria to an electrifying climax on "Non voglio morir." Sir Ernest MacMillan's son, Keith, who was the recording engineer for some of Lois's earliest Hallmark recordings, reportedly said that her voice was so powerful he had to locate the microphone a good twenty feet away from her to avoid distortion in the pickup. William Steinberg must have been satisfied that she had the goods for Verdi. In 1961, Lois told radio host Pat Patterson, in an interview on CBC's "Trans Canada Matinee," that she was signed to do a recording of the Verdi *Requiem* with Steinberg in the following year. Lois was not usually one to count her chickens before they hatched, at least not on national radio, but that recording, unfortunately, never took place.

In September 1958, after the Vancouver International Festival, Lois and Weldon packed their bags yet again, for a long trip that began in England with performances in London (Strauss's *Four Last Songs* under Sir Adrian Boult at the Proms), moved on to France (the Montreux Festival), then to Italy (two performances of the *Missa Solemnis* at La Scala), took in the Netherlands, and concluded back in England (Elgar's *The Kingdom* with Sir Malcolm Sargent, another *Missa Solemnis*, with Sir John Barbirolli at the Royal Albert Hall, then the *Four Last Songs* in Bournemouth). The great highlight of this trip, however, was their first visit to the Soviet Union in October, between her appearances in Italy in September and the Netherlands in November.

Good luck and careful background negotiations on Lois's behalf preceded her first visit to the Soviet Union. Still engaged in the Cold War, post-Stalinist Moscow in the mid-1950s was only beginning to make tentative gestures towards the West. The Soviets probably saw Canada, with its much lower international profile, as a safer recipient of cultural overtures than the United States, its archrival and chief competitor in matters cultural and scientific, as well as military. The American pianist Van Cliburn had stunned the Soviets, and the international musical world, by his upset victory at the first international Tchaikovsky Competition in Moscow in April 1958; Leonard Bernstein, conducting the New York Philharmonic, would cause controversy with some of his public comments during the orchestra's visit to the Soviet Union in 1959. However, in 1957, before these contentious, high-profile events, the Soviet Ministry of Cultural Affairs invited its first two Canadian guests, Québécois conductor Jacques Beaudry, and Glenn Gould, to the Soviet

Union. The arrangements for Gould's visit were handled by Walter Homburger, the Canadian impresario who ran Toronto's International Artists concert series and would, in 1962, become the Managing Director of the Toronto Symphony Orchestra. Homburger had travelled with Gould on his 1957 tour, and was a strong supporter of Lois and her career. Gould so impressed the Russians that they asked what other Canadian artists he might recommend. Gould and Homburger mentioned Lois's name. When Gosconcert, the official government concert agency that controlled all visits by musicians to the Soviet Union, issued an invitation, Lois leapt at it. Homburger worked out the details on her behalf and by January 1958, the tour was already being reported in the Toronto papers. Her Moscow debut would take place on October 2.

In 1958, isolation and repression still dominated every aspect of Soviet society, including its musical life. Too obvious a curiosity about the West might smack of disloyalty, could be dangerous, so audiences in Moscow, one of the major musical centres of the world, knew virtually nothing of Western artists. With Western recordings almost impossible to come by, they weren't even abreast of recent developments in performance practice, changing tastes in concert repertoire, or the postwar sound of classical music-making. Their musical horizons remained where they had been twenty years or more ago, fixed by a controlling regime that feared the influence of all things foreign, all things modern, all things tainted by capitalism. They were the generation of the Cold War, children of the post-Revolution, and ripe for revelation.

Their tastes had been formed by the glorious musical tradition of their own past, reflected in part by the architecture of their principal concert hall, the Great Hall of the Moscow Conservatory. Once through the classically elegant, yellow stucco portico (the façade of one of Moscow's eighteenth-century royal palaces), concert goers ascended a magnificent marble staircase to enter one of the great concert halls of the world, acoustically perfect, with cream coloured decoration set off by white stucco mouldings and plush seats. The vast stage, big enough for a full symphony orchestra, was dominated by ranks of pipes from the huge organ at the rear. The setting was both inspirational and intimidating. Any musician presuming to appear on this stage had the eloquent standards of the hall itself, its architecture and musical tradition, to live up to. Would Lois, on that October night in 1958, be up to the challenge? Would anyone in Moscow even care? At best, only two-thirds of the hall's seventeen hundred seats were occupied. She was an unknown from Canada, parachuted into Moscow's most prestigious concert venue with little advance publicity. Thanks to official Soviet indifference, her reputation, though growing steadily in Europe and North America, had not preceded her. What could the audience members expect?

Certainly not what first caught their attention. As the slight figure made her way from the stage door, all the long way to centre stage, there was a collective intake of breath. Her left leg appeared to be stiff, of little use to her. It had to be swung laboriously from the hip with every step. Nothing had prepared them for the sight of such an obvious disability. Their hearts went out to her as she moved slowly, purposefully, to her place, followed at a discreet pace by Weldon, a tall lanky man, handsome, intense, obviously a good deal older than she. Once she had established herself securely in the bend of the grand piano, she raised her glance to meet theirs. A second collective intake of breath. She was so pretty, with serious eyes, her pale skin set off by the elaborately styled, abundant dark hair, and with the sentimental ball gown she had chosen, with extravagantly full crinolines and yards of overskirt. Visual pleasures were in short supply in the Soviet Union in 1958. Without having heard her sing a note, the Muscovite concert goers felt disposed to like the stranger before them.

But as soon as she began to sing, irrelevant considerations of appearance and sentiment evaporated. Here was revelation, singing unlike anything the Moscow audience had heard in the last twenty years. Some of the repertoire was unfamiliar — the English songs of the seventeenth and eighteenth centuries, songs by Mahler and Strauss, British folk songs, but even the familiar repertoire — Handel, Bach, the German Romantics — was sung with a restraint, an elegance of taste, a shapeliness of phrasing and a depth of feeling that made it new and exciting. Audience members could not contain themselves. Her singing took them out of the old-fashioned musical conventions of the past, out of the hardships of their Cold War lives. Her singing breathed into them new possibilities of youth, of freshness, of vigour. Instantly, they took Lois Marshall to their hearts.

Almost fifty years after the event, at least three individuals could recall vividly the excitement of that evening. Alexander Tumanov was then a young vocal student in Moscow. He would become so enamoured of Marshall's singing, and eventually so enthused about her compatriots, like Maureen Forrester, that he immigrated to Canada, thinking the country that could produce the likes of them would provide a welcoming environment for an aspiring musician like himself. Not all his hopes would be realized, but he brought with him a treasured pirate tape of Marshall's Moscow debut, a poor recording, but a powerful testimony to the fact that memory has not exaggerated the event. Peter Roberts and Doris Crowe, both attached to the Canadian Embassy in Moscow at the time, also remembered the instant impact of her performance.

All three agreed on a story that had also been told about Glenn Gould's Moscow debut a year earlier. Perhaps it was the way of a Moscow audience when assessing an unknown artist. Perhaps it was their only way of getting the word out about a Western newcomer. At intermission, people stormed the few telephones in the lobby to call their friends and tell them to drop what they were doing and come to the concert hall. When Marshall returned to the stage after intermission, it was noticeably fuller than it had been before. She sang a generous, by today's concert standards huge, program. Tumanov thought then how tired she must have been, not just from singing, but also from the long and exhausting flight to Moscow. With six more concerts and the rigours of 1950s Soviet travel in prospect, another singer might have been anxious to conserve her voice. But apparently Marshall hadn't reckoned with a Russian audience's implacable demand for encores, or the exhilaration of the evening itself. According to Tumanov, she refused to spare herself.

> She wanted to sing more and more, and the more she sang, the more she wanted to sing. So the atmosphere was huge excitement. In one of the encores, the "Musetta Valse" from *La Bohème* by Puccini, she was in very good voice. She sang Musetta with such a freedom, such a

joy, it was really a woman who was relishing her life. And then she goes up to the top note. I believe that this is B natural on the top. And when she came to it, she wanted to hold this note like a *fermata*, and I presume that when they rehearsed it, when they did it in other circumstances, she was supposed just to pass this note and go down. But she wanted to sit on it and Weldon wanted her to get off of this note. So we could hear in the accompaniment, how he *pushed* the next chord to chase her out from this place.

The Moscow audience, used to the strictest formal etiquette between performers on the concert stage, to a society that frowned on public displays of spontaneous affection, sensed that there might be a more intimate relationship between the young singer and her much older accompanist, as indeed there was. Alexander Tumanov once more:

The relationship between Lois Marshall and Weldon Kilburn on stage was different than the usually stiff and very formal communication between a singer and an accompanist.... I would say that philosophically, she opened for me a new world. She represented the inner freedom which was an absolutely overwhelming concept, because we all were captives within our country. When we heard her, we felt this inner freedom which they had, saying what they wanted, relating to whom they wanted, and this was a huge thing.

As initially planned, the 1958 tour called for only one performance in Moscow, followed by appearances in Riga, Leningrad, and Kiev. But that opening Moscow recital, broadcast over state radio and television, transformed Lois instantly from an unknown Canadian singer into a celebrity. "I can hardly describe it," Lois recalled later. "The audience stood and cheered and cheered. They were broadcasting the program over radio and TV, and even the TV technicians crowded round me and actually cheered my performance. It was wonderful." In Riga, they gave her the same tumultuous reception. On the street outside the concert hall, strangers greeted her and congratulated her. The Leningrad concerts sold out long before she got to town. Even before she had left Moscow, a return engagement had been added. Gosconcert rescheduled a symphony concert, originally booked into the Great Hall of the Conservatory on October 23, to make way for Lois. From Kiev, she returned to Moscow in even greater triumph.

Lois and Weldon on the stage of the Great Hall of the Conservatory for Lois's Moscow debut, October 2, 1958. The event was broadcast on Soviet television.

Credit: From the collection of Cindy Townsend.

For this second concert, the Canadian embassy rallied to host a large diplomatic reception, with Lois as the guest of honour. But the party had to be thrown together on relatively short notice. Both the Ambassador, David Johnson, and the Chargé d'Affaires, Marshall Crowe, were out of Moscow on previously scheduled diplomatic business, leaving the junior in the Embassy, Peter Roberts, in charge. Roberts himself would later serve as Canada's Ambassador to Moscow, and later still as the Director of the Canada Council. An indispensable member of the Embassy staff at the time was George Costakis, a Greek national whose family had lived in Russia for generations, and whose lively interest in the arts gave him informal contacts with a host of Russian artists and musicians. Costakis approached Marshall Crowe's wife, Doris, who remained behind in Moscow, with the information that people in Moscow's musical circles anticipated Lois's return eagerly, and wanted the opportunity to meet her. Might the Embassy host a reception for her after the concert? Doris Crowe and Peter Roberts thought this a good idea, and set about arranging a party. Their guest list included large numbers of Moscow musicians, as suggested to them by Costakis. In order to get some diplomatic mileage out of the event, they also invited Max Frankel, the Moscow correspondent for the *New York Times*. Frankel was delighted by the invitation. The day before the party, news had come in via the wire service that Boris Pasternak was to receive the 1958 Nobel Prize for Literature. This would be the perfect opportunity to interview Moscow's cultural elite, in an informal setting, about their response to the exciting announcement.

The events of the day itself demonstrated instead the power of the Soviet state to invade every aspect of the private life of its citizens. If there had previously been a slight thaw in Soviet cultural relations with the West, the public announcement of the Nobel Committee's decision, on the very day of Lois's Moscow recital, plunged relations into the deep freeze once again. The Khrushchev government could not countenance such international recognition for a writer who was discredited by the authorities in his homeland. Under pressure, Pasternak would eventually, famously decline the honour offered him.

The government couldn't risk unscripted comments from its artists on such a delicate subject finding their way into the Western press. On the day of the party, the regrets, all worded identically, came pouring in from the musicians and artists who had so wanted to meet Lois. It seemed that all the prominent musicians in Moscow had been mysteriously called out of town on the same day. "It was," as Doris Crowe later described it, "as though they had all been written by central casting."

And, as Roberts recalled, "You didn't, if you were a Russian, go lightly to foreign embassies. The Soviet police would stop you at the door on the way in, and perhaps, on the way out. They might even visit you later, at your apartment." Given the tensions caused by the Pasternak announcement, who could blame the vulnerable Soviet citizenry for keeping a low profile under duress? The politics of the Cold War had intervened, to put a damper on the celebrations for Lois.

Fortunately, Lois herself knew nothing of this at the time. Her concert was jammed (presumably by many of the same artists who would find themselves "out of town" as soon as it concluded). Her appearances outside of Moscow had accustomed her to some of the ways of Russian audiences — the rhythmic clapping, the insatiable appetite for encores, the interruptions to the program while baskets of flowers were presented at the footlights, the spontaneous little gifts, some of them handmade, the handwritten notes with expressions of admiration and love, the heartfelt requests that she return to Russia again — but one of the conventions of Russian concerts still perplexed her. At every concert, an "announcer" accompanied Lois and Weldon onto the platform and, in a pompous, elocutionary style, spoke the name of each selection before it was sung, accompanied by a brief summary, in Russian, of the lyrics, despite a printed program being provided. Understanding none of the announcer's introduction to one of her folk songs of the British Isles, Lois was taken aback when the audience involuntarily tittered. The announcer had solemnly intoned the Russian equivalent of, "He loves her but she does not love him. Both are unhappy." The poignant third verse of "Ae Fond Kiss," which by now was Lois's signature folk song, a piece she sang with heartfelt longing and almost unbearable regret, in fact, bids farewell in these rather more poetic words:

> Fare thee weel, thou first and fairest;
> Fare thee weel, thou best and dearest.
> Thine be ilka joy and treasure,
> Peace, enjoyment, love, and pleasure.

Even such disruptions to the atmosphere by the announcer, however, could not dampen the audience's enthusiasm for Lois. In the second half of the program, as a departure from the standard soprano repertoire, she included Manuel de Falla's *Siete Canciones Populares Españolas* (*Seven Popular Spanish Songs*), usually sung by mezzo-sopranos or contraltos. Alexander Tumanov remembered the absolute sensation Lois created, especially when she reached "Polo," the concluding song in the set.

> And suddenly, in the "Polo," the first note was like a knock on your head by a hammer. It was like a gypsy crying, screaming. We heard the rage of a woman in despair. And for me it was a woman dancing in despair, just turning around, raging, screaming, not with a clear soprano voice, but with something like an animal in her voice. And when she finished, it was such a rapture of applause I thought that the hall would be destroyed.

In the audience, Doris Crowe and Peter Roberts sat with the Soviet pianist, Sviatoslav Richter, at that time one of the most eminent figures on the world concert stage. Roberts took the opportunity to ask him what he thought of Lois's singing. "Miraculous," said Richter. Emboldened, he went on to ask Richter how he thought Weldon had played. "Not the way she sings," came the answer. Neither of them followed that train of thought any further.

The post-recital party at the embassy was still on, albeit with a smaller turnout than anticipated. One Moscow musician, a conductor accompanied by his glamorous red-headed wife, did show. It turned out he really had been out of town on the day of the recital, on a flight back to Moscow, and had come to the party straight from the airport, unaware of the Soviet directive that he be otherwise engaged. Peter Roberts escorted Lois from the ornate grandeur of the Great Hall of the Conservatory to the Canadian embassy, which he described as "a lovely, old, soft, eighteenth-century building." As they were leaving the stage door of the concert hall, crowds of young concertgoers pressed on Lois as she made her way to the embassy car, surged round it as it pulled slowly away, hung

Lois at a party in her honour, following her Moscow debut, 1958. Lois's interpreter is seated behind her.

From the collection of Cindy Townsend.

onto the door handles and called out, "Encore, Lois, Encore!" A hundred years earlier, they would have unhitched her horses and pulled her carriage through the streets. It was like the departure of a legendary diva in the Golden Age of song.

Within the Soviet Union, however, Lois's 1958 appearances were not breaking news. Without a functioning free press, informed critical response for any cultural event was scarce. The Moscow dailies did not review concerts, unless there was a particular political point in doing so. The cultural journals, such as *Soviet Music* and *Soviet Culture*, notorious for their long delays in publishing accounts of performances, routinely omitted the date of the performance in question, to avoid calling attention to the time lag. Accounts in their pages sometimes read more like flowery, abstract appreciations than specific reviews of an actual concert. After the Pasternak embarrassment, there was even less incentive to provide a press record of a Western artist's accomplishments. Reuters news agency, however, managed to get an assessment from one informed observer at Lois's October 23 recital. "Words fail to express my admiration. In the more than 20 years since I heard Marian Anderson in Moscow, I have not gotten such pleasure from singing…. Lois Marshall captivates one by her high culture and genuine artistry." Nina Dorliak's admiration counted for something. She was one of Soviet Russia's prominent sopranos (virtually unknown in the West, of course) and a leading professor of voice at the Moscow Conservatory. She was also Sviatoslav Richter's wife.

Lois would make six more trips to the Soviet Union during her career. On her second visit there, in January 1960, a chance encounter at an airport resulted in a detailed, first-hand account of the difficulties Lois had to face in travelling to an iron curtain country. On January 6, 7, and 8, Weldon and Lois attempted to fly from Brussels to Moscow. In the Brussels airport, they happened to meet an American freelance journalist, Richard Gehman, whose account of their travel woes, published in Toronto's *Star Weekly* (May 28, 1960), gives a vivid record of one arduous, unglamorous incident in the life of the touring artist.

All three travellers were booked on the Russian state airline, Aeroflot, for the January 6 flight to Moscow. Lois and Weldon arrived at the Brussels airport in plenty of time for the noon departure, checked in at the main terminal, and then walked the inordinately long distance to the departure lounge, burdened with all the carry-on and parcels of the international traveller. In the lounge, they were told that the flight would be delayed. They toiled back to the terminal, then, when their flight was called again, returned to the departure lounge. Now the flight was cancelled because of poor visibility in Moscow. Another walk back to the terminal, followed by a bus ride to the cheap hotel in which passengers were being accommodated overnight. When Lois went to hang up her coat, the rickety wardrobe fell over on her, and she had to call Weldon to come to the rescue.

Early on the morning of January 7, after another long walk from check-in to departure gate, followed by an hour-and-a-half wait, Weldon and Lois were allowed to clamber laboriously up the steep exterior staircase into their aircraft. For an hour they sat in the damp, unheated plane, and then received instructions to disembark and return to the terminal. Aeroflot fed them lunch on the ground, during which they discovered, too late, that a Sabena Airlines flight had just taken off for Moscow. After lunch, Aeroflot called their flight and they hiked down to the departure lounge one more time, to be told that the flight was, once again, cancelled. Another night in the same cheap hotel. After a great deal of upheaval, Lois at least managed to retrieve some of her music from their checked luggage for score study, so that her second night of delay would not be completely wasted.

On January 8, they finally managed to take off as scheduled and arrived in Moscow after the three-hour flight that had now taken them three days to accomplish. In Moscow, after the wearying process of clearing customs, a cultural attaché met them with flowers and the news that they were leaving that evening for Leningrad, a twenty-four hour trip by train. Lois would have barely a day to recover and rehearse before her first concert, in Leningrad's Great Hall of the Philharmonic.

Gehman's account emphasizes two important things. First, Lois took on all this exertion and inconvenience in good humour, without complaint, without any of the aids that today's air traveller takes for granted — no moving sidewalks, no same-level entry to the aircraft, no electric courtesy carts inside the terminal — and without relying on a wheelchair or any other accommodation for her disability. Second, though she was silent about it, she did so at a cost, as Weldon revealed in private conversation with Gehman. "Her leg is paining her now, I know. It always does when she has been on it too long, and she's been on it much too long today."

If the Russians loved her in 1958, they worshipped her in 1960. In Leningrad, after all the foot stomping and the clapping and the last of the many planned encores, the audience continued shouting for Schubert's popular "Ave Maria." Lois and Weldon finally complied and after she had finished, in Lois's own words, "There was a silence in the hall that I couldn't possibly describe. We felt it was the only way we could have ended such an evening." Her Leningrad admirers presented her with two white lilac trees, over four feet high, in full bloom. (They even promised impetuously to ship them to Canada so she could plant them in her garden on Golfhaven Road.) In Moscow, the audience mobbed Lois at the footlights, pressing flowers on her and calling out, "We love you, and we are waiting for you." Long after she had retired to her dressing room and the crowds awaiting her there, the hall remained half filled with lingering fans. As Lois reported in one of her letters to George Kidd, the Riga audiences delighted her by "their universal appreciation of our work as a team. They do not focus their attention on the voice or the piano, but listen to every song as a whole thing. A good ensemble is as essential to the audience here as it always is to the performers." And in their Riga hotel, where the elevators stopped running at midnight, the elevator operator remained patiently at his station until Lois and her party had finished their post-performance dinner at 1:15 a.m., in order to spare her climbing four flights of stairs. Among the anonymous gifts delivered to Lois's hotel was a miniature candelabrum, with a note painstakingly worked out in English: "This gift is in case the lights of the world should go out, and I do not believe they will, for there is more good people in the world as bad."

Such spontaneous outpourings of love from the fans were Lois's greatest reward, since the Russian tours did little for her bank account. Gosconcert covered travel and accommodation for visiting artists, but it adhered resolutely to its socialist schedule of fees for concert artists, paltry by North American standards, and it paid those fees in Russian rubles, which could not be taken out of the country. Essentially, Lois performed in Russia for the few souvenirs she was able to buy with her fees, and for the experience. Some of the souvenirs turned out to be overpriced. On one of their trips, Lois and Weldon bought a small gold and silver cordial set, with decanter and glasses. When they got to London on the return journey, Weldon took it to Christie's, hoping to have it valued conservatively by the world-renowned fine art auctioneers in order to get it through Canadian customs with minimal duty. "I'm afraid I've got rather bad news for you," said the discreet appraiser at Christie's. "They're not really worth what you paid for them." And he set the value at five pounds for the lot.

As was customary for visitors to the Soviet Union, Lois and Weldon had an interpreter assigned to them for their visits. Lois mentioned their interpreters in one of her 1960 letters home to the *Toronto Telegram*'s George Kidd.

> We have a charming interpreter, Larisa, who is very good fun, and we had a wonderful reunion with our Tamara, who was with us last year and whom we simply loved. So we had, in fact, two interpreters while in Moscow. Tamara and Larisa have been to all three Moscow concerts and the following parties at the Canadian Embassy.

Tamara drew an affectionate set of caricatures of the visit and presented them to Lois as a gift, which Kidd published in his column of February 15.

Weldon's son, Nicholas, later painted a different picture of the couple's relationship with their interpreters. He believed that Weldon's roving eye had alighted on one of them in particular, whom he found extremely attractive, but close proximity to Lois at every moment of the tour allowed him no opportunity to act on his inclinations. Weldon, apparently, did not equate personal devotion with sexual fidelity. Though his love for Lois was deep, his care and compassion for her authentic, and his admiration for her genius unqualified, such considerations seem to have placed few restrictions on his pursuit of sexual enjoyment outside of their relationship. He had behaved thus during his marriage to Marion, after all, and little had changed, even though he had left Marion for Lois. Whether Lois guessed any of that at the time can never be known.

Lois's tours of the late 1950s included important studio recording sessions as well as performances. The Beecham discs and the oratorio LP with Anthony Bernard and the London Symphony Orchestra had been made during her first trip to London in 1956. On her second, in 1957, she recorded a disc of operatic arias with Eduardo Pedrazzoli and the LSO once again (studio sessions September 18–20, 1957). Some selections from the oratorio collection and three tracks from the operatic recital (one Handel and two Mozarts) have been reissued on the *Lois Marshall Arias* CD by CBC, but the most interesting of the repertoire from the operatic disc has virtually disappeared. The LP itself may never have had a North American release. This rare recording now circulates among a few die hard Marshall fans, chiefly by means of taped copies, often of poor quality because of frequent recopying.

This operatic recital is, at best, a frustrating, inconsistent hint of what might have been. Lois, who occasionally battles a somewhat breathy tone and intrusive vibrato, seems constrained, and rises only intermittently to the dramatic heights of which she was capable. Pedrazzoli's conducting, often slow and lacking energy, may account in part for the constraint of Lois's performances. The recording levels on the disc are harsh and unflattering to the timbre of her voice. The short duration of the recording sessions, only three days, suggests a hurried project. Even her later folk song LP, which involved only piano accompaniment, apparently took five days in the studio. But for all that, the operatic album abounds in rare treasures. "Hark the ech'ing air" (Purcell), well-known in Lois's other recordings with piano accompaniment, gets the full orchestral treatment. "Parto, parto," from Mozart's *La clemenza di Tito*, which she often performed in recital with piano accompaniment and clarinet obbligato, showcases her fabulous, confident coloratura line. And here is documentation, at the very least, of the operatic repertoire she programmed so often, but for which she is seldom remembered — "Non mi dir" from *Don Giovanni*, "Tacea la notte placide" from Verdi's *Il Trovatore*, "Leise, leise, fromme Weise" from Weber's *Der Freischütz*, "Casta diva" from Bellini's *Norma* (a glorious performance to which most of the critical reservations previously expressed do not apply), even "In questa reggia" from Puccini's *Turandot*. This LP, however inadequate in some respects, lays to rest any doubts the skeptic might have about Lois's ability to perform the Italian repertoire convincingly and preserves for the record the Lois Marshall of large, dramatic, operatic ambitions.

A year later, in September of their 1958 trip to London, Lois and Weldon made what was probably the most popular of her recordings, although to date it has never been reissued on CD. *Lois Marshall Sings Folk Songs* was recorded for EMI and released in North America on the Capital label. With Lois in superb, youthful voice, and Weldon providing sensitive support of the highest musical standards, the LP presents sixteen of the folk songs of the British Isles that Lois had already made a staple of her recital repertoire. Lois performs with an eloquent simplicity that touches the emotional depth of these songs, as it did the hearts of thousands of her fans, in the concert hall or glued to the speakers of their record players. For generations of those fans, her stately, serious performance on this disc of Robbie Burns's "Ae fond kiss" has never been equalled. On those rare occasions when it is broadcast today, it still has the power to stop listeners in their tracks, a testimony to a voice and a way of singing now silent.

But despite its popularity, *Lois Marshall Sings Folk Songs* was the last of Lois's European studio recordings and almost her last work for a major commercial label. At a time when the burgeoning recording industry and the brave new world of high fidelity had the power to create a worldwide reputation and market for classical musicians, a time when records made a singer's name and sold her concert appearances to a record-buying public, Lois's recording career languished. Even her later North American records, many of them concert recordings rather than studio sessions, received limited promotion and distribution.

Lois often regretted that recording technology was not advanced enough to do her justice in her heyday. Her voice certainly could pose problems for the recording engineer. But as Carl Morey, former Dean of the Faculty of Music at the University of Toronto and creator of the three-part CBC radio documentary on Lois, "Hark the Echoing Air" (broadcast in 1983), has pointed out, the voice itself was unusual: "There was a kind of silvery whiteness to the sound that I think a lot of people did not find appealing." Detached from her stage presence, divorced from the electric atmosphere she and Weldon could generate before a live audience, Lois's sound lacked the qualities that made other singers easily marketable on record. She was a performance artist, not a studio artist, and in her heart of hearts she knew it.

Once, while Lois was still a teenager and her brother Fred was home on leave, a friend of his brought a primitive version of a tape recorder to one of the musical evenings at the Marshall home. Fred recorded an enthusiastic rendition of Rodolfo's "Che gelida manina," from *La Bohème*, strong on passion but a little weak on the concluding high C. Lois allowed herself to be talked into recording Mimi's responding aria, "Si, mi chiamano Mimi." Hesitantly, she got down on the floor in order to sing directly into the machine. When she heard the playback, she fell into deep despair, unable to believe that what she heard was any approximation of her voice. The assurances of Fred's friends that this was exactly the way she sounded only deepened her misery. Lois suffered, in exaggerated form, the disillusionment that many people experience on first hearing a recorded version of their own voices. There seemed to be a complete disjunction between the internal impression she had of her own sound, resonant and full, and the pallid, strangulated sound of the reproduction. This early experience exposed the central insecurity of the singer's profession: you can never truly know the most important thing about yourself, how you sound to others, how you sound "out there." God forbid it should be what the tape recorder tells you.

Lois's disappointment with her recorded sound probably contributed to her later dissatisfaction with the recording studio. Certainly the strongest recordings of her mature career remain those that were taped live — Schubert's *Die schöne Müllerin*, or her recital of three Schumann song cycles, both recorded in concert at Hart House at the University of Toronto. Even if their audio quality cannot match the controlled conditions of the recording studio, live records such as those capture the spontaneity and continuous drama of a Marshall performance as no studio sessions have done. For similar reasons, Lois's enduring, virtually secret legacy remains the treasure trove of tapes from her CBC broadcasts, an archival record that spans her entire career, from the Scarlatti Christmas concert in 1947 to her Hugo Wolf recital with Greta Kraus in 1981. Unlike most studio recordings, these live performances fix in our imaginations a moment in time, an evening when Lois, unedited, actually performed these feats, when an audience heard and applauded, when ordinary people, touched by what they had heard, lined up after the concert for just a word or two with the woman who had moved them so deeply.

Lois's international touring of the late 1950s had made her a public figure back home, her international exploits eagerly reported in newspapers across the country. The summer of 1959 could be thought of as her royal summer. On Canada Day she dined with Queen Elizabeth and Prince Philip at a state dinner in Rideau Hall in Ottawa, one of a host of citizens invited to represent a broad spectrum of Canadian achievement and experience. The guest list included Lawren Harris, Maurice Richard, Celia Franca, Claude Bissell, and Robertson Davies, as well as leaders in business, labour, religion, and politics. After dinner, when the ladies withdrew to the long drawing room, Lois enjoyed some private conversation with the Queen. Not many of the guests were so lucky. Most had to content themselves with a brief, formal presentation to the royal couple before dinner, and conversing with one another.

Just two weeks later, on July 15, Lois performed for the royals in Vancouver. Her Majesty had agreed that the new Vancouver Civic Auditorium could be named in her honour, and Elisabeth Schwarzkopf, the great German soprano and EMI recording star, a headliner at the Vancouver International Festival, had been invited to sing on this gala occasion. But Schwarzkopf, recovering from surgery, suddenly cancelled her entire North American tour, so Niki Goldschmidt turned to Lois. Her old friend, Sir Ernest MacMillan, conducted her in arias from the Handel oratorios *Judas Maccabeus*, *Solomon*, and *Samson*. A cynic might be tempted to reflect on the double standard implicit in this sequence of events. Lois made the A-list at the state social occasion for distinguished Canadians, but when star power was required, she got the nod only as a substitute for the indisposed international artist. Her newfound Russian fans would have been very puzzled.

The new decade began with even greater international exposure — an extended tour of Australia and New Zealand. In the fall of 1959

On July 1, 1959, Lois was among the guests at a formal dinner in Ottawa for Queen Elizabeth and the Duke of Edinburgh. She is pictured here at Rideau Hall with Celia Franca, founding Artistic Director of the National Ballet of Canada.

Credit: York University Libraries, Clara Thomas Archives and Special Collections, Toronto Telegram *fonds, F0433, image no. ASC05189.*

Lois was occupied with her Boston *Tosca.* December 1959 was filled with bread-and-butter performances — a recital in Winnipeg, *Messiah* in Toronto, even, contrary to her expressed preferences, a Beethoven Ninth in the CBC's complete Beethoven symphonies cycle, with the Russian-born Efrem Kurtz conducting the CBC Symphony and the Mendelssohn Choir. Then, in January 1960, Lois and Weldon embarked on the longest of their tours to date, an eight-month marathon that took

them first to Russia, and then, via London and the Netherlands, on to
Australia and New Zealand. While in London, Lois fielded newspaper
enquiries about rumours that she was being courted by Covent Garden,
and even the Metropolitan Opera. "It's only talk. I don't know whether
I want to or not," Lois parried the reporter's questions. Perhaps she
dragged her feet because of the role under discussion — another Queen
of the Night. Despite her operatic experiences with Sarah Caldwell, the
major houses still seemed unable to think of her in any but the most
static of roles. In any case, the talk came to nothing. Lois never sang in
either house. By mid-February, she had moved on to the Netherlands
(her fourth visit to that country in five years) for eight concerts there.
From the Netherlands, she undertook the arduous thirty-three-hour trip
to Australia, touching down but not even leaving the plane in Karachi,
Calcutta, Singapore, and Bangkok.

Discussions about a possible tour of Australia went back a full ten
years. Paul Malone, an Information Officer in the Canadian Embassy in
Washington had raised the possibility with Lois after her very first appearance there, at the Washington Sesquicentennial in July 1950. Malone
had helped to arrange a tour of Australia for Sir Ernest MacMillan in
1945 and hoped to do the same for Lois. (Perhaps Sir Ernest had put a
bug in his ear?) At that time, the Australian Broadcasting Corporation
sponsored the visits of many foreign artists to Australia, whose appearances they then broadcast over radio and television. Canadian embassy
officials in Canberra raised the matter directly with Charles Moses, the
Corporation's Managing Director, who suggested 1953 as the earliest possibility, given the long lead time needed to arrange such tours.
The invitation, however, took even longer than that. By 1960, Lois had
achieved a worldwide reputation, and Australia had an ambitious new
artistic venture to promote. The Corporation invited Lois to open the
first Adelaide Festival of Arts, followed by an extensive tour. Originally
planned for twelve weeks, it eventually stretched to almost sixteen.

The outdoor opening concert of the Festival, on March 12, attracted
an audience of forty thousand people. (Lois herself estimated a mere
25,000, but the *London Times* of March 14, 1960, reported the higher
figure.) It was a sweltering summer night in Adelaide. Backed by the

combined Sydney and Melbourne Symphony Orchestras, conducted by Henry Krips and by Nicolai Malko (with whom she had worked at Grant Park, in Chicago, seven years earlier), Lois trotted out a few of the old chestnuts from her repertoire, ideal festival fare: Mozart's brilliant *Exsultate, Jubilate*, then Puccini's popular "Si, mi chiamano Mimi," and his demanding "In questa reggia." Her tour then criss-crossed Australia, taking her from the far west (Perth and Albany) to the far east (Melbourne and Sydney), north as far as Brisbane on the Gold Coast and inland to Toowoomba. Lois had nearly 140 songs in her active repertoire, meaning in her memory, for the recitals she and Weldon gave on the tour. In addition, she performed frequently with local orchestras, in repertoire ranging from Ravel's *Shéhérazade* and Strauss's *Four Last Songs* to Haydn's *Creation* and Rossini's *Petite Messe Solonnelle* (with Sir Malcolm Sargent in Brisbane). With that exhausting pace it was small wonder that she caught a bad cold in the middle of the tour, and had to sing a few performances at less than full strength.

Her tour of New Zealand, immediately following the Australian one, lasted approximately four weeks, to the end of July 1960. In Christchurch and Wellington, with John Hopkins and the National Orchestra, Lois performed programs that included Strauss's *Four Last Songs*, Falla's *Seven Popular Spanish Songs*, Beethoven's "Ah, Perfido," and Lia's aria from Debussy's opera, *L'Enfant Prodigue*. In smaller centres, she and Weldon presented some of their standard recital repertoire. Weldon was still including a solo piano selection on most of their recital programs, as was customary in concerts at the time. In Auckland, he took on Beethoven's "Moonlight Sonata."

"Weldon Kilburn, an able accompanist, especially in the Falla cycle, was less at ease as a soloist. He began the 'Moonlight' sonata with a casual air, passed on to some good moments and got into sad difficulties of memory in the finale." This reviewer had discovered Weldon's Achilles heel. Throughout his career, he suffered from stage fright so extreme it undermined his ability to play from memory. According to some, this weakness alone had stood between Weldon and a distinguished solo career. As an accompanist, or member of an ensemble, he could control his nerves, but as a solo performer he always ran the risk of succumbing to them.

In a new country, no matter how good her advance publicity, Lois had to build her audience from scratch. Her recital program in Auckland, for example, drew "an audience which in numbers, if not in enthusiasm, was an insult to an artist of this stature." The forty thousand who heard her in Adelaide's Elder Park had evidently come for a civic event, as much as for Lois. When she gave a recital in Adelaide's Town Hall just one week later, the auditorium was only half full. But that audience heard Lois at her best. John Horner, reviewing for the *Advertiser* (March 21, 1960), described in loving detail her way with the lengthy "Alleluias" at the end of Purcell's "Evening Hymn." He elaborated on her decision to ignore the *accelerando*, or quickening of tempo, that editors of the score often suggest in order to solve some of the singer's problems of breath control.

> Scorning such aids, Miss Marshall held herself proudly and measured out each dotted crochet and quaver in full at the original tempo, growing louder and louder the while and broader in style, producing in the end an effect of such regal majesty and power as only one singer in a generation has the equipment even to attempt.

His keen observation brings a vintage Marshall performance back to life, and serves as a reminder of how different the character of her Purcell was from the less weighty, more delicate and instrumental sound favoured for his vocal music today. And though she held herself proudly, the reviewers couldn't help commenting on her unusual stage deportment and mannerisms. In Sydney, "these included the quite extraordinary range of vigorous head movements and facial expressions by which Miss Marshall supplemented the voice's demonstration of the depth of the feelings which possessed her as she sang" and "the rather gasped intakes of breath and a pulsation of the tone in sustained notes."

At a different concert, as another reviewer noted, "On some occasions she would jerk her head to a whole bar of music, timing herself for entry."

Vignettes such as these capture the surprise, the wonder, and at times the discomfort of observers encountering Lois for the first time.

They strip away the insulating familiarity that by now conditioned the responses of her regular audiences, who were used to her platform manner. Lois had a great voice, though not a perfect one, as the roundabout description of her vibrato quoted above points out. She had extraordinary communicative powers, over a wide range of repertoire. But her stage presence was always a surprise. Spectators were often taken aback, before they were won over.

In *This Is Your Brain on Music*, the McGill University neuroscientist Daniel Levitin cites recent scientific studies that show that "... nonmusician listeners are exquisitely sensitive to the physical gestures that musicians make." He describes the ordinary listener's ability to detect the musician's expressive intent by attending to gesture and movement. Full musical appreciation, he argues, comes through this combination of auditory and visual stimuli. If this positive correlation applies then its reverse may also hold true. The negative, or at any rate unexpected, visual stimulus of some of Lois's stage mannerisms could have complicated the initial responses of members of her audience. They had to become accustomed to what they saw, before they could be fully attuned to what they heard.

That was not a long or difficult process. Experiencing Lois for the first time, reviewers in Australia and New Zealand outdid themselves in their efforts to compare her to great singers of the present and the past: Victoria de los Angeles (who had recently toured New Zealand), Dorothy Maynor, Lotte Lehmann, Conchita Supervia (the legendary early twentieth-century Spanish soprano and definitive interpreter of Falla's songs — Lois would have been pleased). But such efforts to locate her on a map of vocal artistry were futile. Artistically and vocally, she was a law unto herself. With only Weldon's musical guidance and support, she fearlessly made each work she sang an expression of her own remarkable individuality. It took the accounts of strangers to remind her home audiences that Lois was unique. She belonged to no conventional school of singing. She stood outside the schools.

CHAPTER SEVEN

1960 to 1967 —
Wagner and the Vocal Crisis

The human voice issues from two small bands of muscle tissue, the vocal cords or vocal folds, located in the larynx. In their resting position, the vocal cords are separated from each other. Singing or speaking requires that the cords be brought together and then set vibrating by the controlled passage of air through them. The quality of the sound depends on breath support and resonance, but the essential activity is muscular. As such, it is subject to the normal process of aging. For the singer, this process typically affects the overall range and suppleness of the voice, an older singer losing the ability to reach the highest (and sometimes the lowest) pitches of which she was once capable, and often also losing the ability to control the vibrato, or sound of vocal "wobble," when singing a single, sustained pitch. Listeners describe the natural aging process as the singer's voice becoming darker with age. In the older singer, maturity of musical experience and depth of interpretation often compensate for this gradual fading of basic vocal equipment, this sense that the older voice has lost its youthful bloom or become somewhat tarnished with age and use.

But because singing is essentially a muscular activity it can also lead to specific, unanticipated episodes of muscular strain, quite apart from the normal aging process itself. Over time, bad habits may creep into a singer's vocal production; illness, fatigue, or simple overuse of the vocal cords may cause them to react physically and impair or even prevent the normal activity of singing. Individual singers respond in widely differing ways to signs of such vocal strain. Some are able to "sing over" a cold or even a bout of laryngitis, by which they seem to mean that they use a lighter, less strenuous approach to activating the vocal cords and manage to sing successfully by using less voice than they normally would. Both Beverley Sills and Maureen Forrester gave perfectly creditable performances while suffering from laryngitis that made it difficult for them to speak normally. Other singers, however, feel completely undermined when their voices fail to perform to maximum capacity and can do themselves greater harm if they attempt to soldier on. A singer's relationship to her voice is a complex combination of physical response and psychological reaction. Serious muscular strain poses a constant occupational hazard for any singer, and especially for a singer as active as Lois.

As she moved into the prime of her career, during her mid and late thirties, Lois unwittingly moved towards a major vocal crisis, an episode of severe vocal strain that silenced her singing for a prolonged period of recovery. Though she returned to as full and active a career as ever, that experience eventually affected her vocal self-confidence. Gradually, the daredevil Lois who would tackle anything gave way to a more careful, sometimes more hesitant artist, who no longer had the absolute confidence that had characterized her in her youth. Furthermore, after this crisis, the normal signs of aging, as they began to appear in her voice, affected Lois's spirit more deeply than they might another singer. A robust voice wasn't just basic artistic equipment for Lois, it was an essential part of her identity. Practically speaking, it was also her meal ticket and, increasingly, it was Weldon's as well.

Unlikely as it seems, Weldon's name had remained on the faculty of the Royal Conservatory throughout the years of extended absences, touring with Lois in Europe, the Soviet Union, and Australia. On their return from New Zealand in the late summer of 1960, however, all that changed. Weldon's name appeared in the Conservatory *Yearbook*, its annual prospectus for students, for the last time in 1959–60. Thereafter, he coached independently, from his own studio, and was listed, in 1961 and 1962, as head of the voice faculty at the Brodie School of Music and Modern Dance on Eglinton Avenue in Toronto, a school founded in 1961 by saxophonist Paul Brodie and his wife Rima, a dancer and artist. The radical design of Brodie's school (flexible, non-standard lesson lengths, no formal examinations, no diplomas or certificates), suggested a degree of rebellion against the strictures of Royal Conservatory practices that appealed to the maverick in Weldon. As an independent coach, he continued to attract an impressive roster of singers, both senior students and established professionals.

Weldon's progress to this position of independence and respect as a vocal pedagogue had not been easy. At the Conservatory, because he had never had a professional career as a singer, some of the members of the voice faculty, like Ernesto Vinci, considered Weldon an interloper. Not until 1951, after his student had won both "Singing Stars of Tomorrow" and the Eaton Graduating Scholarship, did Weldon's name appear as a member of the Voice faculty there. Prior to that, his appointments had been in Piano, Accompanying and Vocal Coaching — a minor distinction to an outsider, perhaps, but a hotly defended one in the ego-driven world of the Conservatory.

Weldon's formal departure from the Conservatory confirmed the fact that his career was now tied inextricably to Lois's. His reputation as a vocal pedagogue depended in large part on her fame, and a significant portion of his personal income now derived from her engagements. He received accompanying fees from Lois, since her contract with Columbia obliged her to cover her accompanist's expenses, and would have been entitled to charge her for coaching and preparation time as well, though there is no record of any such formal arrangement between them. With or without formal acknowledgement, their partnership, which had long been both artistic and romantic, was now a business partnership as well.

Following her return from Australia and New Zealand in the fall of 1960, a solo recital at Massey Hall on November 18 confirmed Lois's stature as an international star of the first order. Lois had sung at Massey Hall many times in the past, but never as a solo attraction in Walter Homburger's elite "International Artists Greater Artists" series, and never advertised with the powerful tag line, "Only Toronto appearance this season." "International Artists" carried the same cachet in Toronto that "Sol Hurok Presents" did in the United States. "It was the only major series that was in existence at the time," Homburger later commented, "and it was held in the biggest hall and I tried always to get the top artists to come. And so I guess from that point of view it became a prestigious event." John Kraglund estimated that two thousand people crowded Massey Hall to welcome Lois home. As she had done in her Russian debut, she treated the Toronto audience to Musetta's Waltz from Puccini's *La Bohème* as one of her encores. Reviewing the performance in the *Toronto Star*, John Beckwith heard it as a personal statement, as well as a musical tour de force.

> Musetta's Waltz Song from 'Boheme,' done as the third of four encores, carried Miss Marshall's usual depth of feeling, and moreover — what might not have been predicted — an exceptional understanding of Musetta's free-love radiance. The piece brought the audience, already enthusiastic, to its feet with shouts of approval.

Internationally, Lois was keeping distinguished company, as befitted her stature. Her other prestige engagement, in December 1960, was with the famed Beaux Arts Trio at the Smithsonian Institute in Washington. The Beaux Arts Trio, founded in 1955 and active with its original pianist, Menahem Pressler, until 2008, was already acknowledged worldwide as the standard-bearer among small chamber ensembles. This concert was Lois's first collaboration with its then cellist, Bernard Greenhouse, who would be one of her most frequent musical colleagues in years to come. On this occasion Lois performed, with Weldon, Schumann's song cycle, *Frauenliebe und Leben*, and with the Trio, three of Handel's "German Arias" and the little-known *Rococo Trio* for soprano and trio by Hermann Zilcher, a twentieth-century German composer. Paul Hume, writing in the *Washington Post* (December 3, 1960), called the Zilcher "a monument to banal clichés, [with] phrases so fatigued that the mind, dazzled by Haydn and Handel, refuses to believe they are seriously meant." This weak composition, he went on to say, was "topped by a kind of Everest performance unstintingly given by singer and players. Miss Marshall fairly outdid herself in glorifying the music." Hume had long been one of Lois's strongest supporters, but the Everest metaphor suggested something more than the usual praise, that Lois was now an artistic force in her own right, the kind of musician whose performance could redeem even a negligible work.

But almost immediately after the recognition of these important engagements, Lois's career took a surprising step backwards. The lure of opera, and her friendship with Sarah Caldwell, drew her into professional company and artistic circumstances that she would have been better to avoid. Columbia Artists had picked up Caldwell's production of *La Bohème* for the Community Concerts circuit in small-town Canada and the United States. In February 1961, Lois hit the road for a six-week tour. In sharp contrast to her earlier experience, this time *La Bohème* tried her to the uttermost. The entire tour was done by bus, a mode of travel Lois loathed. The difficulties of mounting the steep, narrow stairs of a bus's entry and finding a comfortable position for her legs in the cramped seats during the long trips took an especially hard toll on Lois, given the nature of her disability. But it took more than mere discomfort to get Lois to complain. In her view, the musical experience, despite Sarah Caldwell's presence in the pit, was bad. Only at the final performance in Boston did they have a decent orchestra. Caldwell herself did not conduct all the performances outside of Boston. And except for Lois, even the cast members, including her Rodolfo, changed during the tour as well. With such lack of continuity, musical standards inevitably suffered.

Reviewers in the American regional centres, where fully-staged performances of opera were a rarity, loved it. "If an applause meter could have been installed in Aycock Auditorium last night it would have become overloaded and blown a fuse," said the *Greensboro Daily News*. Even Boston's *Christian Science Monitor* reviewed the show favourably, perhaps not surprisingly, since the Boston performance had the benefit of Boston Symphony players in the pit.

But Udo Kasemets, the Canadian composer and reviewer for the *Toronto Star*, called a spade a spade when he caught the production at the Community Concerts series in Hamilton, Ontario. He had only praise for Lois's performance, acknowledging her as the highlight of a production that, in his view, was lamentable and entirely unworthy of an artist of Lois's calibre. "Except for the simple, practical sets, designed by David

Hays, the whole production was outright provincial," wrote Kasemets. "The orchestra, led by Sarah Caldwell, hardly ever played in tune and the cast included only a few singers of vocal proficiency and acting ability." Out of charity, his review omitted the names of any other participants in the fiasco. In the two years since the original production, Sarah Caldwell's trademark attention to detail had been lost. The revival played as a cynical exploitation of an earlier success, in which Lois unwittingly got trapped as the headliner. At least that experience finally taught Lois to resist the temptation of opera simply for the sake of the opportunity itself. Not until the very end of her career did she venture onto the operatic stage again, and then in circumstances worthy of her artistry.

Lois's career passed one other milestone in 1961, her last recording for a major international label. In the fall of that year, she appeared in concert in New York with the American duo-piano team of Arthur Gold and Robert Fizdale. By this time, Gold and Fizdale had achieved world fame as the leading practitioners of the exacting art of duo-piano playing, with a reputation for the discovery of forgotten repertoire and the commissioning of important new works for two pianos. They would go on to win respect for their biographies of two figures of *belle époque* France, Misia Sert and Sarah Bernhardt, and would also publish a quasi-autobiographical cookbook, a reflection of their love of elegant entertaining and gastronomy. With Gold and Fizdale, Lois performed in a work for two pianos and vocal quartet that the duo-piano team had unearthed in the New York Public Library and wanted to bring before the American public. Robert Schumann's cycle of songs, the *Spanische Liebeslieder*, Op. 138, has since found a place in the vocal repertoire, but in 1961, in its vocal quartet version, it was unknown in North America. The other singers at New York' s Town Hall were Regina Sarfaty, Léopold Simoneau, and William Warfield, and this cast also recorded the work for Columbia Records. In 1963 Columbia released it, the first recording ever made of the work, along with a performance of Brahms's more familiar *Liebeslieder Waltzes*, Opus 52 (for the same combination of forces, but without Lois) on side two. Lois's contributions (one solo song, one duet with Sarfaty, and the final quartet) are charming, and the disc, though re-released in 1985 in the

"Chamber Music from Marlboro" series, is now one of the most difficult of Marshall's recordings to locate.

From that point on, the recording studio and the operatic stage, the two easiest ways to maintain a high profile in the world of professional music, had little impact on Lois's career. Within Canada, however, her frequent radio broadcasts and occasional television appearances kept her before the wider public. And from that point on, her live performances on the concert and recital stages defined her, as an artist known to connoisseurs for a specialized and highly demanding repertoire.

During this period, her memorable, if fleeting, collaboration with Glenn Gould strengthened this reputation of Lois's as a musician's musician, by matching her with one of Canada's acknowledged musical giants, an artist renowned for his unwavering musical intelligence and integrity. At the Stratford Festival in July 1962, with Gould at the piano, she departed from her standard repertoire with a performance of *Das Marienleben*, Paul Hindemith's song cycle on the life of Mary, the mother of Jesus. The actor John Horton served as narrator, reading English translations of the German texts by Rainer Maria Rilke. Udo Kasemets in the *Toronto Star* (July 30, 1962) noted the potent combination of Lois's "emotional capacity and sheer humanity" with Gould's "profoundly analytical mind."

"The most unforgettable moment," he wrote, "came with Mary's lament at the cross. Here Miss Marshall not only sang of, but actually turned into, a mother possessed by grief and agony."

John Kraglund, writing on the same date in the *Globe and Mail*, was equally enthusiastic. Despite the critical response, however, the work had limited popular appeal. Hindemith had composed the cycle in 1922–23, and revised it later in his career. Gould, already blazing his own trail as one of the directors of the music program at the Stratford Festival, chose the earlier version for this performance as being far more exciting than the later version sanctioned by the composer. In Canada, in 1962, it all counted as arcane, modern music, far off the beaten path of the ordinary concertgoer. Lois never again had the opportunity to perform it. She made plans to record it with Gould in 1971, but, after repeatedly postponing the recording date, eventually backed out of the project.

On October 15, 1962, while Lois was on another tour of Russia, CBC televised a program, "Glenn Gould on Strauss," which had been recorded earlier for its *Festival* series. On this program, Lois and Gould perform some of Richard Strauss's most popular repertoire in his lush, post-romantic vein ("Beim Schlafengehen," from the *Four Last Songs*, and the concert favourite, "Cäcilie"), as well as a less frequently performed group of songs, the three *Ophelia Lieder*, in a sparser, more transparent compositional style appropriate to the mental derangement of Shakespeare's Ophelia. Gould provides the commentary on the program. Lois's "Beim Schlafengehen" has been commercially released in the Sony edition of Gould's recordings; "Beim Schlafengehen" and "Cäcilie" were issued on videotape and laserdisc in Sony's "Glenn Gould Collection." The *Ophelia Lieder* have never been made available commercially.

The complete show, on audio transcript at Library and Archives Canada, documents the fascinating collaboration between these two artists. In "Cäcilie," Lois and Gould appear not to have reconciled their interpretations completely. She uses a restrained sound, thinner and more contained than most artists bring to this tempestuous work, but Gould seems to prefer the more voluptuous style, and overpowers Lois on the climaxes. In the three *Ophelia Lieder*, however, the two artists are of one mind and working on the same plane of artistic accomplishment. Gould matches his touch to Lois's delicately-spun sound. Together, they achieve a tentative, slightly crazed effect, ideal for the subject matter. In the remarkable rhythmic complexities of the second song, singer and pianist are in perfect lockstep, their unity something felt between them not just calculated in rehearsal. Clearly, though Lois contributes nothing to the television commentary, she understands the character of this music as profoundly as does Gould.

These excursions into less immediately accessible repertoire harkened back to the youthful Lois, unafraid of musical challenge, ready to expend enormous amounts of preparation and rehearsal time on a single performance of a work, but her response to her collaboration with the eccentric and temperamental Gould betrayed, as early as

1962, something of the insecurities that would haunt her later career. Reflecting on their collaboration after the fact, Lois revealed a modesty bordering on insecurity about the value of her own contribution to it.

> He was so incredible in the strong passacaglia type things, and yet the freer and more lyrical things, *he* said, anyhow, that he had some trouble with [them] and that I sang them instinctively. He said he learned something from that, which was very interesting. I wouldn't have thought Glenn Gould would ever learn anything from me, but there you are.

In striking contrast to Gould, Lois's understanding of her art was not abstract and seldom articulated in any way other than through her performing. To the end of her life, she remained intensely uncomfortable when asked to talk about her singing or to comment analytically on any of the works she had performed. She spoke most revealingly when she spoke of the practicalities of music making, including, once again, of Gould as a collaborator.

> He was a little difficult … but he was very sweet … we discussed everything and he accommodated me when it was necessary. I think the hardest thing for … someone like Glenn, who's not used to singers, is that they can't get used to the fact that you have to breathe. And breathing, whether you like it or not, does take a fraction of a second. And it holds things up sometimes.

Modesty like this, perhaps tinged with a hint of awe at the analytical fluency of a talker like Gould, contributed to Lois's often-quoted, and famously misleading assessment of herself as "just a singer." As she put it herself: "I think of myself as a singer. I'm not a great intellectual, but I can sing and I know that. So I think I'm just a singer. And if I am remembered at all I guess I would like to be remembered for bringing people some pleasure." That self-deprecating comment helped Lois to avoid conversations she found uncomfortable, but anyone who thought it a sufficient assessment of her achievement as an artist had simply been deceived by her conversational sleight of hand. "Just a singer" she may have been, but she was the kind of singer who inspired the admiration of the foremost musical colleagues of her time, Glenn Gould among them.

Between the two appearances with Gould, one in person, the other on CBC television, a critical family matter interrupted the hectic pace of Lois's career. Too frequently, she missed the major family occasions while on the road, leading the life of the touring celebrity while her sisters looked after domestic matters. In August 1962 she was on the road again, but fortunately much closer to home, performing Haydn arias at the Stratford Festival, when her mother was hospitalized for cataract surgery. While recovering from the surgery, Florence Marshall, then seventy-six years old, suffered a heart attack. Lois, scheduled to appear at the Peninsula Music Festival in Fish Creek, Wisconsin, cancelled the engagement at the last minute to come to her mother's bedside. In one of the ironies that her private relationship with Weldon sometimes created, Weldon's daughter-in-law, Ilona Kombrink, replaced Lois in Wisconsin.

Lois made it back in time to see her mother, but after a few days of hospital visits it was over. Florence Marshall died on August 15, 1962. Three days later, the family celebrated her funeral mass and buried her in Mount Hope Cemetery, where her husband David had been buried twenty-one years earlier. For the past ten years, Lois's relationship with her mother had been largely long-distance, with many letters from Lois on tour and much maternal pride from Florence back home for her famous daughter's accomplishments. Florence, however, had little appreciation for the kind of music Lois sang and practically no comprehension of the world of professional music. If, by her adult years, Lois had little in common with her mother, their relationship had nevertheless provided her with a vital link to the childhood and family past that had been so deeply affected by her frequent stays in the hospital and the early death of her father. Now that connection was broken. Though Lois stayed in Toronto through the funeral and the interment, she took little time to come to terms with the sudden, unexpected loss, or to adjust to new family structures as they emerged following the death of the matriarch. Just one month after the emotional upheaval of the hospital visits and the funeral, she was back in the Soviet Union for a month of appearances in Riga, Kiev, Moscow, and Leningrad. The life of the professional artist allowed little time for personal grief.

For this Soviet tour, Lois appeared in each city both in recital with Weldon and in a concert appearance accompanied by full orchestra. In Moscow, the orchestra was the Moscow Philharmonic, led by the eminent Russian conductor Kyril Kondrashin, and the repertoire included Richard Strauss's *Four Last Songs*. Strauss composed these lyrical outpourings, filled with melancholy retrospect and calm resignation, in 1948, the year before his death. Their unabashed melodic beauty and rich orchestration evoke an earlier world, untouched by the dissonances of the Second World War, but from the other side of the abyss, recognizing that that world has passed forever. If, as the Russians told her, Lois was the first singer to perform these songs in the Soviet Union, then she had the rare privilege of introducing her Soviet audience to repertoire that has spoken poignantly and personally to all who reflect on the passage of time and the shock and disruption of world events. She gave no sign of slowing down before her demanding Russian audiences. In addition to the *Four Last Songs*, the Moscow program included Beethoven's concert aria "Ah, Perfido," Mozart's *Exsultate, Jubilate*, and "Parto, parto" from *La clemenza di Tito*, a marathon by any standards.

It was likely on this trip that Lois and Weldon made her two recordings for the Russian label, Melodya: another version of their popular folk songs of the British Isles and a small-format LP consisting only of Schumann's *Frauenliebe und Leben*. Very few copies of these records found their way into specialized record shops in Toronto in the 1960s, to be snapped up by collectors and then disappear from view. The Schumann disc, in particular, was one of Lois's favourites of all her recordings, but even she had trouble obtaining a copy. Both recordings are vintage Lois Marshall. They give a vocal snapshot of her as a mature artist, confident in both her interpretive and her vocal powers, all the more valuable because of their likely historical position, just before the vocal crisis that very nearly finished her career.

Lois returned from the Soviet Union in the fall of 1962 to head into a busy Christmas season of *Messiah*s in Winnipeg and San Francisco. Then, in January 1963, she began preparations for one of her Toronto appearances with Heinz Unger and the York Concert Society. Unger had planned something of a departure for Lois's part of the program, a substantial grouping of Wagner arias consisting of "Dich theure Halle," from *Tannhäuser*, Elsa's dream, from *Lohengrin*, and Senta's ballad from *Der fliegende Holländer*, not the most demanding of Wagner's work for soprano, but in combination a real workout. Lois used to perform "Dich theure Halle" fairly often, had sung Elsa's dream at least once, and had done scenes from Act III of *Die Meistersinger* at the May Festival in Cincinnati, but all much earlier in her career. Singers who specialize in Wagner, whose work is notorious for the stamina it requires and the demands of power and sustained delivery it places on the human voice, usually have naturally heavier voices than Lois's, and, if wisely guided, build up to the most demanding Wagner roles strategically, over time. Wagner had played no part in Lois's recent vocal strategy. She had never programmed that much at one time. Indeed, there is no record of her performing any Wagner at all in the years immediately preceding this 1963 concert. Her voice had matured and settled, and had been subjected to intensive use in a comparatively lighter type of repertoire. Whether it would have the weight and power for such a concentrated dose of Wagner, given the development of her career thus far, was an open question.

On January 22, 1963, before a student audience in Massey Hall, Lois sang all three arias at the open rehearsal for the concert. John Kraglund, in the *Globe and Mail*, reported her to be in good voice and looked forward to the next night, when, he believed, she was to add Elisabeth's prayer from *Tannhäuser* to the mix. On the 23rd, Lois appeared, but performed only "Dich theure Halle" and Elsa's dream, abandoning the more taxing aria from *Der fliegende Holländer* and any additional selections from *Tannhäuser*. Kraglund reported the alteration to the program as necessitated by laryngitis and commented that she handled the two arias with "a great deal of vocal beauty and remarkable emotional intensity, seemingly only a trifle troubled by low notes."

Udo Kasemets, in the *Star*, provided more detail, and a more vivid sense of the effort and sacrifice that went into Lois's attempt to fulfill at least part of her obligations.

> … she was forced to handle her voice with more than customary caution. One also was aware that her low notes were less rich than when she is in good voice.
>
> But much graver things than a throat impairment have to happen before Miss Marshall's voice loses its beauty, clarity and communicative power. She is such a great artist, so secure technically and profound musically, that even when fighting a physical handicap, she is capable of electrifying her listeners.
>
> Tumultuous applause and consistent bravo-calls gave witness of how affectionately Miss Marshall's heroic action and artistic performance were received by the far less than capacity audience.

Though Lois had wanted to cancel, Unger, without counting the cost to her own vocal stamina, had talked her into saving the day. The main item on the program, Mahler's Symphony No. 9, was little known at the time, and hardly a drawing card. Unger needed Lois's star power to support this adventurous programming. Lois had sung over laryngitis before, but on this occasion she challenged her voice — already tired from years of uninterrupted, strenuous use — just a little too much. She would eventually pay the price of pushing her vocal cords beyond their limits.

Initially, she appeared to make a good recovery from laryngitis, and filled engagements in Canada and the U.S. before departing on a European tour in March. On that tour, however, she encountered vocal problems more severe than any she had ever experienced before.

In the middle of one of her Dutch concerts, trying to ignore the warning signs she had noticed earlier, she finally could not go on. For the only time in her career, she failed to complete a concert as scheduled. Then she made one of the most difficult decisions of her life; with the help of her doctor, she convinced her tour manager, who wanted her to continue at all costs, that she had to cancel the rest of the tour. Lois returned to Toronto and, for the next six months, on her doctor's orders, neither sang nor spoke.

Her problems were so serious that Weldon feared Lois's career might be finished. Nodules on the vocal cords, the dread of all professional singers, are small growths on the cords, the result of irritation to the vocal cords because of overuse or prolonged misuse. They can be removed surgically but, with the surgical procedures that were standard at that time, at a risk to the singer's voice that Lois could not countenance. Lois jokingly told her sister, Rhoda, that things were so bad she had nodules on her nodules, but she may have been exaggerating for effect. Close friends who knew about her condition believe that she came close to developing nodules, but just managed to avoid them. In any case, her enforced silence allowed her vocal cords time to heal. Although she could have spoken, and one would not have known from her speaking voice that anything was the matter, Lois carried a pad and pencil about with her and, for the prescribed six months, communicated with those around her only in writing.

Characteristically, she never spoke publicly about the frustrations of this period of her life. There is evidence, however, that she chafed under these unnatural restraints, and even contemplated a return to the concert stage much earlier than her doctor had ordered. At the end of April, little more than a month into her regimen of silence, she cancelled an important engagement with the Cleveland Symphony at the University of Western Ontario on just twenty-four hours' notice. She was to have sung the Canadian premiere of Poulenc's *Gloria*, and evidently acknowledged the impossibility of it only at the last moment.

Her enforced hiatus entailed other major cancellations in the spring and summer of 1963. A celebrity recital in New York's Judson Hall, a concert performance of Purcell's opera, *Dido and Aeneas*, at Stratford,

Bach's *Mass in B Minor* in New York, even another Stratford collaboration with Glenn Gould, this time songs by Mahler and Schoenberg — all had to be sacrificed to the slow process of vocal convalescence. And while she remained inactive her income dried up completely.

Long after she had returned to full professional activity, this vocal crisis continued to haunt Lois. Heretofore, her approach to stage fright had been a combination of apprehension conquered by steely resolve. She had drawn energy from nervous tension and, like a high-strung racehorse, had performed well under pressure. Now she became skittish, and shied away from challenges that previously would only have made her nervous. "I actually think this was the beginning of the end of my top notes. After that I was *afraid* when I would get up around high C — being *worried* was bad enough."

Weldon noticed the change in attitude, and even in retrospect scoffed at her apprehension, though he acknowledged its effects.

> … [it] created a psychological block about singing high pitches, I think, and gradually she started taking off arias that would require anything above, say, a C, and then gradually lower than that. And I still think that this whole business of being a contralto and a mezzo stems from that. I think basically it's all psychological. I don't think there's a darn thing wrong with her voice.

Because the long-term damage was more to Lois's resolve than to her abilities, audiences would not hear the results of this vocal crisis of 1963 for some years. Nevertheless, the Lois Marshall who sailed out to meet every vocal challenge head-on, who thrived on the adrenalin rush of testing her own limits, who believed that anything was possible, however difficult, imperceptibly began to give way to a more measured and cautious artist, matured and slightly chastened by experience.

Lois prepared her return to the major concert stages carefully, with performances in smaller centres, removed from the critical spotlight, of familiar repertoire, well-established in her voice. She first ventured out with the *Four Last Songs* at a concert of the Hamilton Philharmonic in early November. She must already have regained some of her old confidence, because she also programmed "Pace, pace, mio dio" from Verdi's *Il Trovatore* and the "Air des Bijoux" from Gounod's *Faust*, not the kind of programming calculated to get any singer through her obligations with a minimum of effort. Then, in early December, she took on the familiar challenges of *Messiah*, not in Toronto, but in Winston-Salem, North Carolina. The reviewer for the *Winston-Salem Journal* appeared to be unaware of any recent vocal crisis. In fact, she thought Lois sounded even better in 1963 than when she had last performed *Messiah* in Winston-Salem, well before any vocal difficulties.

> ... in my report of Miss Marshall's previous appearance, I said I looked around for the angel, so moving was her recitative, "And the angel said unto them." I can go that one better this time — I looked for the whole "multitude of the heavenly host" when she reached that point.

These excursions served as preamble to Lois's real comeback, as soloist for a major engagement that would come under the full critical scrutiny of the international press. On December 4, 1963, the Toronto Symphony Orchestra made its official debut at Carnegie Hall in New York. The orchestra had appeared in Carnegie Hall twice before, in 1953 and in 1954. On the first of those occasions, however, it had been guest-conducted by Leopold Stokowski, the famous American conductor, as part of the special concert devoted entirely to Canadian music in which Lois had performed Godfrey Ridout's "Two Mystical Songs of John Donne." On the second, it had accompanied the Mendelssohn Choir (again with Lois as soloist) in its back-to-back performances of *Messiah* and the *St. Matthew Passion*. This time, under Walter Susskind, who had succeeded Sir Ernest MacMillan as Music Director in 1956, the Toronto Symphony Orchestra appeared on the strength of its own reputation as part of the International Festival of Visiting Orchestras series. For such an occasion, the TSO needed a soloist of international calibre, closely identified with its own performance traditions but well enough known to New York audiences to act as a draw. Lois was the logical choice. Much rode on the success of this engagement, both as a test of the orchestra's abilities in the international arena and as a confirmation of its reputation back home.

She sang Strauss's *Four Last Songs*. "The Canadian soprano sang with a vocal richness and a kind of troubled, tense calm that suggested the irresolution and *Angst* inherent in the painful beauty of these last echoes of a great tradition," said Eric Salzman in the *Herald Tribune*.

Ross Parmenter, in the *Times*, echoed his praise.

> In grace and purity of musicianship, she provided the high point of the program. Always an artist of intense projection, she has mellowed a bit with increasing maturity, and last night one was struck by the velvety quality of her voice. There was a flawless flow of line, too.

His critical stance acknowledged Lois as an established artist, and confirmed the wisdom of the orchestra's choice in identifying Lois as an artist with whom it had a special, longstanding relationship.

If Parmenter knew anything about the major interruption Lois's performing career had just suffered, he said nothing. One of his comments, however, echoed eerily the remarks Kraglund and Kasemets had made about her handling of her lower register in the Wagner concert, just before those serious vocal difficulties.

> A slight reservation was that some of her lower tones were a little hard to hear, but this, in part, was because Mr. Susskind's accompaniments, in being rather loud for such gentle music, were neither very sensitive nor particularly atmospheric. Most of the spell-weaving was left to the soprano.

Though Lois would now worry more and more about her high notes, critical ears detected hints of a problem in her lower register instead. Only one reporter, Ralph Thomas, a staff writer for the *Toronto Star*, made mention of Lois's period of enforced silence, and treated her New

York appearance as the comeback that it was, a glorious refutation of the rumours that had been circulating that "her career was finished."

Fortunately for the interests of historical analysis, a pair of recordings preserved on tape in the CBC collection housed at Library and Archives Canada provides a revealing "before and after" record of the effects of these vocal difficulties on Lois's voice. In both, she sings music by Bach, in Montreal's Redpath Hall, accompanied by the McGill Chamber Orchestra under Alexander Brott. One took place just before her enforced silence, the other shortly after her return to the stage. A comparison of the two reveals a great deal about Lois's vocal problems and about her indomitable musicianship in the face of them.

On February 25, 1963, a month after the difficult Wagner performance of January 23 in Toronto, and prior to her departure for the European tour she would have to abandon, Lois sang Bach's Cantata No. 202, the *Wedding Cantata* ("Weichet nur, betrübte Schatten"), in Montreal. From the insecure opening entry of the voice, something is clearly wrong. She sings the first few minutes of the cantata tentatively, almost *mezza voce* (half voice). Either she is saving herself, or her voice will not respond as she wants it to. (One thinks back to her strenuous warm-ups, and her almost pathological desire to ensure the full responsiveness of her voice before even setting foot onstage.) Three or four minutes into the piece, and her voice sounds fuller and more responsive, but the trills and ornamentation which she would normally throw off with panache are curtailed and hesitant. Not until the second recitative and aria do the old Marshall sound and coloratura flexibility reassert themselves, and even then, in one of the sustained, *piano* passages in a hushed upper register, her tone thins out far more than intended. That uncomfortable moment provides a measure of Lois's difficulties, and of her artistry. Had she sacrificed the dynamic range, and barrelled through the passage at a robust *mezzo-forte*, as many singers experiencing vocal difficulty would have done, she could likely have maintained the quality of her sound. To Lois, however, the musical effect remains more important than the beauty of her own tone. She risks exposure in order to keep true to her conception of the music. Especially in hindsight, the tape testifies unequivocally to the severity of the problems Lois was facing.

Almost a year later, on January 25, 1964, with her successful Carnegie Hall concert behind her, Lois returned to Redpath Hall to substitute for an indisposed Elizabeth Benson Guy, again at a concert by the McGill Chamber Orchestra. This time she sang Bach's fiendishly difficult solo Cantata No. 51, "Jauchzet Gott in allen Landen." From the very opening of the recording of this concert, Lois commands strength, clarity and beauty of tone to equal, if not vanquish, the silvery sound of the baroque trumpet, with which she shares extended duets. There is only one hint, repeated when the musical phrase repeats, of vocal problems past. On the ascending coloratura run on the word "jauchzet," Lois thins out her sound and then cuts short the final note, clearly beyond her comfortable range. But this problem does not faze her in the least. In all the rest of this taxing work, her voice is strong, supple, beautiful, not remotely threadbare. After about fifteen minutes of strenuous singing, this cantata ends with a series of repeated phrases on the word "alleluia." She throws out the text with brilliant, energetic attack, and sustains the brilliancy of her sound throughout the enormous range of the phrase, from bottom to ringing top. She declaims the final "alleluia" triumphantly, resoundingly, its last echoes in Redpath Hall drowned out by the "bravos" of the audience. For any other singer, a return to Bach after such a severe vocal crisis would have been a daunting experience; for Lois, it was a homecoming.

After Redpath Hall, in the spring and summer of 1964, Lois resumed her previous level of touring and concert activity. *Four Last Songs* (with the York Concert Society in Toronto and on CBC television), the Verdi *Requiem* in Winnipeg, an appearance at Massey Hall with the Dovercourt Citadel Salvation Army Band, another tour of Russia (in May and June 1964), Puccini arias in the open air at the Canadian National Exhibition bandshell (with her old friend Sir Ernest MacMillan conducting), the "Seven Early Songs" by Alban Berg at Stratford (another marked departure from her usual repertoire), a program of operatic arias and duets with tenor Richard Verreau in Montreal — the list goes on. The only hint of

On March 28, 1964, at Toronto's Massey Hall, Lois appeared as special guest at
the Salvation Army's seventeenth annual Tri-Festival of Music.

a change, perhaps an indication of her future direction, occurred in some
of her recital programming where, for the first time as far as the records show, she introduced into her repertoire Cherubino's two arias from
The Marriage of Figaro, in the mezzo-soprano range. And of course she

Lois with her friend and mentor, Sir Ernest MacMillan, performing in the bandshell at the Canadian National Exhibition, July 5, 1964.

Credit: Courtesy of GetStock.com.

continued to appear frequently with the Toronto Symphony Orchestra. Lois's strong association with the TSO, acknowledged in their selection of her as their soloist for the Carnegie Hall debut, stretched back to the very beginning of her professional career, in 1948. By its end, she had played a role in the major period of expansion and development of the orchestra's history.

In their thirty-seven year association, Lois appeared at least 125 times with the TSO, in Toronto, on tour, and in frequent radio broadcasts on the CBC. The orchestra's original home, Toronto's Massey Hall, became a second home to Lois. She was moved to defend its acoustics publicly, in a letter to the editor of the *Toronto Star* in 1964 when acoustical renovations were under discussion, and made a special appearance as a soloist in Mozart's *Toy Symphony* when the "Old Lady of Shuter Street," as Vincent Massey had nicknamed the hall, celebrated her hundredth birthday in 1994. When the TSO inaugurated its new home, the Arthur Erickson-designed Roy Thomson Hall, in 1982, Lois was there, as soloist in one of the celebratory concerts.

She was too young to have sung with the Symphony's first Music Director (Luigi von Kunits, Music Director from 1923–31), but she sang frequently with the next, Sir Ernest MacMillan, during his twenty-five year tenure with the orchestra (1931–56), and also with the following four, Walter Susskind (1956–65), Seiji Ozawa (1965–69), Karel Ančerl (1969–73), and Sir Andrew Davis (1975–88), and with Victor Feldbrill, who, as Resident Conductor, bridged the gap between Ančerl's death and Davis's appointment. That succession of conductors guided the orchestra from its beginnings as a supporting ensemble for the famous visiting artists who attracted subscription ticket buyers, to a recognized orchestra with its own musical identity, vying for recognition as one of North America's major orchestras and for attention on the world stage. After Susskind, the youthful dynamo, Seiji Ozawa, rejuvenated the orchestra's sound, shattered its reputation for stodginess, and allowed its promoters to market a cosmopolitan glamour that had never before been associated with Toronto the Good — all before Ozawa's appointment to lead the Boston Symphony catapulted him into the select ranks of international superstar conductors. Karel Ančerl, a survivor of the death camps at Terezin and Auschwitz, brought to the orchestra his maturity of experience and depth of knowledge of the European orchestral tradition. His untimely death after only four years in charge cut short an association that had already inspired the orchestra and its audience, and for which many held out even higher hopes. By the time Davis arrived, attracted to Canada from England on the strength of the orchestra's growing reputation, the TSO had long since stepped out of Sir Ernest's Victorian shadows, into the twentieth century.

Lois was part of that exciting transition, not only a mainstay in traditional music like the annual *Messiah*, but also a participant in groundbreaking performances of important new repertoire. The Symphony's frequent collaborator, the Mendelssohn Choir, recognized her special place in their history by making her their honorary president in 1984, and presenting her with a scroll commemorating her fifty-five separate appearances as soloist with the choir, many of them with the TSO as well. Nor was she simply the famous celebrity, parachuted in like a high-profile visitor. It wasn't the guest conductors who sought Lois's services, but rather the orchestra's music directors, its in-house conductors, and the Mendelssohn's conductors, for whom she clearly became part of the team, a colleague who shared the musical values and performance traditions of both ensembles.

Not surprisingly, the Toronto Symphony Orchestra and the Mendelssohn Choir turned to Lois for one of their most important and prestigious joint ventures, the November 1964 Canadian premiere of Benjamin Britten's passionate anti-war statement, the *War Requiem*. Walter Susskind conducted, and the male soloists were Canadian Victor Braun (already well-launched on his international career) and Britten's long-time collaborator, Peter Pears, for whom the tenor role had been composed. Elmer Iseler, the newly-appointed conductor of the Mendelssohn Choir, prepared the chorus for this daunting assignment. In future years, Lois's career would be as strongly associated with Iseler himself as with the Mendelssohn Choir, which he conducted until 1997, the year of Lois's death.

For a two-year-old work, the *War Requiem* came with a lot of emotional baggage. Toronto audiences anticipated its Canadian premiere as a major event, a musical pilgrimage, not just a night out at the Symphony. Its first performance had taken place in 1962, to consecrate the new Coventry Cathedral, finally completed as a memorial next to the ruins of its medieval predecessor, which had been destroyed by

German bombs during the air raids on Coventry in the Second World War. Canadians felt a close link to the historic site. In 1948, Lois had participated in a Toronto performance of *Messiah* that raised funds for the organ in the planned new cathedral. To augment the *War Requiem*'s powerful historical significance, the Canadian premiere had already been preceded by an enormously influential British recording that captured the pacifist ideals of the composer and the political turmoil they had provoked. By stepping into the soprano role in the *War Requiem*, Lois knew she would be measured, in a work of great emotional resonance for her audience, against a recorded performance that was widely considered to be definitive.

Britten, who had left England for the United States before the outbreak of war and then returned in 1942 to claim conscientious objector status, conceived the *War Requiem* as a statement of his anti-war sentiments. As such, he wanted its solo performers to symbolize reconciliation among the nations that had been such bitter opponents. It was a daring and difficult project to undertake at the height of the Cold War, as subsequent events bore out. Britten composed the soprano part with his personal friend, the Russian Galina Vishnevskaya, in mind. Vishnevskaya, just one year younger than Lois, had prevailed over wartime hardship and Soviet politics to become the leading dramatic soprano of the Bolshoi Opera in Moscow. She was also the wife of the Soviet cellist, Mstislav Rostropovich, himself a famed dissident who was frequently in trouble with Soviet authorities. The other two soloists were the British tenor Peter Pears and the West German baritone Dietrich Fischer-Dieskau. The Soviet authorities could not countenance such overt political symbolism, and refused Vishnevskaya permission to participate because it would have involved her singing in a Christian church, with a West-German. British soprano Heather Harper took her place at the premiere. However, Vishnevskaya's clarion interpretation of the role was well-known from the first recording of the work, released in 1963, when the Soviet authorities did allow her to sing. Despite Vishnevskaya's absence from the 1962 Coventry premiere, the music critic for the *Times* of London recognized Britten's potent, difficult message of peace and reconciliation.

> One could wish that everyone in the world might hear,
> inwardly digest and outwardly acknowledge the great
> and cogent call to a sane, Christian life proclaimed in
> this *Requiem*; yet the work is so superbly proportioned
> and calculated, so humiliating and disturbing in effect,
> in fact so tremendous, that every performance it is given
> ought to be a momentous occasion.

The first Canadian performance took place on November 10, the second on Remembrance Day, November 11, 1964. The TSO replaced its usual house program with a large-format souvenir edition, on the front a stylized depiction of the Coventry cross of nails, which had been fashioned from the relics of the destroyed cathedral. On the inside there was a photograph of the altar, with the inscription, "Father, Forgive," erected in the ruins. Even before the first notes had been heard, the audience was prepared for a momentous occasion.

Anyone lucky enough to be in that audience, as I was, can still remember vividly just how momentous it was. Britten's amalgam of traditional liturgical text with the war poetry of Wilfred Owen created the powerful sense of bitterness, sorrow, and reconciliation that provided listeners with an avenue of access to the music itself, still radically unfamiliar to our ears. Britten's pacifism expressed itself eloquently in a personal, rather than political, response to war. Lois proved herself a worthy collaborator with Peter Pears, who brought with him all the authority of his personal connection to the composer and his experience in previous performances of the work. The spiritual intensity that had always marked Lois's approach to music made her an ideal interpreter of the soprano role, and distinguished her from the more dramatic approach of her Russian predecessor on the recorded version. Britten composed the *Requiem* so that the soprano solos, high in *tessitura* and strong in emotion, elaborate the liturgical Latin texts, while the male solos comment on these texts more colloquially, in Owen's powerful words. John Kraglund caught the mood of opening night, and the importance of Lois's contribution to it, in his review for the *Globe and Mail*.

> ... if all else had gone wrong, this performance would
> still remain memorable for the Lacrimosa, with Miss
> Marshall soaring effortlessly to the fantastic heights
> of the heartbreaking solo line over the subdued mur-
> mur of the choir, before the lament was interrupted by
> Pears' more realistic but equally moving solo beginning:
> "Move him, Move him into the sun...."

In 1969, under its new Music Director, Karel Ančerl, the TSO repeated the work, but by then much had changed, both in Britten's musical reputation and in Lois's voice. Associations with the circumstances of the British premiere no longer exercised such a reverential hold on a Canadian imagination. The *War Requiem* itself had undergone severe, revisionist criticism, led by no less a figure than Igor Stravinsky who, according to *Toronto Star* music critic William Littler, had accused Britten of "passing off artifice as art."

John Kraglund still admired the work itself, but pointed out the difficulties Lois now had with the high-flying soprano part. Because of problems with orchestral balance, "... there were periods in both the Sanctus and the Libera Me where Miss Marshall's valiant efforts were almost inaudible." Even more tellingly, "elsewhere Miss Marshall made a moving and musical contribution, despite brief struggles with high notes." The normal process of aging was now having an audible impact on Lois's voice, and Kraglund, no matter how tactfully he phrased it, could not ignore the matter.

In the fall of 1965, Seiji Ozawa became the Music Director of the Toronto Symphony Orchestra and wasted no time getting acquainted with its favourite soprano. She appeared under his direction that September with the TSO in Ottawa, the first of many collaborations with Ozawa on tour and in Toronto. Even after he left Toronto for Boston at the end of the 1968–69 season, he continued to call on Lois, especially when he programmed Berlioz's *Damnation of Faust*, which she performed with him in Toronto, San Francisco, Saratoga Springs, New York, and Lenox, Massachusetts (the last two times at summer festivals with the Boston Symphony). In October 1965, when Ozawa and the

TSO went to England and France for the orchestra's European debut, they brought Lois along as the distinguished guest artist for key engagements in London and Paris. In London, Lois sang Maurice Ravel's cycle of three songs, *Shéhérazade* and, as an encore, Fiordiligi's technically challenging aria, "Come scoglio," from Mozart's *Così fan tutte*. The London concert was taped as part of the 1965 Commonwealth Festival, and a copy of the performance is available in the CBC collection of Library and Archives Canada. The performance of the Mozart, in particular, has become the stuff of vocal legend.

As a record of a live performance, the tape provides a vivid reminder of the impact Lois's physical disability had on an action as simple as coming onstage. Judging by the length of the welcoming applause, it took twenty-five to thirty seconds for her to make her progress from first setting foot onto the stage to taking her place by the conductor's podium, longer than even a vainglorious diva would allow for milking the applause. In later years, as this progress became even more difficult, friends in the audience sometimes feared that the applause would fail to cover her entire entrance.

Vocally, one is struck immediately by the darkness and weight of Lois's mature voice, in dramatic contrast to the lighter, girlish sound she could still command for Purcell, Bach, or the Marguerite of Berlioz's *Damnation of Faust*. The Ravel emphasizes these womanly qualities in her voice. "Come scoglio," however, demands both coloratura agility and dramatic power, and the ability to span the extremes of mezzo and soprano ranges without stumbling on the break between the two. Lois's riveting performance delivers on all fronts, with passion, drama, and authority. Her voice is strong, secure, and confident. She provides no evidence of the fears that she admitted to feeling after her vocal crisis, but it is worth noting that the dynamic range of the aria, *mezzo-forte* and upwards, would be easier for her to sustain than prolonged *pianissimo* singing at the same pitches. Like any canny professional, Lois was suiting her choice of repertoire to the condition of her vocal equipment.

Almost immediately after her return from London and Paris, in the fall of 1965, Lois even got to perform the Poulenc *Gloria*, which she had had to pass up, reluctantly, at the height of her vocal crisis in 1963. With Elmer

Iseler and the Mendelssohn Choir, she sang it in Massey Hall on October 20 and then ten days later in Boston, when the Mendelssohn appeared at the International Choral Festival celebrating the 150th anniversary of the Handel and Haydn Society. Chameleon-like, Lois once again took on the coloration of a high soprano, completely convincingly, by all accounts. The *Toronto Star* spoke of "her radiant soprano" and the *Globe and Mail* singled out "her stellar performance, despite the impossible demands of her part."

Meanwhile, Lois was somewhat uneasily taking on the role of national public figure, which she shouldered a little less gracefully than she had the role of globe-trotting musician. Back in December 1964, CBC television had broadcast a special produced by Franz Kraemer, called "Masters from Soviet Russia." Parts of the show had been taped in Toronto in January 1964, when the Soviet violinists David and Igor Oistrakh had come to town to play the Bach double violin concerto, the Beethoven violin concerto, and the Mendelssohn violin concerto with the Toronto Symphony Orchestra, all on one glorious subscription concert. For the television program, father and son played Vivaldi and a Bach sonata for two violins; cellist Mstislav Rostropovich played Tchaikovsky and Bach.

Lois, as Canada's best-known cultural ambassador to the Soviet Union, introduced the program and provided occasional commentary. The studio musical tapings were augmented with footage of Lois sitting in the audience seats of Massey Hall, ostensibly enjoying a live performance. A review of the videotape, available in the collection of Library and Archives Canada, provides a revealing glimpse of the development of Lois's public persona, and its gradual estrangement from her private personality.

Aside from the musical performances on it, the videotape is a contrived affair, typical of the heavily-scripted pseudo-spontaneity of broadcasts of the period. Lois's demeanour owes much to those conventions. By the time of the taping, she was thirty-nine years old, and her figure had filled out. Without a rigorous program of diet and exercise, the concert artist's life is not conducive to keeping in shape. Lois loved rich food and good drink, and even if time had allowed, her disability made a regular program of physical exercise a greater challenge than it is for most. Here, aided and abetted by the CBC's scriptwriters and designers, Lois plays up the matronly image with a brocaded dress, a heavy necklace, an elaborate coiffure, a plummy elocution, and stilted diction and commentary. (Why in heaven's name does she pronounce Teresa Stratas's name as Shtratas?) The camera presents — Lois Marshall, *grande dame*.

Lois had favoured an austere, formal look for her personal publicity from her student days. She rarely smiled in any of her official portraits. A turned-up coat collar, a bit of drapery, an elaborate fur piece, tended to erect a slight barrier between subject and viewer, as did her serious, slightly challenging gaze. The image of *grande dame* emerged, then, as a logical extension of this formality. Almost to the end, Lois preserved a protective public posture. For the camera, she cultivated an air of formal reserve and rigid respectability, which kept the viewer at a safe, respectful distance as surely as the wigs she eventually adopted concealed her gradually greying hair.

At the end of "Masters from Soviet Russia," however, while the credits roll, the camera cuts to unscripted shots of Lois in the audience, applauding enthusiastically and apparently passing comments to the person in the next seat, out of camera range. These do not look like the staged events they must have been. Lois's engagement in the music seems authentic. The sequence reveals a smiling, spontaneous, approachable Lois, quite at odds with the stilted CBC personality of the show proper. In miniature, this television show captures the dichotomy that came to characterize Lois's life as a national treasure. Her official role, and her intense desire for privacy, led her to construct a respectable, carefully manicured, and highly polished version of herself for public consumption. Underneath, revealed only in the comfort and security of private encounters with close friends, there lurked the earthy, slightly rowdy Lois of Ellerbeck Street, the Lois who relished a good dirty joke and could tell one with the best of them, who delighted in sly parodies of friends and professional rivals, who loved a stiff drink and a good party. And every once in a while, in unguarded moments, glimpses of that private Lois could break through the obscuring mists of her public persona, to give outsiders a momentary feeling for the warmth and sunshine that lay behind.

Lois receiving the Order of Canada from the Governor General of Canada, His Excellency, the Right Honourable Roland Michener, April 26, 1968.

Credit: Dominion Wide Photographers, Ottawa.
From the collection of Cindy Townsend.

Lois's emergence as a national figure in Canada was accompanied by the honours attendant on such status. In 1965, the University of Toronto gave her an honorary doctorate of laws. Instead of delivering a convocation address (Lois would have cringed), she performed a program of nine songs. The *Globe and Mail* of June 5, 1965, ran her picture, in full song and resplendent in academic regalia, on its front page. On April 26, 1968, Governor General Roland Michener presided over Lois's investiture in the Order of Canada. Lois entered the Order at the level of Companion, the highest level in the Order, but in the second list, not the first. Maureen Forrester's investiture as Companion had taken place in the inaugural year of the Order, ten months earlier, amid all the publicity of Canada's Centennial celebrations. These little rivalries mattered. In her autobiography, *Out of Character*, Forrester made much of the fact that she was the first artist to be named a Companion of the Order.

With advancing middle age, Lois also experienced some of the hazards to which her disability made her vulnerable. In November 1966, Lois, alone at home in her house on Golfhaven Road, went into the kitchen to make herself a cup of tea, a perfectly normal activity, but one fraught with peril for Lois. Somehow, she fell to the floor, unable, no matter how she tried, to pull herself up again or get to a telephone. The record player

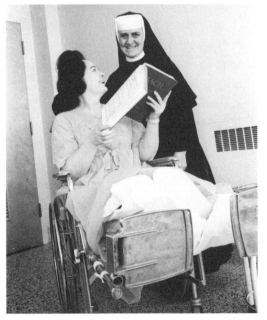

In 1966, Lois prepares to give a thank-you recital for the staff of the Scarborough General Hospital, who cared for her after she fractured her hip.

Credit: *York University Libraries, Clara Thomas Archives and Special Collections,* Toronto Telegram *fonds, F0433, image no. ASC05190.*

in the other room, stuck in a groove, kept repeating itself maniacally as she lay on the floor in pain for three hours. Finally, she managed to make enough noise to attract her sister, Pat, still living in the house next door.

Lois had fractured her hip. Her doctor sedated her and admitted her to Scarborough General Hospital, where she remained for over a month. After initial recovery, she managed to practise in the hospital's chapel and, on December 29, returned to it to give her first performance after her fall — a thank you for the staff of the hospital. Lois performed sitting in a wheelchair. And in a wheelchair she sang at Massey Hall with the Toronto Symphony Orchestra on January 11, 1967, and again with the TSO on tour in Florida on the 14th and the 17th of January. In order to board the plane for Florida, Lois, seated in her wheelchair, had to be hoisted up on the lift used for loading the catered meals into the aircraft. She accepted it all calmly, her days of being hypersensitive about her disability now behind her. When she asked Seiji Ozawa if he would mind her appearing in a wheelchair, he reportedly replied that she could lie on her stomach for all he cared, as long as she was prepared to sing. In Miami, she came down with the flu and arrived at the concert hall just as a nervous Ozawa and the TSO were finishing their first number, late, in her wheelchair, somewhat under the weather, but ready to perform nonetheless. For these comeback appearances with the TSO she had programmed, surely with a touch of irony, Aida's aria, "Ritorna vincitor!"

On March 23, 1965, Lois sang, for the first time in her career, the complete Berlioz song cycle, *Les Nuits d'Été*, at Massey Hall with the York Concert Society. The concert was to have been conducted by Heinz Unger, but had to be led instead by his understudy, Hans Bauer, as a memorial. Unger had died suddenly a month earlier, just one hour after completing a rehearsal of his beloved Mahler for a CBC taping. He had been a loyal supporter of Lois's career, presenting her on ten different occasions, either with the York Concert Society or under other auspices.

An even more personal loss came with the death of Frederick C. Silvester, Lois's beloved "Freddles" from her early days at Bloor Street United. Silvester died on June 24, 1966. The private funeral took place a few days later, but Lois sang at the public memorial on October 19, held, of course, at Bloor Street United. Silvester was sixty-five years old when he died, Unger sixty-nine. Their deaths served as reminders of the extent to which Lois's career and professional life had thrown her into the company of an older generation. Weldon himself was sixty in 1966, closer in age to Silvester than he was to Lois.

The most significant brush with mortality, and the most ambiguous, came two years later, on July 26, 1968, with the death of Marion Kilburn. The fact that Weldon and Marion had been living separately for at least ten years had remained publicly unacknowledged. Marion's death notice listed her as the wife of Weldon Kilburn, mother of their four children and grandmother to their eight grandchildren. To the end, some façade of respectable married life prevailed for the public's benefit. Now all that had ended. Weldon was free to marry, if he pleased.

CHAPTER EIGHT

1967 to 1975 —
On the Road with the Bach Aria Group

On December 1, 1965, Lois made her debut as the soprano member of the Bach Aria Group, a small vocal and instrumental ensemble specializing in the works of Bach, which was already a fixture on the New York musical scene and the North American touring circuit. It would become her musical home for the next fifteen years. She had always enjoyed working in close musical collaboration with instrumentalists. As she sensed her days of vocal pyrotechnics becoming numbered, she found an artistic niche for herself in this small ensemble work with like-minded colleagues committed to a joint musical enterprise. Though her solo recitals and orchestral appearances continued, the overall trajectory of her career from the mid 1960s onward tended once again towards the music of Bach, as it had done at the very beginning of her performing life.

The Bach Aria Group had been founded in 1946 by William H. Scheide, scholar, musicologist, philanthropist, and collector of rare books and manuscripts. As a young man, Scheide looked for a way to make a significant contribution to American musical life, and decided to do so by promoting the performance of music from the cantatas of Bach, an enormous and, in 1940s North America, largely untapped reserve of masterworks. Much of this repertoire could be performed with a chamber group of five instrumentalists (flute, oboe, cello, violin, and keyboard) and four singers, but each one had to be a soloist of the highest calibre. Scheide reckoned, correctly, that the abundance of beautiful solo writing for each player and singer in these ensemble works of Bach would attract musicians of the first rank, who had little opportunity to explore the repertoire in their regular concert careers. He also sweetened the pot by offering his musicians the security of long-term employment at competitive salaries, with a performance schedule that still allowed them the freedom to pursue other engagements. The group came to enjoy commercial success, and even had a regular show on American radio in its early days, but Scheide's private philanthropy guaranteed its long-term stability.

William H. Scheide, Artistic Director of the Bach Aria Group, at the keyboard of the lovely portative organ built for the Group in Germany in 1969.

Credit: From the collection of
Kim Scott.

Scheide's culture, learning, and religious sensibility were as deep as his philanthropy was generous. His name has long been associated with Princeton University and with the Legal Defense Fund of the NAACP. Lois had a copy of his scholarly theological work, *The Virgin Birth: A Proposal as to the Source of a Gospel Tradition*, inscribed "To Lois with love, Bill," among her effects when she died, and Scheide himself spoke feelingly about her for this biography in 2005, when he was in his early nineties. He never conducted the group, though he did admit, "I may have said occasionally, could you do it this way?" As Director of the group, however, he devised the programs, wrote out performance parts from the full score, organized the seasons, and travelled to every performance.

Yehudi Wyner, for many years the pianist with the group and both a performer and composer himself, characterized Scheide as "a man of absolutely comprehensive, global understanding and command," who could identify at sight a fragment from a single instrumental line of any of the cantatas, which run to 249 entries in the catalogue of Bach's works. His phenomenal memory remained sharp decades after his active association with the group had ended. When I spoke to him in 2005, he could identify any of the cantatas by number, quote the text from memory, and comment in detail on the relationship between text and music in key passages. The Bach Aria Group was no idle self-indulgence of a wealthy dilettante; it was a crusade by a connoisseur to resurrect a neglected repertoire.

In the Bach Aria Group of 1965 Lois found a distinguished group of musical colleagues. Robert Bloom, the oboist, joined the group at its inception after a stint as first oboe in Toscanini's NBC Symphony. At Bloom's death, in 1994, colleagues characterized him as "one of our greatest singers ... who happened to play the oboe." Bernard Greenhouse played cello in the Beaux Arts Trio, of which he was a founding member. Lois had sung with Greenhouse in her concert with the Beaux Arts Trio at the Smithsonian in 1960. Oscar Shumsky, a colleague from Lois's Stratford days, had played violin in the NBC Symphony under Toscanini and, like Samuel Baron (flute), taught at New York's Juilliard School of Music. Paul Ulanowsky taught and coached at Yale University and had a distinguished career as vocal coach and accompanist. Yehudi Wyner replaced him as pianist for the group in 1968. Of the vocalists when Lois joined the group, three were Canadians — the Regina-born bass-baritone Norman Farrow, who had been with the group since its inception, contralto Maureen Forrester, and Lois herself. The tenor at the time was the British Richard Lewis. When Lois joined, she replaced Eileen Farrell in the soprano spot. Until 1973, when personnel changes began to occur more frequently, Lois worked with these musicians on a regular basis, rehearsing about three programs a year, which they performed first in New York and then on the North American touring circuit. Lois appeared with the Bach Aria Group 241 times before she finally left it in 1980.

In the solo recital work of her mature career, Lois scaled new heights. During Canada's Centennial Year of 1967 she was a favourite featured artist at concerts across the country. The centennial called attention to Canada's relative youth as a nation, to the separation between its brash new culture and the far older traditions of the Europeans who had colonized the land. Lois's performances bridged this cultural gap.

On February 2, and again on April 7, 1967, CBC radio broadcast Lois and Weldon in one of its Celebrity Centennial Concerts, recorded at the Salle Claude Champagne of the Vincent d'Indy School of Music in Montreal. The recital itself took place sometime during the busy month of recovery from her fractured hip, in January 1967, when Lois was still singing from a wheelchair. It was a searing performance.

On this occasion, she introduced into her repertoire one of Henry Purcell's most dramatic and passionate hymns, *The Expostulation of the Blessed Virgin Mary*. The words, by Nahum Tate, a minor Restoration poet, depict a moment of rest for the Holy Family during the flight into Egypt. Mary calls on Gabriel, the angel of the Annunciation, to protect her child from the wrath of Herod and to give her some word of comfort, but she calls in vain. Her former heavenly visitor makes no response, and Mary concludes her soliloquy torn between a mother's fear for her child's safety and a mystic's temptation to doubt her earlier revelation. Purcell's music rises above Tate's highly conventional rhetoric to unite these contradictory elements, the spiritual and the carnal, faith and doubt, in a heart-rending cry of longing and pain. To a modern sensibility, the work is dangerously overwrought, almost embarrassing in its exposure of raw human longing and fear. Furthermore, it depicts a situation so far beyond the imaginative capacity of contemporary secular society as to appear implausible, even ridiculous. The concertgoers at the Salle Claude Champagne would have been ill-prepared to have their hearts lanced by such a frenzy of maternal and religious torment. Only a supremely confident artist, unafraid of emotional self-revelation, committed wholeheartedly to the artistic conventions of another culture and another era, could hope to carry it off.

As preserved on tape in Library and Archives Canada, the performance, an explosion of fierce, petitionary zeal, confirms Lois's stature as just such an artist. She shapes the phrases of Purcell's declamatory recitative into something operatic, almost Italianate. For an English-speaking audience, the clarity of her enunciation gives these grand musical emotions a firm textual support. In its liberal use of *rubato* to vary the tempo, its sheer size and range of emotional extremes, her performance contravenes almost all the conventions of Baroque performance practice as they are known today. And yet, despite all that, it achieves an undeniable sense of conviction. It sounds idiomatic. With Weldon's impeccable musical support, and in the spirit of Emmy Heim's insistence on finding a way through to the intention of the composer, here Lois dedicates every fibre of her own musical personality to discovering the nature of Purcell's Virgin Mary. By some alchemical process, she convinces the listener that she speaks this musical language as Purcell understood it, that the state of psychological and spiritual torment she depicts is simply the state that Purcell intended to dramatize. Lois takes the listener out of the familiar pastoral domain of Purcell's nymphs and shepherds, into the world of high tragedy.

Experiencing Lois's performance of this work, even on a tape recording, is like contemplating Bernini's famous sculpture, the *Ecstasy of Saint Teresa*. In both, the ornate decorative conventions of Baroque art are so fully realized, inhabited with such conviction, that they pull the audience beyond the brilliant surface display and plunge it into a direct confrontation with the spiritual and psychological realities that lie beneath. By this music-making, Lois enacts another century's understanding of human nature. (This was the quality of her singing that also made her such an outstanding interpreter of Handel.) Through the old-fashioned conventions of the Baroque era, she speaks idiomatically — fluently, intimately, and urgently — to her modern audience. Lois interpreted the masterworks of the old world to an audience in the new, and did so entirely as a citizen of that new world, trained and formed on its shores. Her example helped to establish the musical culture of western Europe for Canadian audiences, and for future Canadian artists, as a legitimate part of their own heritage, no longer just a remnant of colonial imitation and aspiration. By a combination of her belief in herself and her belief in the musical traditions of western Europe, Lois gave the nation a new confidence in its own cultural possibilities. It was her centennial gift to Canada.

Singing with such intensity and personal identification with the subject did not come cheaply. It entailed an expense of spirit and a drain on physical resources. More and more in the late 1960s and through the 1970s, as Lois entered her mid-forties, she who had never had to consider such matters before, came to count the cost. But instead of conserving her energies, parcelling out her resources in limited quantities in order to make them last as long as possible, instead of giving reduced performances that, to the casual listener, would still pass muster, Lois continued to sing the only way she knew how — extravagantly. For her, an economical performance was simply not worth the candle. She gave her all every time, and when it was a good night the results were as spectacular as ever. But when she could not summon the physical, vocal, and psychological resources to work full out, her audience began to hear the difference.

Lois heard it long before any member of her audience did. For more than a decade she wrestled with the changes to her own capabilities that age and her strenuous career forced upon her. She began to spend her vocal capital.

There was, for example, a tenuous performance of the Beethoven Ninth with Seiji Ozawa, the TSO, and the Mendelssohn, taped in Toronto in September 1966 for telecast on Canada Day 1967. Given the occasion, and the nationalist symbolism of the vocal quartet, Lois could hardly have refused the engagement, despite the much earlier stipulation on her repertoire sheet that she would no longer perform this particular work. Her absence from a group of soloists that included Maureen Forrester, Léopold Simoneau, and Donald Bell would have been conspicuous enough to cause comment. As ever, there was at least one moment that amazed attentive listeners with its musical taste and technical command, in this case a perfectly modulated diminuendo on an upward scale where most sopranos have to maintain or increase volume to support the ascent. But as the vocal rigours of the last movement took their toll, Lois's stamina failed. On a review of the soundtrack, one hears her resorting to *mezza voce* and stealing breaths in obvious places, just to make it through the assignment. Once, her ability to float, angelic, in the upper reaches of her range had won her Toscanini's praise; on this occasion she sounded like a mortal singer.

As inconsistencies like these began to creep into Lois's performances, the problems many critics had noted with Weldon's playing increased as well. In July 1967, Lois and Weldon performed in recital in the foyer of Toronto's new City Hall. The concert was recorded for broadcast on CBC's Centenary Concerts series. John Kraglund, in the *Globe and Mail* of July 5, 1967, praised Lois to the skies, but said bluntly that Weldon "… gave a performance which, if not always a distinct liability, was almost never an asset."

Kenneth Winters, music critic for the *Toronto Telegram*, and a fervent admirer of Lois's art and Weldon's contribution to it, used the occasion for a short essay on Weldon's failings, and the gap in level of performance that now separated the two artists.

> … he is playing sufficiently badly to put his default well past overlooking. Moreover, he seems aware of it, and a good deal of tension — not unmixed with waves of self-exasperation and stubborn courage — now emanates from his half of the performance of any item on a Marshall-Kilburn program which requires technical strength or mercurial delicacy from the pianist. Clearly this can't go on, for it spoils too much that doesn't survive spoiling.

In 1952, John Kraglund had succeeded Leo Smith, who reviewed Lois's Eaton Auditorium debut back in 1950, as music critic of the *Globe and Mail*. Kraglund himself had studied music theory and criticism with Smith. Kenneth Winters, experienced as both a pianist and a singer, had the music critic's desk at the *Telegram* from 1966 to 1971, after which he did numerous CBC radio broadcasts and eventually became one of the editors of the *Encyclopedia of Music in Canada*. Along with William Littler, music critic at the *Toronto Star* from 1966 to 1991, these critics gave a seriousness, prominence, and consistency of viewpoint to music criticism in the Toronto press that it had not previously enjoyed. Kraglund's and Winters' blunt criticisms of Weldon's performance thus carried weight. They would have been widely read and discussed by those who followed the musical scene in Toronto.

Sadly, revisiting the tape of this performance confirms the accuracy of their harsh criticisms. One item in particular stands out, Mozart's "Parto, parto" (from *La clemenza di Tito*), an aria the two had performed many times. Weldon has problems with some of the passage work early in the aria, and by its final minutes he virtually falls apart. He seems to lose his sense of what key he is in, drops notes, resorts to sketching large sections of the accompaniment as though he were a rehearsal pianist, not an onstage collaborator, and at the very end, barely able to hold himself together, offers Lois no support at all. Needless to say, his difficulties sabotage her performance. Passages that should cause her no trouble suddenly become difficult, and at one point in the chaos, she too wanders off pitch and loses her way. She redeems herself in other parts of the program, and Weldon manages to pull himself back from the precipice, but the problems are undeniable. Kraglund and Winters did not exaggerate.

There were reasons for the dramatic deterioration. At sixty, Weldon suffered health problems that had aged him prematurely. A heavy smoker from his youth, who smoked even through voice lessons in the cramped and unventilated confines of his studio, Weldon developed emphysema that frequently racked his body with coughing fits. His hard-drinking ways (he had been a frequent drinking buddy of Healey Willan, legendary for his consumption of scotch) had done little to steady his hand or sharpen his acuity. And his battle with performance nerves never abated. Weldon could work miracles in the studio or the rehearsal hall, but could never be completely confident of duplicating them in front of an audience.

There was one more circumstance of his partnership with Lois that must have affected many a performance, though it does not help to account for this one. Weldon had made himself a martyr to his own virtuosity and to Lois's expectations of him. Collaborative pianists routinely accompany in a variety of keys to accommodate the range and vocal condition of the singers they work with. Most commonly, they establish the preferred key in rehearsal and either transpose the accompaniment themselves, in advance, or obtain an arrangement in the required key. In rehearsal an accommodating pianist will transpose at sight, but depending on the key relationships involved that can be a tricky business. Few would undertake to transpose at the keyboard during a performance.

Weldon had such musical and technical command that he could transpose accompaniments on request. Mary Morrison remembered how useful this talent became as Lois's voice underwent change and she worried more about its responsiveness and range.

> Weldon could transpose at the drop of a hat. I know that Lois would go into a concert and on the night, or maybe even just before they were to start a group of Lieder, she'd say, "I want this in such and such a key." And he would do it. He *could* do it. He was quite amazing. If she didn't feel up to doing it in a high key, he could transpose. There are not many pianists who would, or could.

But even a talent like Weldon's might get into trouble with a tricky transposition for a complicated score, and onstage there was no place to hide. Perhaps some of his flaws as an accompanist stemmed from this devotion to Lois's needs. The audience would never know and if catastrophe struck, Weldon, not Lois, would have egg on his face.

Like Lois, Weldon could still pull off a fine performance under the right circumstances. In February 1968, less than a year after the City Hall debacle, he returned to top form for a recital at New York's Hunter College, greeted effusively by the *Times*' Donal Henahan.

Lois Marshall, who could make "Frère Jacques" sound like a cry from the heart, gave an extraordinarily moving song recital at Hunter College Playhouse last night.... Weldon Kilburn, her accompanist, spun out the piano postlude [to Schumann's *Frauenliebe und Leben*] superbly, resisting the temptation to upstage the silent singer at this important point.

The rest of the difficult program included Strauss's *Ophelia Lieder* (the same ones Lois had done on television six years earlier with Glenn Gould) and Berlioz's *Les Nuits d'Été*. But again, the niggling comment that was creeping into more and more of Lois's reviews: "The Berlioz put strain on Miss Marshall's top notes, and suggested she might be either coming down with a cold or recovering from one." No matter how the reviewer sugar-coated it, Lois's vocal difficulties now caused frequent comment.

Within three weeks of the death of Marion Kilburn on July 26, 1968, Lois left Toronto for an appearance in Dubrovnik with the Bach Aria Group, the beginning of a tour that included three concerts in Israel and a stop in Spain. Before her departure, however, she gave her sister, Rhoda, an invitation list and a set of detailed instructions. The list included family and friends, and most of the prominent names in professional music in Toronto. Rhoda puzzled over two names tucked into the middle of the list — Liz and Phil. Lois explained her little joke on her return. Since everyone else was being invited, the Queen and Prince Philip might as well receive an invitation too. She didn't want to leave anyone out of the celebrations when she and Weldon married.

The small private ceremony took place on Weldon's sixty-second birthday, September 9, 1968, at St. Paul's Anglican Church on Bloor Street, with Lois's sister Pat and Pat's husband as witnesses. Though most of the details of the wedding, including its location, were kept out of the papers, it was anything but a modest affair. The lavish reception following

Lois and Weldon at their wedding reception, September 9, 1968.

Credit: York University Libraries, Clara Thomas Archives and Special Collections, Toronto Telegram *fonds*, F0433, image no. ASC05188.

the private ceremony spilled out of Lois's house and backyard over into Pat's. A huge marquee and covered walkway, erected for the occasion, connected the adjoining properties. Caterers hovered solicitously, and bartenders attended liberally to the needs of the throng. Sir Ernest and Lady MacMillan were there. So was Seiji Ozawa. Weldon's brother, Peter, Chair of the Board of the Orchestre Symphonique de Montréal, brought along Zubin Mehta, just recently retired as its Music Director. And, of course, there were old friends from the Conservatory days, like Reginald Godden, Weldon's fellow teacher and musical colleague from the Five Piano Ensemble more than twenty-five years earlier. Even by Lois's exacting standards, it was a hell of a party. But more than just a party, this celebration placed a seal on the central relationship of her life, one that had never, until now, been permitted to display such a public face.

Lois soon discovered that at forty-three, with her career still in high gear, she had married an old man who required care. Within a month of the wedding, Weldon suffered a mild heart attack. Reginald Godden replaced him as Lois's accompanist when she appeared at York University on October 6. Weldon was sufficiently recovered by the end of January to accompany Lois in a Montreal recital, but in general she spent much of the time following her wedding doing work that did not directly involve Weldon — travelling with the Bach Aria Group and fulfilling orchestral engagements. While Weldon remained her coach, her performing identity gradually began to separate itself from his.

Nevertheless, their collaborations during this period, though less frequent, included some of their finest work together. In May 1969, at Massey Hall, they recorded an LP of selections by Schubert, Henri Duparc, and the Canadian surgeon and composer Welford Russell, along with some of their ever-popular folk songs of the British Isles. The disc was part of the CBC "Serious Music" Series (SM 101 in this case), given low-key distribution in Canada by London Records on their budget Ace of Diamonds label. The generous selection of Schubert songs gives a glimpse of some of Lois and Weldon's favourite recital repertoire. Weldon is completely assured at the piano, his delicate touch and musical sensibilities always to the fore. In Schubert's "An die Musik," he supports Lois's flowing *legato* line with a graceful, crisp, slightly detached accompaniment that sends the old chestnut dancing on its way. Lois is radiant in Russell's exquisite setting of "Come hither, you that love," a song which should be in every Canadian singer's repertoire but is virtually unknown on our concert stages. The recording, never reissued on CD, has been unavailable for decades.

In November of the same year, they performed a Sunday evening Hart House recital at the University of Toronto. An undergraduate named Stephen Adams attended, and, thirty-four years later, could still reconstruct the evening from memory.

> The program was astonishing. She started — yes started — with the *Four Serious Songs*. Then came a group of three Mahler, including the huge "Um Mitternacht." After intermission, she sang *Dichterliebe*. All of it was intense, every note heartfelt. Then, to top it off, she gave three encores, as unexpected as could be. She rattled off Purcell's "Hark the echoing air" with virtuoso speed — and brightness — after all the heavy German

Lois and Weldon on November 16, 1969, before a capacity audience in the Great Hall at Hart House, the University of Toronto, scene of many of Lois's most important recitals.

Credit: Robert Lansdale, courtesy of University of Toronto Archives and Records Management Service.

stuff. Then a folksong ("Go Way from My Window," as I recall). And finally, would you believe, the last of the Falla popular songs, with a convincingly Iberian harsh chest voice.

Once again, despite Weldon's failing health and Lois's vocal inconsistencies, the old magic was at full force.

Weldon's musical contributions were not confined to his work at the keyboard. In May 1970, Lois made one of her infrequent excursions into contemporary music. For a special CBC concert of Canadian works, the composer Oskar Morawetz decided to write a piece specially for Lois. He chose a short passage from *The Diary of Anne Frank*, a prayer for Anne's young friend, Lies Goosens, and set it as a nineteen-minute work for soprano and orchestra. As usual, Weldon coached Lois as she prepared this new material. He also involved himself in the discussions with the composer that frequently precede the premiere of a new work. In a letter to Lois after the performance, Morawetz thanked both Weldon and Lois for their contributions to his composition, and mentioned that he had incorporated one of Weldon's suggestions regarding diction into the score. Morawetz's *From the Diary of Anne Frank* attracted the attention of Anne's father, Otto Frank, in Switzerland, who sent the composer a family heirloom as a memento and cabled flowers to Lois for opening night. Lois would record the work for CBC, with Lawrence Leonard and the Toronto Symphony Orchestra, and perform it again with Karel Ančerl and the TSO in Toronto, New York, and Washington, DC.

Though they made two more international tours after they married, Lois and Weldon's travelling days together were drawing to a close. In the fall of 1970 they took their last trip to Russia, playing to Lois's established audiences in Riga, Leningrad, and Moscow. In the summer of 1971, Lois travelled again to New Zealand, where most of her engagements were with orchestra. By now, Weldon's deteriorating health and his problems with alcohol were putting serious strains on their relationship. On that trip those strains began to show. Lois found it difficult to take on the care of another person, especially when she needed to conserve her energies for her own work. It was all she could do just to ensure that her own physical needs would be accommodated when she travelled. She lost patience with Weldon when he insisted on accompanying her on the tour. She later confided to her friend, Doreen Simmons, that she would have preferred to travel alone, and work with an accompanist provided for her there, rather than have the added responsibility of looking after Weldon throughout the tour. The old adage, "Marry in haste, repent at leisure," had in their case reversed itself. The marriage that had been contemplated for decades began to unravel just a few years after the ceremony.

The end came suddenly, fraught with painful melodrama. Following the trip to New Zealand, Lois did a small tour with Ozawa and the Boston Symphony, performing Berlioz's *Damnation of Faust* at Tanglewood and Saratoga. Weldon stayed in Toronto. When she returned, Lois discovered that another woman had been sharing the house with Weldon in her absence, *her* house, as she continued to think of the home on Golfhaven Road that she had purchased thirteen years ago. The brazen effrontery of Weldon's actions pushed Lois over the edge. That night, she threw Weldon out of her home, and from that moment cut off all contact with him. Neither party filed for divorce at the time, but in 1979, when Weldon finally did so, the application stated that he and Lois had lived "separate and apart since September 9, 1971" — the third anniversary of their wedding, and Weldon's sixty-fifth birthday.

How much did Lois know? Did she turn a blind eye or was she really in the dark? From the time she was a student, Weldon's reputation with women was well-known around the Conservatory, even if it was seldom acknowledged. By all accounts, his pursuit of other women did not stop during the years preceding their marriage, although it may have abated somewhat. And of course he had never legally severed his relationship with his first wife. It seems that Weldon indulged his appetites whenever he got the chance, and that he fell in love with Lois anew every time she gave one of her radiant performances. Music, romance, and sex concoct a heady brew. That's why opera holds such sway over our imaginations. Though Lois seldom performed opera, her own romantic life seemed to be caught up in one. Unlike grand opera, however, hers had no stirring final curtain, no tumultuous curtain calls. She simply and swiftly drew a veil over the most important relationship of her life and refused to speak of it, regardless of the emotional cost of rewriting her personal history in this way.

There had been good times, and not only onstage. Working together with a demanding musical intelligence such as Weldon's, whatever friction it may have entailed, gave Lois the greatest professional and personal satisfaction she could imagine. If prolonging that relationship well beyond student days cost her some degree of artistic independence, she never complained. In return she received a lifetime of collaboration, coaching, and support, without which her artistic identity might not have flourished as it did. And she had enjoyed romance and simple intimacy with Weldon too. Years later, the soprano Monica Whicher, one of Lois's students, gave her a small gift, a copy of Paul Gallico's sentimental novel *The Snow Goose*, on impulse, just because she thought

Lois might like it. In thanks, Lois offered a rare glimpse into her personal life. *The Snow Goose* had been a favourite of hers and of Weldon's, she told Monica. She recalled how they had read it to each other in bed, and how she had cried.

But now her tears were bitter, as she berated herself for her own gullibility. Nicholas Kilburn remembered a difficult conversation he had with Lois after the separation. "I thought that once we were married, it would all stop," she told him. That comment suggested that she had been aware of infidelities throughout, but after learning that they had been conducted under her roof she could no longer choose to ignore them. Perhaps her bitterness was directed as much at her own naïveté as it was at Weldon's infidelity. She needed to get some distance from her situation.

Work could provide only so much distraction. She had a December tour with the Bach Aria Group that kept her busy until Christmas, but the Group's winter itinerary happened to be sparse that season, with only three concerts in their post-Christmas calendar. In February 1972, she was called to substitute for an Argentinian chamber group, Camerata Bariloche, at a Community Concert in Peterborough, Ontario, and for the first time confronted the problem of finding a new accompanist. By now Lois had developed such a dependency on her accompanist, for every kind of support, that the choice had a personal as well as musical dimension. She turned to Stuart Hamilton, an old acquaintance who would become the most regular of her accompanists for the remainder of her career, and a staunch friend and loyal supporter to her death.

She had first encountered Stuart in July 1948, when, as a scholarship piano student just arrived from Regina, he participated in Gerald Moore's Conservatory summer school class on accompanying. Lois was one of the singers provided for the piano students to work with. Stuart's outrageous sense of humour ("I was a little brat in those days — I guess that hasn't changed a lot,") appealed to Lois, and they struck up a friendship. In later years, he took some lessons from Weldon, sometimes at the house on Golfhaven Road, and the acquaintance continued, although Stuart and Lois had not worked together since the classes with Moore in 1948. By 1972, Stuart had established himself as a vocal coach and accompanist in Toronto. In 1974, he would found his highly successful

Opera in Concert series, which later provided Lois with one of her last major performance opportunities. After retiring from active performance, and from Opera in Concert, Stuart became a nationally-known figure on radio as the irreverent, sardonic intermission quiz-master on the summer editions of CBC's *Saturday Afternoon at the Opera*. He seemed to know every major figure in Canadian music of the last fifty years personally, and had attended more performances of obscure operas than all of his panels of experts combined. Above all, he had a warm heart and a generous disposition, two qualities Lois had great need of.

In February 1972, when Lois phoned and invited Stuart to play for her, he didn't ask why Weldon couldn't, and Lois offered no explanation. Such was her need for privacy and her friend's respect for it. Stuart's recollections of the concert in Peterborough further demonstrate the extent of his personal concern for her, as well as his sense of humour. The stage, a typical Ontario high school auditorium, was up a flight of steps, and there were no bathroom facilities at stage level. At intermission, Stuart was appalled to discover that Lois had no intention of negotiating the stairs to find a bathroom.

> "Lois, that's terrible. You can't sing a whole concert wanting to pee!"
>
> She said "Yes, I can. I've done it many times." And so the poor woman got through that whole long concert.
>
> I said, "Lois, I'm going to go and get you a pail or something!"
>
> She said "Don't you believe it. I'm not peeing in any pail."
>
> And I said, "Well that's ridiculous. I can't stand the idea of your just — "
>
> She said, "Never mind. I know what I'm doing. You just go and sit over there and shut up."

By this stage of her career, Lois did little rehearsing, although she still warmed up compulsively. She had expected Stuart to do his own preparations, and they put the recital itself together on the fly. They opened with a song of Purcell. Stuart, hearing her as his musical partner for the first time, was overwhelmed.

> I have never in my life heard such a brilliant perform-
> ance … she made it into such a miracle, I thought, "My
> God, what am I doing on the stage with this woman?" …
> I never really did get used to what she could do when she
> was at her best. There were a couple of times when she
> was so "on" that I was ashamed to be with her, because I
> didn't think I was anywhere near where she was. It was
> like being with a rocket and trying to hold on.

Over the years, Stuart provided unfailing companionship for Lois on their tours, talked her through musical crises and failures of confidence, and tried his best to accommodate her demands. But he wouldn't transpose at sight. Once, for the Lethbridge stop of her farewell tour, Lois made a last-minute request to sing her entire recital in lower keys. Stuart could comply only because he scoured the music stores in Calgary for lower settings (of complicated works by Schumann and Mahler), drove to Lethbridge, and practised frantically all day. It would have been only one of the many small ways in which Lois's rupture with Weldon affected the professional routines she had become used to over more than twenty years.

March and April 1972 brought with them a pair of Easter *Messiah*s in Winnipeg and a few higher profile engagements. Karel Ančerl took Lois to New York and Washington with the Toronto Symphony Orchestra, in *From the Diary of Anne Frank*. This time around, Stuart did the preparatory coaching with her. But before that, in late March, she returned to Carnegie Hall for one performance of Handel's opera *Rinaldo*, part of the New York Handel Society's project, not at all common at the time, of working through all the Handel operas in concert. Its conductor, Stephen Simon, dedicated much of his career to reviving the music of Handel, which he did with performances like these, with published editions of Handel works, and with a series of recordings. In the *New Grove Dictionary of Music and Musicians*, his contribution to the Handel revival is acknowledged more for its enthusiasm than for its historical authenticity. But his work played its part in helping to bring Baroque repertoire into the prominence it enjoys today. In *Rinaldo*, Lois sang the role of Almirena, and it may be the only time in her career that she sang publicly the haunting aria, "Lascia ch'io pianga," well-known outside its operatic context as a concert and recital favourite. Donal Henahan reported that her performance of it was "breath-catching in its vocal warmth and emotional power." She also sang the opera's "Bird Song" ("Augelletti che cantate"), accompanied by a recorder ensemble, not the modern woodwinds that would have been favoured by most symphony orchestras of the time. This brush with the now-common practice of using original instruments for the performance of Baroque music gave Lois the closest contact she had with the Baroque revival of the late twentieth century, which would transform performance practice for the repertoire that had formed the core of her career.

Now that she no longer had a regular travelling companion, Lois also faced the problem of the post-performance reception. During the *Rinaldo* preparations, a colleague asked if Weldon was bringing her to the party. Lois sidestepped the reference to Weldon and said she was coming with a friend, one of the other women singing in the Handel Festival. At this response, eyebrows shot up, but nothing was said. Lois learned only later that her date for the evening was a lesbian, and that her response had created quite a stir among the gossips. Lois enjoyed a joke on herself, and later told this story to Stuart Hamilton, to great comic effect. Despite her enjoyment of innuendo and off-colour jokes, however, her attitudes towards sex were completely conventional and decorous. She could exhibit a quaintly Victorian prudery about explicit sex in movies or on television, for example, completely at odds with her raunchy sense of humour. Perhaps it was a remnant of her now-abandoned Roman Catholicism, or simply a characteristic of the generation in which she grew up.

On May 1, 1972, Lois and Maureen Forrester appeared at the Guelph Spring Festival (another Nicholas Goldschmidt enterprise) in an evening of solos and duets. The two had sung many times together, most frequently in the Bach Aria Group, but this was the first time

that Canada's most famous female singers had headlined a joint recital.
Predictably, their star power caused a huge commotion, and they toured
the program extensively over the next three years. Yehudi Wyner, the
pianist from the Bach Aria Group, and a friend of both the singers,
accompanied in Guelph and later for the broadcast from Mt. Orford,
but Stuart Hamilton toured with this program as well. It was distinguished not only by its star quality, but by its adventurous programming. Monteverdi's rarely-heard "Interrotte Speranze" and sacred
music by Clari and Schütz rubbed shoulders with more familiar songs
by Schumann and Brahms, and with a group of Canadian and British
folk song arrangements especially commissioned from composers Keith
Bissell and Robert Fleming. But the two encores really brought down
the house. Lois and Maureen had been singing the soprano-alto duet
from Bach's Cantata No. 78 ("Wir eilen mit schwachen doch emsigen
Schritten") for years in the Bach Aria Group. As encore material, it displayed both a bravura technique and a spiritual joy that set feet tapping
and sent their recital audiences out of the concert hall humming. But
not before they had enjoyed the comic excesses of Rossini's "Cat Duet,"
a vocal cat fight set entirely to the word "Miauw," that Lois, a cat lover
all her life, could sink her fangs into, complete with a feline high C she'd
held in reserve to the end of the concert.

The Mt. Orford performance was taped, and received limited release
as an LP from RCI (Radio Canada International), but no trace of it
exists now, except for pirate transcriptions. Forrester's more heavily pub-
licized duet disc with Rita Streich, which included much of the same
German repertoire, came out seven years later and cornered the admittedly limited duet market.

But by Lois's professional standards, the year after the breakup of
her marriage was a slow one, with too much liberty to reflect on recent
unhappy events. To try to remove herself from her Toronto environment, which reminded her at every turn of Weldon and their years
together, Lois agreed, quite uncharacteristically, to a long-term commitment whose obvious advantage was a complete change of scene.
She accepted an appointment as Artist in Residence on the Music
Faculty at Ohio State University in Columbus, Ohio, for the 1972–73

academic year. Her duties involved teaching in the Faculty and singing
a few concerts at the University. As Lois understood matters, Ohio
State wanted an artist with an active performance career, who would
fit teaching around her regular engagements, and Lois, with her busy
performance schedule, certainly fit this description. But in practical
terms, her students needed someone who would be available for regular
lessons, not an intermittent mentor. Despite the fact that Lois pulled
up stakes in Toronto and took an apartment in Columbus for the year,
her performing commitments came into conflict with her responsibilities as a teacher. Nor did she find the musical standards there to be
at a fully professional level. And to compound these stresses, she was
intensely lonely. She had needed to escape Toronto, but in Ohio she
found herself far too isolated. Even the presence of her beloved cat,
personally chauffeured down to Columbus by Lois's nephew, couldn't
dispel the loneliness. It was a deeply unhappy year. Lois appeared as
soloist in the *Christmas Oratorio* while she was in Columbus, but the
bright spot of her year there came at the end of April, when, with
Stuart at the piano, she gave a solo faculty recital in Thurber Theatre.
The local critic had to resort to exclamation marks and capital letters
to express her admiration sufficiently. "It was an Event! As a matter of
fact, it was the Event of the Season! And in a season that had a wealth
of fine concerts and brilliant soloists, that's going some."

On her return to Toronto from Ohio State University, a mournful
duty awaited her. On May 15, 1973, she sang at the service celebrating the life of her dear friend and mentor, Sir Ernest MacMillan, who
had died nine days previously. The service took place in Convocation
Hall, where, just over twenty-five years earlier, Lois had first sung the
St. Matthew Passion under Sir Ernest's leadership. With the alienation
from Weldon, the deaths of her mother, of Frederick Silvester, and now
of Sir Ernest, the passage of time was steadily robbing her of the people
who had been the fundamental supports of her life and career for over a
quarter of a century.

Though Lois's career now settled into a somewhat predictable pattern, largely defined by her commitments to the Bach Aria Group, vestiges of her old adventurous spirit occasionally resurfaced with excursions into new repertoire, some of it in new languages. On April 27, 1974, she appeared as soloist with Mario Bernardi and the National Arts Centre Orchestra at the St. Lawrence Centre's Town Hall in Toronto in the Canadian premiere of Shostakovich's Symphony No. 14, settings for soprano and baritone of eleven poems on the theme of death, by four different poets. Lois hired a language coach and learned the work, phonetically, in Russian. A week and a half later, she switched to High Church Slavonic for Andrew Davis's debut concert with the Toronto Symphony Orchestra, the first TSO performance of the *Mša Glagolskaja* (Festival Mass) by Janáček. Critics received the Shostakovich with much of their old enthusiasm for Lois's musicianship and artistry, but turned distinctly lukewarm when it came to the Janáček. Both the *Star* and the *Globe and Mail* noted that Lois had difficulty coping with the *tessitura* of the soprano part.

Almost every Toronto review now carried some such caveat about Lois's upper register, and it bothered her. Around this time, Kenneth Winters, the critic who had taken Weldon's playing to task in the 1967 City Hall recital, reviewed a concert by Elmer Iseler's Festival Singers that Lois had been scheduled for, but had withdrawn from because of illness. In his review, he hazarded the guess that the real reason might have been because she found the *tessitura* of the work too daunting. To his surprise, he received a call from Lois, in tears, protesting that she really had been sick. They spoke for a few minutes, by which time Lois had regained her composure, and even her sense of humour, but clearly, his assumption about her abilities rankled.

In this climate, the Bach Aria Group provided a haven for Lois. It allowed her to continue her career with the music of Bach, which had been her artistic life support since she first sang for Sir Ernest. The group's touring routine, which repeated on the road a mix of the repertoire from its three annual New York recitals, made for a great deal of repetition, but it also conserved Lois's energy. She did not need to expend vocal resources learning vast amounts of new repertoire, or varying it from night to night. Within the group, Lois found a regular social outlet that offered a degree of solidarity, friendship, and support, though she maintained her personal privacy and extended close friendship only on her own terms. And, perhaps most important of all, membership in the group provided financial security for Lois at a time when her income from other sources was dwindling. When Yehudi Wyner joined in 1968, three years after Lois, his annual salary as an instrumentalist with the group exceeded the salary he then received as a full-time member of faculty at Yale University. He believed that the vocal soloists may have been paid at an even higher rate. Though Lois had once earned some of the highest fees in the business, her income had brought with it no long-term security — no benefits, no pension plans, no safety net for retirement. The Bach Aria Group gave her financial security while she remained in the group, and, along with her other American touring, qualified her to receive American Social Security benefits after her retirement, at a time when she experienced real financial hardship.

Socially, the Bach Aria Group offered a hothouse kind of camaraderie, the dynamics of friendship always subject to the demands of artistic ego. They did much of their North American touring by car, and Maureen Forrester, who liked to choose her own routes instead of following obediently in convoy, often drove, with Lois as one of her passengers. They had opposite temperaments. Lois was private and slow to share intimacies, Maureen, five and a half years younger than Lois, immediately gregarious. Lois's long and noisy warm-ups drove Maureen crazy; Lois, for her part, couldn't fathom how Maureen could eat a hearty meal, do a few seconds of vocalizing, and then stroll casually onstage, ready to perform. Thrown together by circumstance, they developed a relationship seasoned by professional respect, with a peppery dash of healthy professional rivalry to keep it interesting. At a reception following one of the concerts in Israel, Lois noticed Maureen chatting up the concert promoter and commented in an aside to Bill Scheide, "Maureen's trying to line up more engagements for herself."

According to Stuart Hamilton, who toured with both women, "They admired each other, but Maureen resented Lois's spirituality and Lois resented Maureen's commercial successes."

From his vantage point at the keyboard for the Bach Aria Group, Yehudi Wyner had a chance to observe the professional respect and co-operation that characterized their relationship. "I never heard anything but a kind, supportive and loving word from either of them about the other." But he too recognized that Lois brought a "kind of realized conviction and matter of testimony and faith" to her art quite different from Maureen's more practical musicality. In Wyner's analogy, "Maureen was our Aaron and Lois was our Moses." Maureen may have had readier eloquence, but Lois, at least in Wyner's view, had the more direct access to the very fount of her artistry.

But for all its specialization in sacred repertoire and its elevated sense of purpose, the Bach Aria Group, entirely male except for the alto and soprano soloists, was also a bunch of guys on an extended road trip. Lois, with her sharp wit and risqué sense of humour, fit in comfortably. That sense of humour also formed a convenient shield that permitted her to be part of the group without sacrificing her lifelong need for privacy. Yehudi Wyner counted himself a particular friend of Lois's, yet even he didn't know much about the painful breakup of her marriage. On the Midwestern tour of 1971, just a few months after Lois broke with Weldon, the group let down its hair in a bawdy mock newspaper review which described a fictitious performance of a "newly discovered" Bach cantata (No. 69 S), every musical term laden with sexual double entendre. The piece was read out at a Christmas party on the road, in either Chicago or Terre Haute, just before they all separated for the holidays. One paragraph opened with Lois and Richard Lewis, then the tenor soloist, "coupled in a highly dynamic duet," and descended from there. The rigorously egalitarian parody spared no member of the group its lewd and fanciful inventions. One can imagine the public reading of this "review," fuelled, no doubt by alcohol, the camaraderie of long acquaintance, and the anticipation of the holiday break to come. Did Lois enjoy it as much as the rest of them, given her recent confrontation with Weldon about his infidelity? It seems unlikely that the rest of the group knew about this event in any detail. Had they been aware of Lois's recent trials, this bit of undergraduate humour would have seemed tactless at the very least. As it was, she kept her own counsel, and even these

close professional associates had only a dim, and often delayed, awareness of her marital situation.

Bill Scheide, the group's founder and artistic director, shared Wyner's
admiration for Lois. He made it his special concern to see that travel and
accommodation arrangements would take account of Lois's disability.
But while he recognized her musical gifts and her aptitude for Bach, he
responded even more to her "very sweet personality and unpretentious
airs," as he put it many years later. Wyner, like other members of the
group, knew nothing of Scheide's sentiments, but, seeing his devotion
and tenderness towards Lois, suspected he might be falling in love.

The suspicion was correct. One day in the late 1970s, after Scheide's
own marriage had ended in divorce, tested in part by the strains of his frequent touring with the group, he entertained Lois on a visit to Princeton,
where he lived. Scheide was a collector and a connoisseur, so the visit
began with a personally-guided tour of the Scheide Library, a substantial
addition Scheide had built to Princeton University's Firestone Library
to house his personal collection of rare books and manuscripts. Scheide's
grandfather, an associate of John D. Rockefeller, had amassed the family
fortune in the Pennsylvania oil industry and by age forty-one had made
enough money to retire and devote himself to his real passion, reading
and collecting rare books and manuscripts. Scheide's father continued
collecting, and Bill Scheide himself further augmented the collection's
emphasis on musical manuscripts with major purchases on the international market. On his mother's death, he moved the collection from
the family home in Titusville, PA, to its present location in Princeton.
The story of the collection was as impressive as the beautiful room that
now housed it.

In the part of the collection devoted to music books and manuscripts, Lois could hold in her hands a fragment, in Bach's own hand, of
his cantata, "Ein feste Burg," an autograph letter by Bach, a Beethoven
sketchbook, or an early printed copy of Wagner's *Ring*, inscribed by
Wagner himself. But what interested her most intensely, even more than
the Gutenberg Bible for which the collection was famed, was the opportunity to examine an autograph manuscript of the Schubert song, "Die
Sterne," signed and dated by the composer himself. ("Die Sterne" had

been a specialty of Adolphe Nourrit; Chopin played it on the organ at a memorial service for the great dramatic tenor in Marseilles in 1839.) This experience allowed Lois direct contact with the musical tradition to which she had devoted her life. Emmy Heim had impressed Lois with her personal connections to the European tradition; now Scheide made it possible for Lois herself to touch Schubert's hand.

After the tour of his collection, Scheide ushered Lois into his own house on one of Princeton's most gracious streets, a home of culture, tradition, and understated affluence. It was an entire world away from her humble beginnings on Ellerbeck Street. On the wall near the fireplace hung a small photograph of the Thomaskirche in Leipzig, Bach's church, and above it an oil portrait of Bach himself, by Elias Gottlob Haussmann, dating from 1748. Other beautiful works of art were displayed on the walls of the spacious living room, which also housed a grand piano and a Baroque pipe organ, both of which Bill enjoyed playing, and played well. Bill Scheide had spread his riches before Lois, riches not only of the world, but of the mind and of the spirit, and now he offered them to her. He asked Lois to marry him and share his home. "Oh I couldn't," she replied, "I'm just a singer."

Lois told very few, if any, of her intimate friends about the proposal, and confided her motives in refusing to no one. Despite the refusal, Bill Scheide maintained an abiding affection for her. "I will always cherish her memory in a very special way. There's no doubt about it," he said almost a decade after Lois's death. He did eventually marry, a woman of great humanity and understanding, and continued the life of the scholar, collector, and philanthropist well into his nineties. He and Lois remained professional colleagues and friends, but did not maintain regular contact after she left the Bach Aria Group in 1980.

The 1970s brought two major rites of passage in Lois's professional life. August 1973 marked the end of her association with Columbia Artists. She had had a pretty good run. Over the twenty years Columbia had represented her, she had seen her concert fee double, from one to two

thousand dollars, but it had not mounted anywhere near the five-fig-
ure range a singer like Forrester would eventually command. And after
twenty years, Columbia no longer provided the type of representation
she needed. Initially, when Lois had been a hot property and Columbia
promoted her aggressively, her career flourished. But as her novelty as
a new singer on the scene waned, and particularly when her recording career failed to take off, it began to settle into a routine. The really
savvy artists with huge international reputations took personal control
of their publicity. Forrester hired her own public relations agent to keep
her name in the news, and advised Beverly Sills to do the same when the
two were appearing in Handel's *Giulio Cesare* at New York City Opera.
But Lois couldn't be bothered with such details. She never hired her
own agent, never shopped around for more aggressive management, and
relied entirely on the public relations arm of Columbia Artists to generate press. By the time her contract with Columbia ended it was too
late for her to move up to a bigger agency, too late for her to learn the
ropes of effective self-promotion. Lois needed dedicated management.
Though she had other representation after Columbia, she never again
received the kind of promotion any career needs, even the career of an
established artist, to keep a performer before the public eye. In her final
decade on the stage, just at the time when Forrester was shooting to
ever greater prominence, Lois settled into her performance routines and
watched her own career winding down. Her old fans remained faithful
to her, but her days of conquering new audiences were past.

On February 8, 1975, two years after the break with Columbia, completely by chance Lois made the decision that enabled her to prolong
her career for almost a decade after her soprano days were over. On tour
in El Paso, Texas, the Bach Aria Group convened a morning emergency
meeting. Helen Watts, their alto, had contracted such a ferocious cold
that she would not be able to sing that night, and there was no time to
fly in a replacement. What were they to do? The group always brought
spare repertoire along on tour, in case of such emergencies, but they had
already been on the road for over a week and no one wanted to spend
the afternoon rehearsing a revised program. Lois suggested a solution.
"If you'll trust me, I'll do her pieces, because I know them." Not that she

had ever learned this alto repertoire. But, as she put it, she had heard Watts and Forrester before her sing these arias "umpteen times" and felt confident that she could take them on, in addition to her regular soprano assignments.

On condition that she not require a rehearsal with the full group, the other members agreed. So that night Lois sang both the alto and the soprano selections for the program, relying on her phenomenal ear (and doubtless one of her marathon warm-ups) to get her through the new material. Only one substitution was needed. Try as he might, Bill Scheide could not think of a way to have Lois sing a duet with herself, so the signature duet from Cantata 78 had to be dropped. Otherwise, El Paso heard the entire program as advertised. As Yehudi Wyner later described it, "It was a knockout for all of us."

A knockout not only because of Lois's remarkable achievement, but also because it signalled, completely without warning, her interest in the alto repertoire. Typically close-mouthed, Lois had confided to none of her Bach Aria Group colleagues her growing discomfort in repertoire of the soprano range. The shift came as a complete surprise. They recovered quickly enough, however. At the end of the 1974–75 season, Helen Watts left the Bach Aria Group. In October 1975, ten months after El Paso, Lois officially became its alto and remained in that spot for the next five seasons, until her retirement in 1980. As soprano, she was initially replaced by Lorna Haywood and then, for the longer term, by Benita Valente. With these two sopranos, she continued to sing the duets she had sung so often with Forrester and Watts, but she had to keep her wits about her to avoid drifting unthinkingly into the higher parts engrained in her memory by a lifetime of performances as a soprano.

CHAPTER NINE

1975 to 1997 —
Home Again at the Faculty of Music

Lois sang her signature tune, "I know that my Redeemer liveth," for the last time in the December 1975 Toronto performances of *Messiah*. By that time she had come to dread the aria, all the more because of its close identification with her in the minds of her fans. They expected her to live up to their memories of her in the aria, sometimes from decades earlier. Stuart Hamilton remembered one of their last warm-up sessions for it.

> People would walk miles to hear her sing "I know that my Redeemer liveth," because it was so gorgeous. But by the time she was getting tired of being a soprano, it was torture for her.
>
> She went halfway through the aria and she said, "Oh, I can't stand this." And she brought out the score of *Tosca*. We went through the whole of *Tosca* before the *Messiah*. "There," she said, "that's singing. This damn Handel is going to kill me."

After the 1975 *Messiah*s, Lois made the switch official. She gave up much of her old soprano repertoire and listed herself as a mezzo-soprano or an alto for all her engagements, not just those with the Bach Aria Group. Despite the well-developed lower register she had always commanded, critics divided on the question of whether she had a true alto sound or not. To Lois, this kind of debate mattered little. The switch to alto freed her from the tyranny of her reputation as a soprano. It allowed her to choose any repertoire that suited her voice, and to perform it only in the keys in which she felt comfortable. She credited the decision with extending her working life by several years.

The change in designation had a more subtle effect as well. She had been "Lois Marshall, soprano," for so long, that none of her fans ever came to think of her as "Lois Marshall, alto." She became, instead, just "Lois Marshall," a musician you went to hear for the wealth of musicianship behind every performance, and the outpouring of warmth and humanity that rode on her sound, whatever its register. Not "just" a singer, but simply and purely a singer, in her last few years of performing Lois achieved a status unmodified by labels. Even as her voice became less reliable, the artistic freedom implied by her unique status on the Canadian musical scene allowed her a select number of achievements as great as any of the more spectacular accomplishments of her youth. In her artistic maturity, she finally put "Lois Marshall, soprano," behind her and became, uniquely, "Lois Marshall."

In 1976, she revisited the repertoire of British songs and folksongs that had formed a staple of her repertoire, with a recording for the Canadian label Marquis Records made in the spacious acoustic of St. Anne's Anglican Church in Toronto. Under its Byzantine-style dome, with its famous murals by members of the Group of Seven, Lois and Judy Loman, the virtuoso Principal Harp of the Toronto Symphony Orchestra, recorded a selection of the Elizabethan songs Lois had sung in her youth, as well as folk songs in the Kennedy-Fraser and in the Britten arrangements. It was a retrospective act, but not a repetition. Not one track duplicated any of the material from Lois's 1958 folk song record with Weldon, and seven of the seventeen appear to be entirely new repertoire, a few of which Lois would return to, again with Loman accompanying her, in her Toronto farewell appearance.

Elmer Iseler, who, as conductor of both the Festival Singers and the Mendelssohn Choir, had supported Lois throughout her career, stuck with her after her transition to alto. In 1977 he had the inspired idea to engage her for a work she had never done before, Aaron Copland's *In the Beginning*, a setting of the creation story from Genesis for mezzo-soprano and unaccompanied chorus. Copland's 1947 work had been in the Festival Singers' repertoire for many years, with Patricia Rideout originally singing the solo part. The exposed, declamatory opening for unaccompanied mezzo-soprano gives way to exchanges between chorus and mezzo, rife with sound effects depicting the various stages of creation, and filled with tricky key changes and harrowing entries for the soloist. No longer a really avant-garde work by 1977, it was nonetheless a departure for Lois and for her audience. She rose to the challenge magnificently. John Kraglund, in the *Globe and Mail* of January 20, 1977, thought that "... the solo part ... sounded as if Miss Marshall had been created for it.... There were some particularly dazzling moments when the solo voice soared over the choral part and when Miss Marshall's voice climbed smoothly and effortlessly out of the mezzo range to high soprano passages."

Capitalizing on this success, Iseler programmed *In the Beginning*, with Lois as soloist, for two tours by the Festival Singers. The first was a fast-paced run through Saskatchewan in March 1977 — thirteen concerts in seventeen days, touching down in Saskatoon and Regina, but concentrating on smaller centres like Nipawin, Estevan, Weyburn, and Swift Current.

In her early days, Lois had taken that kind of touring in her stride but now she found the pace demanding. On her return in May she cancelled two important Toronto engagements, evidently still tired out from the demands of the tour a month earlier. One was a performance of Mahler's *Lieder eines fahrenden Gesellen* (*Songs of a Wayfarer*) with the CJRT Orchestra (Maureen Forrester replaced her on short notice), the other an evening of duets with counter-tenor Theodore Gentry (Rosemarie Landry stepped in on this occasion). But she managed her scheduled Midwestern tour with the Bach Aria Group in November 1977 and left ten days after that with Iseler, the Festival Singers, and the Canadian Brass for Moscow, Leningrad, Tallinn (Estonia), Kaunas (Lithuania), and Riga (Latvia). In every city she introduced her audiences to the Copland, and sang as well some of the repertoire her Russian fans had heard her do before — selections from Mahler's *Des Knaben Wunderhorn* or Falla's *Seven Popular Spanish Songs*. This second tour with the Festival Singers served as Lois's unannounced farewell to the Russian audiences with whom she had had a lasting love affair. Despite later hopes, she did not visit the Soviet Union again.

In the final decade of her career, Lois, constrained more and more by the unpredictable state of her health, could no longer commit herself to long-term, ambitious projects. However, she did manage to complete, piecemeal, what turned out to be just such a major project, a series of four great valedictory recitals in Toronto, in which she summed up her lifelong understanding of the German song repertoire. The Canadian composer and CBC radio producer, the late Srul Irving Glick, oversaw the recording of all four for broadcast. Posterity owes him an enormous debt for his vision and foresight. CBC subsequently released three of these concerts on LP and later on CD. They stand as the most comprehensive testimony of Lois's mature understanding of the German Lieder that had occupied almost as much of her professional life as the music of Bach. The recordings provide first-hand evidence of the greatness she achieved in her last years of performing, when the odds seemed increasingly stacked against her.

The first of these, in November 1976, teamed her with the pianist Anton Kuerti for complete performances of Schubert's tragic and difficult song cycle, *Die Winterreise*. They performed it three times, twice in Toronto, at Upper Canada College's Laidlaw Hall on November 6 and in the Great Hall of Hart House, at the University of Toronto, on November 7, then a week later on the road, at Trent University in Peterborough. CBC recorded the Hart House performance. Like her earlier collaboration with Glenn Gould, these concerts paired Lois with a star piano soloist of international repute, renowned for his uncompromising standards and idiosyncratic nature. Kuerti had been known to lecture his audiences about their coughing and, on one famous occasion, had asked that young children present be removed from the front rows of the audience, since the program he was about to play was too demanding for their youthful attention spans. Lois had performed with Kuerti twice before, in 1972 at Toronto's Town Hall and in 1974 at Hart House. They had been scheduled to appear together at the Guelph Spring Festival earlier in 1976, but Lois had had to cancel because of illness. In Kuerti, she encountered an independent artist with strong ideas of his own, certainly not a deferential accompanist. When Lois wanted to transpose a song down a semitone to a key more congenial for her voice, Kuerti would argue the point if he thought the transposition damaged the overall key relationships of the cycle. Although they resolved such discussions professionally, and Kuerti generally acceded to Lois's requests, it was, for Lois, not as easy a co-operation as the one she had known with Weldon, and was developing with Stuart Hamilton.

Die Winterreise tells the story of a failed love affair and the male protagonist's descent into despair and eventual suicide. Its twenty-four songs, though beautiful, are almost unrelieved in their gloom and sadness. For both the audience and the artists, the cycle presents real challenges of endurance in its seventy-four minutes. In concert, singers often present it with an intermission, even though doing so breaks the continuity of the cycle. Lois, however, found the reserves of strength to perform it without interruption. Because of its male point of view, women undertake it only rarely, although the legendary Lotte Lehmann had done so and the great Christa Ludwig would record the cycle a few years after Lois. Among female singers, only one who had achieved the reputation Lois enjoyed in the maturity of her career would dare to take it on.

William Littler, in his review of the Upper Canada College performance in the *Toronto Star* of November 8, 1976, recognized it as a landmark. Acknowledging the unparalleled interpretive challenge the cycle presents to even the greatest singers, Littler said that Lois, "… at a surprisingly secure-voiced 52, has entered a select company by bringing to it the wisdom of the heart."

John Kraglund, in the *Globe and Mail* of the same date, admitted, somewhat grudgingly, that the concert was one of the few "that should not be missed in any circumstances," but implied that Lois might be able to improve her interpretation in some future performances. "But all of this is no more than a matter of saying that Miss Marshall was less than perfect in one of the lieder repertoire's most demanding cycles, which she has not yet managed to incorporate fully into her repertoire." Such comment seemed oblivious to the facts. Lois, at this stage of her career, was conquering mountain peaks the best way she knew how, not running marathons. Her endurance would no longer permit her to refine new repertoire by dint of repetition. In appearances like these she was making final statements about her art.

In hindsight, that knowledge inevitably colours our response to the CD of the Hart House performance of November 7, 1976. Knowing about Lois's vocal insecurities and nervousness, the strength and grandeur of her voice, throughout its range, come as a shock and a vindication. Not all the echoing spaces of Hart House's gothic Great Hall are big enough for Lois's sound. Herein lies one of the reasons this performance may not appeal to all tastes, especially not to tastes moulded by the almost irresistible example of Dietrich Fischer-Dieskau, who completely transformed modern performance practice for the Schubert repertoire in the 1960s. The big, burnished sound and resonant acoustics, so much to Lois's liking, make for a performance that is large-scale and dramatic, not intimate and psychological. But for lovers of Lois's sound, here is God's plenty. The combination of exact focus with a pervading liquid quality creates the impression, so typical of Lois's singing, of a voice amplified through tears. (Mary Morrison described that sound as the "ping" every singer strives for.) Her interpretation matches her sound. The consummate musician, Lois shapes each phrase for its full musical value. Despite the psychological complexities of the cycle, every song for Lois is a melody first, then a dramatic situation. Littler noted this quality in his review.

> For like the composer, Marshall addressed herself directly to the texts, narrating them as much as singing them and choosing her vocal colours and dramatic emphases in very specific response to their verbal imagery.
>
> In doing so, however, she managed to avoid the mannered inflections some lieder singers cultivate in their almost syllabic dissection of Schubert's musical settings.

This last comment could have been aimed directly at Fischer-Dieskau's minutely-detailed style. Lois narrates the texts dramatically, but, in contrast to the great German baritone, without resorting to simulated sobs, gasps, or breathy *Sprechstimme*, and always with due reverence for the overarching phrase, rather than the isolated word. Here, in a performance from the end of her career, one can hear not only her early teachers, Weldon and especially Emmy Heim, but also the singers she admired in her youth, the singers of the thirties, their example enriched by all her own musical experience.

Like all of Lois's concert recordings before a live audience, this one captures the excitement of the evening itself, but it has been edited in one important respect. In performance, Kuerti introduced each song with a summary of the words and with comments of his own. Some audience members complained that his commentary prolonged the concert to an unreasonable length. Lois grumbled privately about the interruption it created to the continuity of the cycle, but it did provide her with moments of respite between songs for vocal recovery and preparation. The CBC recording edits out these interruptions.

Two years later, Lois gave the recital that summed up her lifelong relationship with the songs of Robert Schumann. She had been singing his *Frauenliebe und Leben* since the very earliest days of her career, and had had his complete *Dichterliebe* in her repertoire since at least 1960. On October 29, 1978, again at Hart House, she added *Liederkreis*, Op. 39 and presented all three of Schumann's major song cycles in a single evening. As a vocal workout, this recital easily equalled the demands of *Die Winterreise* two years earlier. The three Schumann cycles come in at seventy-seven minutes of music-making, an endurance test few singers would take on in a single evening at any stage in their careers. The Canadian pianist and teacher William Aide, who had joined the Faculty of Music at the University of Toronto that fall, accompanied her.

In the two years since *Die Winterreise*, Lois's voice had aged perceptibly. A review of the CD reveals momentary patches of a threadbare quality, and a bit of a wobble corrupts some of her initial entries. However, as is always the case when listening to Lois, these problems recede as the concert progresses. Lois gains strength and control as she warms up through the recital, of course, but more importantly, she wins the listener over to her way of singing. As the listener becomes attuned to the virtues of her style, minor vocal flaws become negligible in the face of her musicality and complete conviction. In keeping with the psychological, rather than dramatic quality of these songs, Lois consciously adopts a thinner, more attenuated sound than she employed for *Die Winterreise*. In "Du Ring an meinem Finger," however, the fourth song in *Frauenliebe und Leben*, she rises to as full-bodied a climax as one could desire. John Kraglund found it a little too robust "to permit a clear projection of [the] most subtle aspects" of the cycle. But questions of vocal production aside, Lois's "penetration of the emotional truth of the songs" (as Littler put it in his review) carried the evening. Once again, she had presented herself, not as a singing sensation, but as a musician of the first rank, an artist who compelled her audience's attention by the depth and maturity of her musical understanding rather than the superficial glamour of her sound. The Schumann recital, which in lesser hands could have degenerated to a mere marathon of endurance, was a heartfelt retrospective of Lois's engagement with Schumann's art.

The same quality of mature reflection ennobled Lois's recital of Schubert's *Die schöne Müllerin* a year later, in November 1979. Once again tackling repertoire that is traditionally the territory of the male singer, she took her Hart House audience straight to the emotional core of this poor-man's story of love lost and a broken heart. By now, John Kraglund had dropped his niggling tone and recognized the once-in-a-lifetime nature of these recitals. According to him, the three concluding songs "were surely the greatest example of bel canto heard in Toronto in several seasons, and unquestionably the most moving." The CD made from the concert recording reveals just how extraordinary Lois's achievement of this singing line actually was. As she moves through the turbulent songs of the middle of the cycle, their emotional pressure causes more and more split-second breaks in her otherwise plangent sound. Hardly audible, except to the most carefully critical ear, such vocal imperfections can sabotage a performer who dwells on them. Lois refuses to be distracted and fall into this trap, sings through every little vocal crisis and, instead of playing it safe, gambles everything on the last three songs,

taken at unbelievably slow tempi. Gambles, and wins. In this performance Lois transcends the limitations of her instrument and the perils of
artistic ego to achieve a completely selfless performance. Only the music
matters, not the musician.

Lois had as her companion on this journey the remarkable Greta
Kraus. A Viennese musician of the old-school, Kraus had made her
career playing the harpsichord, but had returned to the piano to accompany Lois in a few Mozart songs at Anton Kuerti's suggestion, for the
Northstars Mozart Festival he organized in 1978. Kraus had frequently
been at the harpsichord during Sir Ernest's *St. Matthew Passion*s, and
had even performed with Lois in the Scarlatti *Christmas Cantata* in
1947. Her collaboration with Lois for the Mozart, however, achieved a
new level of sympathetic, intuitive communication between two artists.
At rehearsal, Lois had a cold, and barely hummed through the repertoire,
just listening to Kraus's tempi and muttering, "That's fine, that's fine."
But come the performance, the two collaborated as though each could
read the other's thoughts.

> I don't think I can explain it. I can only say that when
> I play the first introduction and Lois comes in, she
> answers in a way that makes me realize exactly how
> she wants the next part. And when I play it she knows
> where I'm driving. It's a communion which I can't really
> put into words.

Not into words, perhaps, but certainly into music. On the CD of
Die schöne Müllerin, the spontaneity of their teamwork provides a text-
book example of the collaboration that should exist between pianist and
singer. In "Ungeduld," a song with a notoriously demanding accompaniment that seems to allow the singer no breathing room, Kraus starts
the introduction at a tempo somewhat faster than the one Lois wants,
but builds a slight hesitation into the repeated triplet motif to allow
Lois the freedom to establish her own tempo on her entry. With a deep,
audible breath, Lois slows the piano down just a fraction before she
sings her first note. From that point on, the two musicians are in perfect

synchronization, each feeling the freedom the other takes in the music, together bending and shaping the phrases to their will without ever compromising the insistent pulse of the underlying accompaniment. It is a tour de force all the more remarkable for the lightning speed at which these tiny adjustments take place. In later years, Kraus singled out this track from the entire CD as one of the most remarkable moments of her collaboration with Lois, one of the ones most typical of Lois's individual art. For the connoisseur, it may be a technical marvel; for the listener, it remains a moment of unalloyed, unbelievable joy.

The success of *Die schöne Müllerin* made a second collaboration between Lois and Greta inevitable. In March 1981, this time at the Edward Johnson Building's large concert hall, the MacMillan Theatre, rather than at Hart House, the two artists presented an evening of Lieder by Hugo Wolf. The songs of this late-romantic composer (born after both Schubert and Schumann had died) had figured less prominently in Lois's repertoire, and are less accessible to many listeners than those of his forebears. Almost at the end of her performing days, Lois took on the challenge of substantially new repertoire in order to round out her survey of the major German song literature. She had, of course, her old association with Emmy Heim, a great exponent of Wolf's work, to draw on, as well as her new one with Kraus.

An abiding friendship had developed between Lois and Greta in spite of the fact that the two were temperamental opposites, Greta as forthright and blustery as Lois was indirect and coyly evasive. Greta's formidable manner and absolutely uncompromising musical standards terrified many a student during her long life as one of Toronto's foremost coaches and accompanists. Even Lois, whose international reputation outstripped Greta's, fell under this spell. In the early days of their collaboration, as she later confided to her friend Doreen Simmons, Lois had to circle Greta's block in her car several times before she could summon up the courage to climb the front steps of the house and confront Greta for one of their rehearsal sessions. Greta's impatiently scrawled notes on her program for the Wolf recital testify vividly to her brusque intolerance of any deviation from the highest standards of performance, especially her own. Evidently made while she was listening to a playback of the

CBC tape of the concert, her comments are peppered with phrases like: "NO!!"; "no! piano horrible!"; "Lois very good! piano so-so,"; "Beginning not so good. End very good!"; "? no impossible"; many times simply "no"; only occasionally "NOT BAD AT ALL!"; and very rarely, almost with surprise, "GOOD!"

Perhaps these stringent judgements of Greta's decided the CBC against issuing an LP or CD of this fourth major Lieder recital of Lois's mature years. It exists now in the CBC Radio Archives in Toronto and in pirate tapes of the CBC broadcast of June 1981, in their "Great Singers Series." The program challenged its audience with a generous selection of introspective and often moody songs. Some are scarcely melodic, intoning their texts like thoughtful recitative over a delicately shifting piano accompaniment. Only in the final part of the concert did Lois venture into some of the more lighthearted and satirical songs, ending with "Abschied," in which the poet takes his revenge on the pompous critic. As Arthur Kaptainis noted in his review of the concert for the *Globe and Mail*, Lois remained the consummate musician, avoiding the temptation to overact or over-inflect the melodically simple material for the sake of dramatic effect. She "… made an excellent case for a whole evening of Wolf principally because she *sang* every note." That is, she filled every phrase with musical intelligence and vocal beauty.

She was able to sing such a long and demanding program, once again about seventy minutes of music, because she broke the evening with two intermissions and chose her repertoire carefully to avoid taxing her vocal range. Publicly, Lois achieved some of the greatest acclaim of her long and distinguished career for these valedictory recitals; privately, she became ever more conscious of the strain they placed on her physical capacity.

With successes like these — and a fulfilling new collaboration with a musician of Greta's calibre — more recitals, at whatever pace might be comfortable for her, were expected of Lois. She found it all the more difficult, then, to make the decision that confronted her. Only in a letter could she admit freely to the frightening vocal insecurities that forced her to abandon hopes for another major recital and make her formal retirement from the stage. Eighteen months after their Wolf recital, she wrote a carefully-worded letter to her dear friend.

Sept 28/82

My dear Greta,

I am sorry I have not been in touch long before this. I wanted to call you but felt reluctant to talk over the telephone about something as sensitive as this matter is to me. Perhaps I can explain better in a letter — at any rate I shall try.

First and foremost, I think that I cannot do another big Lieder recital. I really am past being able. My voice is undependable now to the point where I am never sure of it from one day to the next. Whenever I have to sing to fullfil an engagement I am committed to, I go through such an agony of anxiety I can hardly bear it. If I do not sing well then I am in despair. What I must do is complete the few contracts I have over the coming year and then simply "close down the shop" as it were.

I would like to be remembered for the good things I have done, most particularly for the work we did together. Indeed those concerts were to me the highest musical experiences of my singing life.

When she wrote this letter, Lois was already embarked on her national farewell, a coast-to-coast tour of twenty-one Canadian cities, strategically spread over fifteen months, to culminate in a gala evening at Toronto's Roy Thomson Hall in December 1982. David Haber Artists Management Inc., a booking agency founded by the former Artistic Director of the National Ballet of Canada, organized the tour with financial assistance from the Touring Office of the Canada Council. Lois insisted on her standard fee of $2,000.00 per performance, and the hard truth was that without Council support her farewell tour would not generate enough revenue to break even. She prepared three programs, two different mixtures of her standard recital repertoire

(Purcell, Falla, some German Lieder, and French art songs) and one of entirely German repertoire (Mahler and Schumann). Stuart Hamilton, her trusted friend, accompanied her at the keyboard and supported her every step of the way.

By now, her command of her vocal powers was so unpredictable that his support was crucial. Some nights were completely secure. On others, Stuart and Jean Latremouille, the official from the Touring Office who doubled as Stuart's page-turner, could hear Lois struggling just to maintain the placement of her voice.

> There was one concert particularly in a convent in Quebec. After the first half she said, "I can't do the rest of it. It's just not going to work." I'm sure it was because she had two martinis the night before at supper.
>
> I said, "You know you shouldn't have drunk that gin."
>
> She said, "Oh, a little gin isn't going to hurt me." Well, you can't drink gin and sing the next day. She was really in trouble.
>
> I said to her, "Well let's just see. You have your intermission and see how you feel and then we'll just do one song at a time. If you feel that you can't do it, then we'll not do it." But of course the spirit and the experience and the desire to perform came back and she did the second half. Really she was better in the second half than she was in the first.
>
> I think she probably thought, "Well, there are only these songs to do." She could see the finish line and maybe she relaxed a bit. She wasn't struggling so hard with her voice. And maybe her voice felt warmed up by the first half. I don't know. But it was obvious. Even Jean, who was turning pages, said he was scared. It was a very scary business. But she pulled herself together and she made it through to the end. And no one in the audience knew.

Lois certainly knew. After the tour was over, she sent Stuart a thank-you note, accompanying, with typical Marshall extravagance, a gift of champagne flutes.

> April 6/82
> Perhaps even more I shall remember the nights when my voice would not respond to my commands — your aware-ness, sensitivity and support on those occasions were something I have never before experienced with anyone.
>
> Thank you darling and after all our crazy fun and nonsense this thanks is truly from my heart and spirit.

Though at times Lois's voice may have seemed in tatters, anything that phrasing and feeling could achieve was still overwhelmingly com-municated, as the distinguished Canadian mezzo-soprano, Catherine Robbin, testified. Before the final Roy Thomson Hall gala, Lois's tour had included an appearance at Hart House.

> When she gave her farewell recital here in Toronto, at Hart House, I had never heard her sing in person and it was very important to me to get down there and hear her. However I was busy doing something else and was only able to get there in time for the second half, to slip into a back seat and hear her sing *Frauenliebe und Leben*, which perhaps explains why I was so late coming round to wanting to sing it myself.
>
> I knew that it would be good. I was quite prepared for that. But I was in no way prepared for the emo-tional wallop of being in the room with that woman and hearing her sing. Now I've thought a good deal about what it was that made it so special and so different. She used her technique totally as a vehicle for delivering the texts that she loved and understood so well. But that's something that all singers strive for. What Lois had was something that was completely unteachable and

unlearnable. She was a great human soul. And when she sang to you, she delivered from her soul to yours, not collectively, but individually to every person in the room and no one went away unmoved.

I went backstage after that recital at Hart House, which at Hart House is the kitchen, because I wanted to put some of that into words. I had no words and I waited in line because there were many people who wanted to see her. And the closer I got to the front of the line, the more I realized that I would not be able to speak, and when there was just one person left in front of me, I slipped away and I never did speak. Now I met Lois on several subsequent occasions but I never had anything like what you could call a normal conversation with her and I never was able to get beyond the feeling that Lois existed on a different plane from us normal mortals. And therefore I was never able to give her the homage that I would like to have done until today.

Reviews of the farewell tour were good, although most celebrated the career more than the night's performance. The concert promoters, meanwhile, saw a melancholy side to the enterprise. In some centres, Lois was a hard sell, and houses had to be papered to produce a respectable audience. Charlottetown cancelled. Montreal didn't come on board at all until an anonymous donor underwrote her appearance at the Church of St Andrew and St Paul and made tickets available free of charge. There were cash flow problems in the middle of the tour. And though Lois expressed to the promoters and the Touring Office her strong desire to return to the Soviet Union, support for such an ambitious add-on was not forthcoming.

None of that mattered. Her loyal public realized that this farewell tour was not about vocal splendour or packed houses. Beverley Rix's account in an Ottawa neighbourhood newspaper, the *Glebe Report*, got it exactly right.

Prompt to the minute, she comes out on stage, a short stout woman in flowing and exquisite red chiffon. She moves awkwardly, limping and leaning heavily on her accompanist's arm and on a heavy gnarled walking stick. Her hair is as abundant as ever, a full curly halo around her face. Her dark eyes are bright. But the lines in her face are deeper and even when she stands at the piano to acknowledge the prolonged applause, every movement seems an effort.

In the foyer at intermission people reminisce about past performances. They remember hearing her sing when she was a very young woman. They have brought programs for her to autograph of oratorios sung in the fifties, when Lois Marshall was the soloist and they sang in the chorus.

We know that we have not come to hear and to criticize one recital. Nor, steeped in nostalgia as we are, have we come just to be able to say we have heard Lois Marshall on her farewell tour. We have come to acknowledge a common bond uniting one generation of Canadian musical life.

There it was in a nutshell. They weren't just fans, or camp-followers. They were an entire generation of Canadian music lovers — the Lois Marshall generation. She had defined their experience of music in Canada, and for them, there simply was no one else.

Lois was fifty-seven years old when she retired, an age when many singers with strenuous careers behind them could still look forward to a few more years of activity. If her retirement seemed slightly premature, it could be attributed in part to the declining state of her health. For most of her life, Lois had refused to allow her disability to slow her down. In her mid-fifties, however, willpower alone could no longer keep her going.

Her increasing weight placed a burden on her physical frame, long since compromised by the effects of the polio virus that had attacked her in her childhood. One hip had probably been weakened by the break she experienced in 1966. And though the diagnosis was not in use during her lifetime, it is highly probable that she began to be affected by what is now known as post-polio syndrome. Recent medical research has determined that, years after initial recovery from the disease, polio survivors can experience further weakening of the muscles originally affected, as well as new weakening in muscles that were initially unaffected. According to a fact sheet posted online by the National Institute of Neurological Disorders and Stroke, as many as 50 or even 60 percent of polio survivors may experience post-polio syndrome. The symptoms include loss of muscle function and fatigue. It would have been a cruel fate for Lois to fight a second battle with her childhood enemy, especially at a time when diagnosis could not explain the medical reasons for her condition. The frequent cancellations during the last years of her career suggest just such a battle. And if post-polio syndrome does not provide the explanation, the critical high blood pressure that afflicted her in her later years does. Lois could no longer confidently predict her ability to perform. Instead, she had to consult her body on the day in question, to see whether it would allow her the enormous physical exertion and emotional stress necessary to appear onstage. For an artist with Lois's sense of professional responsibility, this state of affairs had simply become untenable.

But before leaving the stage completely Lois had the satisfaction of appearing in opera once again. She had done concert performances in the title role of an obscure Massenet opera, *Thérèse*, to help out Stuart Hamilton's Opera in Concert series in 1976 and again in 1981. Massenet operas were one of Stuart's passions. It was also in a concert performance in 1980 that she first took on the small role of the Nurse in Tchaikovsky's *Eugene Onegin*, with the Toronto Symphony Orchestra and a cast of international stars. Lois felt able to appear in the follow-up staged performance of the opera at Ottawa's National Arts Centre in July 1983. The part had minimal physical demands, but just making her entrance presented a challenge. By this time, Lois used a wheelchair to get around,

and the NAC set called for her to enter from a riser elevated above
stage level. Lois would get herself into costume and makeup then wheel
herself into position in the wings, where she chatted and joked with her
friends the stagehands. Just before her cue they lifted her, wheelchair
and all, onto the riser behind one of the side curtains — this was the
woman who had a terror of being lifted in her wheelchair, and would
normally fly into a rage with anyone who suggested it as a solution to an
access problem. She then rose from her chair, steadied herself, and, leaning on a cane, emerged from the wings into audience view for her scene.
Lois steadfastly refused to dwell on might-have-beens, but there was real
satisfaction in this operatic postlude to her career.

When it finally came, full retirement meant that Lois gave up her
last remnants of a regular income. The financial security of her membership in the Bach Aria Group had ended with its last official concert in
1980, when Bill Scheide, having decided that he had accomplished all
he had set out to do, disbanded the group. Having made little financial
provision for retirement, Lois, who had been spending her vocal capital
for some years, now had to dip into her financial capital as well. From
the mid-1980s on, she moved to a succession of apartments, starting out
grandly and then scaling back, financing them by renting out her own
property on Golfhaven Road. By 1988, she had sold her house, her one
remaining piece of capital, and was living on the proceeds of the sale.
The financial future looked bleak.

And as her career wound down, Lois had to face the final reminder of
her failed relationship with Weldon. In 1979, eight years after they had
broken up, Weldon, who wished to remarry, filed for divorce. Lois did
not contest it, and the Decree Absolute was granted on October 25, 1979.

For all these reasons, during and after the prolonged process of her
retirement, Lois retreated into herself. Public recognition did little to
compensate for the loss of professional purpose and professional identity.
She did some work for the March of Dimes Ability Fund, appearing at a
seminar on polio in April 1983, and lent her name to a number of musical
causes, becoming honorary president of the Mendelssohn Choir in 1984.
Indeed, in those later years the honours came flooding in: the Molson
Music Prize, with a cash value of $20,000, awarded at the discretion

of the Canada Council to the most prestigious of Canadian musicians (July 1980); the Toronto Arts Award (October 1987); an Honorary Diploma from the Western Ontario Conservatory of Music (October 1989); the Roy Thomson Hall Award (May 1992); the Order of Ontario and an honorary degree from Mount Allison University (May 1993); the Governor General's Performing Arts Award (November 1993); an Honorary Degree from the Royal Conservatory of Music (November 1994). But such ceremonial appearances were generally simply interruptions to the reclusive way of life she now preferred.

Lois required care, and someone to stand between her and the outside world. From the late 1970s to the mid 1980s, that role was fulfilled by Jon Donald, a young pianist who made Lois's acquaintance through Greta Kraus, for whom he sometimes house-sat. Donald's quick intelligence, charm, and apparently infinite willingness to be helpful recommended him throughout his life to a number of women, some of them rich and prominent, whom he befriended and cared for, in Toronto, Switzerland, and New York. But to those outside the charmed circle he could be difficult, quixotic, and downright mysterious. Donald helped Lois selflessly, taking her to medical appointments, looking after her cats, running errands, even dealing professionally (though not very tactfully) on her behalf with the booking agency Anton Kuerti had formed, which sought briefly to represent Lois. But then, without warning, sometime after the farewell tour, Donald simply vanished from Toronto and from Lois's life — sold his belongings and his house and moved to Europe without telling anyone of his intentions. By the time he returned to Canada and to his family in the mid-1990s, he was a dying man. Lois had no idea what happened to him after he evaporated from her life.

As opportunities allowed, other friends helped Lois to find ways out of the financial hardships and personal depression that threatened to engulf her. One such friend was Carl Morey. In 1983, Morey, at the instigation of CBC radio producer Neil Crory, put together a three-part, three-hour radio documentary called "Hark, the Echoing Air," which broadcast highlights of the recorded legacy from all phases of her career. It also featured recollections and assessments from many of Lois's friends and colleagues — Stuart Hamilton, Greta Kraus, Nicholas Goldschmidt,

Godfrey Ridout, even Weldon Kilburn — and a glowing tribute from the great Dutch soprano, Elly Ameling. In connection with this project, he also prevailed on Lois to attempt some notes towards an autobiography. Although the autobiography never got off the ground, these notes, carefully edited by Morey, are a treasure trove of personal information that would otherwise have been completely lost.

Morey even convinced Weldon, in very poor health by 1983, to cooperate in the radio tribute. The tapes of Morey's interview with Weldon make it clear that Weldon's admiration for Lois and her work remained undiminished by their separation and his subsequent remarriage. After the broadcast, there was finally telephone contact between Lois and Weldon, likely the first since their divorce. Morey believed that Weldon initiated the call, but never learned any details of the conversation. Weldon died just a few years later, on March 6, 1986. The death notice did not acknowledge Lois in any way. According to this official record, it was as though their partnership of thirty years had never happened.

Morey became Dean of the Faculty of Music at the University of Toronto in 1984, and two years later found himself in one of the awkward predicaments such a position can entail. For a 1986 Faculty Artists recital in the University of Toronto's Walter Hall, the featured performer was indisposed, and a substitute had to be announced. On this occasion, the featured performer was a special favourite. Patricia Kern, who was teaching at the Faculty of Music, had enjoyed a stellar career in both England and Canada. She was to be paired with the Orford Quartet in a performance of the seldom-performed *Il Tramonto* by Ottorino Respighi, the early twentieth-century composer best known for orchestral works like *Ancient Airs and Dances* and *The Fountains of Rome*. Serious music lovers looked forward to a special evening — a rarity performed in intimate surroundings by some of Canada's finest musicians. But Kern was sick, and the announcement had to be made.

Audience members feared the worst when Morey, rather than the featured artists, first took the stage. "We regret that Patricia Kern will be unable to perform tonight," he began, and paused for the inevitable rustle of disappointment. "In her place," he went on, "we are pleased to present — Lois Marshall."

There was, in Morey's own words, "an audible collective intake of breath, a gasp of pleasure and surprise from the whole audience quite unlike anything in my experience." Small wonder. Since her official fare-wells, Lois had all but vanished from the concert scene. She had not yet begun to teach at the Faculty. No one could have counted on this. Until the very moment of the announcement, neither could Morey. The arrangements for Lois's last public appearance as a singer had come right down to the wire.

Morey had had only a few days' warning, and had tried every sub-stitute artist he could think of, to no avail. Under those circumstances, he had nothing to lose. Lois had performed the Respighi several times before, once (in 1971) with the Orford, with whom she had even recorded it. She might say yes, and if she didn't, he was no further behind than he had been. He made the phone call.

"No," Lois said at once. She wouldn't know until she woke up in the morning whether she would actually have a singing voice that day. Morey gently persisted, and eventually got her to agree to think about it on the day of the concert. The Orford prepared a Beethoven quartet as last-minute backup.

Saturday morning, February 8, 1986, dawned cold and windy, with snow that would persist all day. Lois thought she might indeed have a voice, and, despite the difficulties of getting around in the storm, agreed to come to the hall in the late afternoon to do a run-through with the quartet. But she still made no promises. After the run-through, she would make up her mind.

In 1986, accessibility renovations to the Edward Johnson Building had not yet included direct access to the backstage area of Walter Hall, which is located one floor below street level. There was no possibility of Lois's using the artists' entrance that led directly backstage, via a steep stairwell. She had to use the public elevator to the foyer, then make her way slowly along the broad, shallow steps that run down the side of the raked seating area, then up a few more steps to the stage itself. For the pre-concert run-through, fortunately, she could make her entrance unobserved, without having to thread her way through waiting audience members. But once she was in the theatre, she was in it to stay, unless she wanted to treat them all to the spectacle of her toilsome exit.

The run-through went well, the answer was finally "Yes," and Lois retired to the artists' room backstage, to rest and wait for her appearance in the first half of the concert. After Morey's announcement, she entered from the wings, and took her place at the podium that had been provided for her, really a substantial structure in the guise of a music stand, on which Lois could lean for support.

It hardly mattered how she sang. That she sang at all was miracle enough. That she sang when everyone, including Lois herself, assumed she had performed for the last time before an audience. That she sang before this particular audience, in a school closely connected to the one where she had been a student herself. The Faculty of Music had inherited the professional training function pioneered by the Conservatory's Senior School. Lois's portrait as 1950 winner of the Eaton Scholarship hung prominently one floor above Walter Hall, in the main foyer of the Edward Johnson Building, one of the earliest in a large display of distinguished alums of the Senior School and then the Faculty. Her audience that night included aspiring professionals of the future, with members of the University of Toronto Concert Choir, slated to perform in the second half of the concert, scattered throughout the hall.

Among them was Monica Whicher, for whom Lois's name was part of family lore. Not only had Monica's father been a soloist in Sir Ernest's *St. Matthew Passion*s with Lois, but her mother, as a young vocal student at the Conservatory, had sat on the floor outside of Weldon's studio, eavesdropping on Lois's lessons for inspiration. Raised on recordings of Lois Marshall, Monica had never before heard her live, but what she heard now was, for her, no faint echo of the past.

> There was still a core sound that was so completely Lois that it spoke to me in the gut and elated me at the same time. I didn't feel short-changed at all, thinking that this was a remnant. No, I felt that this was the real

deal, a real artist with an incredibly unique and uniquely earthy sound.

At intermission Monica, dissolved in tears, retired to the basement washrooms of the Edward Johnson Building in order to compose herself. For her, the highly emotional synthesis of things personal and things musical in Lois's unexpected appearance triggered the most personal of responses. She could barely summon up the courage to speak to her after the event, but when she did, she was struck by Lois's shy and self-deprecating response. She deflected the conversation to speak of how well the Concert Choir had performed.

For Lois, the final challenge that evening was getting out of the auditorium without attracting attention. She waited backstage through the second half of the concert, waited through the applause, waited until the hall had emptied completely, and then, unobserved, made her way out the way she had come in. A combination of professionalism and personal pride forbade her to break the spell her music had created, and made her reluctant to expose her movement difficulties to the eyes of casual observers. Making the long, tiring day even longer was small price to pay for maintaining the illusion. She finally headed out into the snow, and back to her apartment.

Sometime after this unscheduled farewell appearance, Carl Morey suggested to Lois that she do some teaching at the Faculty of Music. Initially, she was hesitant. She had had earlier appointments as a voice teacher, none of them very satisfactory. In addition to the year at Ohio State, Lois had been listed on the faculty of the Conservatory from 1953 to 1957, but given her hectic concert schedule at the time, she was "on leave" for the last two of those years. In the fall of 1976, the Faculty of Music issued a press release, "Lois Marshall Joins Faculty of Music Staff," which noted that she had already been on the staff of the Conservatory since the preceding year. Again, there is no indication that these appointments involved much actual teaching. By 1986, however, the main entrance of

On January 17, 1986, Jon Vickers presented a lecture on Peter Grimes *at the University of Toronto's Faculty of Music as the first Wilma and Clifford Smith Visitor to the Faculty. Pictured at a reception following the lecture, with Lois in the foreground, are (left to right): Stephen Smith, Jane Smith, Greta Kraus, Mary Morrison, Jon Vickers, Hetti Vickers, and Carl Morey.*

Credit: From the collection of Cindy Townsend.

the Edward Johnson Building had finally been modified to provide an entrance ramp for the disabled. Getting to and from work would not be the challenge it had once been. At Morey's suggestion, Lois decided to give teaching one more try.

The regular routine of teaching was good for her, but the logistics were complicated. Lois would not leave the house without first doing an elaborate and time-consuming make-up. By now, she had given up driving, and had to allow additional time for the schedules of the Wheel-Trans bus service for the disabled. Getting out of the house and to work on time was such a production that Lois tried to fit all her teaching into one or two days of the week, instead of spreading it out. She soon became a familiar sight in the halls of the Edward Johnson Building, waiting in her wheelchair for her studio to become free, always with a book of crossword puzzles at hand to pass the time, ready to exchange a cheerful word with friends. To many of the younger generation of students, unaware of her reputation, she was just a pleasant fixture around the place. As Carl Morey put it, "I think many, many people didn't know who she was. She was just this singing teacher in a wheelchair."

As to her teaching itself, perhaps Catherine Robbin's assessment, though she never studied with Lois, was the most accurate. Perhaps "what Lois had was something that was completely unteachable and unlearnable." Inexperienced students, needing basic vocal technique, could find her allusive and indirect teaching methods frustrating. But for students who already knew how to sing, who were sensitive to example, capable of subtlety, and, above all, who were ready to approach the study of singing through the music itself, not just through their own voices, exposure to Lois's personality was an inspiring experience. Monica Whicher certainly found it so. She and the man who would become her husband first studied with Lois at a Royal Conservatory Summer School session, Lois's first try at the teaching suggested by Carl Morey.

> These five weeks of teaching were the beginning of a new career for Lois, one into which she poured as much passion as she had her singing. What I came to see in very short order was that all the passion in Lois's music was evident in Lois's person. She had an energy that made the everyday extraordinary. One evening, after the summer had ended, Lois called me to express something that moved me profoundly. With tears flowing, Lois explained that with the end of her singing had come an overwhelming sadness. She feared that the particular joy she had felt while singing was gone forever. She then went on to thank Gord and me, two of her new students, for helping to bring back this joy through our music. What moved me was not only Lois's giving, which was evident from the first, but her receiving.

Thus, with discreet help from friends, then more and more on her own initiative, Lois negotiated the "return to the world which so enhanced her last years," as one of those friends, Doreen Simmons, described it. In February 1988, in Toronto's Eglinton United Church, at sixty-three, Lois ventured out as a different kind of performer, as reader at a concert by the Oriana Singers, a women's choir led by another old friend, John Ford. It began a mini-career that exploited her lifelong talent for storytelling and mimicry. She performed as reader or narrator at a number of concerts in London, Ontario, around the time she received her honorary diploma from London's Western Conservatory of Music. In Toronto, with the chamber group Amici, she was the speaker for a performance of Schoenberg's *Pierrot Lunaire* in 1989 and the narrator in William Walton's *Façade* in 1990. In April 1996, CBC radio host Bill Richardson arranged to have Lois and the conductor, Bramwell Tovey, read the narration for Saint-Saëns *Carnival of the Animals* for his request program, *As You Like It*. She had to cancel a scheduled performance as narrator in a program at the CBC's Glenn Gould Studio in January 1997, just before her admission to hospital. Prophetically, the work in question was to have been Schubert's little-known "Abschied von der Erde" ("Farewell to the Earth").

By the early 1990s, Lois had settled in a pleasant but modest apartment on Castle Frank Road, more affordable than some of her previous dwellings, though not adapted for a person with a movement disability. One of her vocal students, Cindy Townsend, provided her with unstinting friendship and endless practical help as she negotiated the challenges of independent living. Along with students like Cindy and Monica Whicher, her inner circle expanded to include Doreen Uren Simmons, a professional pianist and accompanist who initially approached Lois by making a sympathetic phone call after one of Lois's cancellations, and eventually became her studio accompanist and one of the confidantes of her later years. Lois braved the challenges of Wheel-Trans to meet her sister, Rhoda, and Rhoda's daughter and granddaughter, Sarah, for simple pleasures — shopping at the Scarborough Town Mall followed by snacks in the Eaton's cafeteria. Sarah would clamber up onto her

Lois drew this caricature for her good friend, Doreen Simmons, in response to Doreen's frustrations at having to accompany rehearsals for Leonard Bernstein's Chichester Psalms *for the Toronto Mendelssohn Youth Choir in 1986.*

Credit: Lois Marshall. From the collection of Doreen Uren Simmons.

great-aunt's lap and delighted in roaring around the mall on Lois's electric scooter. Lois entertained, on a smaller but still elegant scale, with little lunches of grapes, cheeses, pâté, French bread, served on fine china and silver with linen napkins. There were parties with the old crowd of Toronto musicians. In a fit of extravagance, she and Stuart Hamilton even rented the ballroom at the Four Season's Hotel for a bang-up party on the old scale. By her own admission, Lois had always been "naïve and vague" where money was concerned.

Lois had her life back on an even keel, but not yet on a sound financial footing. Her income from teaching and from her various government pensions barely got her through from month to month, and as the years passed it became clear that she would not be able to remain indefinitely in the apartment on Castle Frank. The cramped kitchen, with counters at the wrong height for a person in a wheelchair, posed particular problems. Doreen remembered Lois's tale of the morning when everything went wrong. As usual, Lois had CBC, her lifeline to classical music and information on world affairs, on the radio as she wheeled about the kitchen, trying to get ready for her day. Whatever she picked up seemed to slip from her hands, and when she wheeled around to try to retrieve it, she drove over the cat, who yowled in protest. Finally, in frustration, Lois let out a bloodcurdling scream of concert hall proportions. In the silence that followed, she heard the CBC announcer saying smoothly, "You have just heard the beautiful voice of Lois Marshall."

Not all her misadventures were so trivial. She began to fall more and more frequently, and though she was careful to have a cordless phone with her at all times, she often had to wait for help to arrive, unable to get up on her own. Some nights she would sleep on the sofa, rather than face the tedious, and potentially booby-trapped rigmarole of organizing herself for bed. The doors on the building's elevator were just a little too small to accommodate her folding wheelchair, so she had to squeeze it together slightly, while still seated in it, in order to drive in, as she often did when confronted with a tight fit. Lois really needed fully accessible accommodation with emergency help nearby. Friends and family began to discuss various options.

In the summer of 1990, while Lois was visiting Doreen's cottage near Owen Sound, she had a major fall and once again broke her hip. She landed awkwardly, in a spot difficult to reach, and Doreen and her companions, unable to move her, comforted her ineffectually, as they waited for the ambulance to make its way to the cottage from the Owen Sound hospital.

While recovering from that fracture, Lois made a snap decision. It concerned only one of her minor vanities, but it spoke volumes about her acceptance of the passage of time. While in hospital she had removed her wig. She now decided that she would not put it on again. She had never been seen in public without the full head of luxuriant dark hair that had always been her trademark. But since she had resorted to wigs to create the effect, her own hair had turned pure white, like her mother's before her. Even her sister Rhoda was shocked. Lois had shed one of the

Lois with Doreen Simmons and her dog, Spaz, at Doreen's cottage in the summer of 1989.

Credit: From the collection of Doreen Uren Simmons.

Lois at her seventieth birthday party in her apartment on Castle Frank Road, January 1995.

Credit: From the collection of Doreen Uren Simmons.

last vestiges of her performing persona, of the image constructed for the benefit of an audience. With this symbolic gesture, Lois's private life could come more fully into its own.

The time came when even the rent on her Castle Frank apartment looked as though it would be beyond her means. If Lois was to continue to live independently, some solution had to be found. A few friends began working discreetly to find it. Together, they approached a private philanthropic foundation with Lois's plight, and asked for help. Lois, they knew, would be loath to accept outright charity. Some other way had to be found to assist her. Thus, in 1991, Lois became the first recipient of a newly-created Lifetime Achievement Award that provided a monthly subvention for a three-year period that covered the rent on her apartment. The award was renewed in 1994 for a further three years. Lois was able to accept the help with gratitude, and with dignity. Her family and those close to her were immensely grateful. She remained in the apartment on Castle Frank, with some degree of financial security, until her death, though her support group was actively seeking more accessible accommodation for her to the very end.

She had begun her life as a storyteller, making up stories for her sisters in their crowded bedroom on Ellerbeck Street, and she ended it the same way, telling stories for children. In December 1996, Lois appeared as a guest of the Toronto Children's Chorus, narrating the tale of *Brother Heinrich's Christmas* by John Rutter for the chorus's Christmas performance at Roy Thomson Hall. Lois was sick at the time of the performance, but appeared rather than let the choir down. Then they asked her to record the work as a fundraising project for the choir. Recording sessions were scheduled for January 18 and 19, 1997, at Toronto's Grace Church on-the-Hill.

By January it was clear that Lois was seriously ill. Rhoda couldn't see how she could attempt the recording session. "Well I have to, I just have to," Lois said. "I feel like my body is leaving me. This may be the last thing I do. And it may be for posterity. They couldn't make the recording if I couldn't do it." So Lois dosed herself with painkillers and Cindy

Townsend and her husband, Danny Nunes, helped her to the church for the recording session on the 19th. Though the temperature outside was well below freezing, the furnace in the church had to be turned off during recording to avoid creating background noise. Lois made it through the long, cold, uncomfortable day and completed her own gift to the Toronto Children's Chorus. It was her last public activity.

Within two weeks she had been admitted to Women's College Hospital for a debilitating series of tests, followed by surgery to remove a growth from her intestine. Cindy and Danny, along with Lois's closest family members, supported her through the ordeal. After the operation, they kept vigil by her bedside. For a day or more they waited for her to regain consciousness and, as the end approached, heard Schubert's Eighth Symphony broadcast on the CBC. Cindy listened to it with Lois, hoping the music might somehow reach her.

On February 19, Monica Whicher, having started her professional career, arrived in Calgary for an engagement. At the end of her day, Monica's husband relayed sad news to her from Cindy. After their conversation, when Monica switched on the television, space and time seemed to fold in upon themselves. She saw first an archival clip from *Peter Grimes*, with her father, James Whicher, in the same shot with Lois, then some stock footage of Monica herself during a coaching session in Lois's studio. It was the memorial item for Lois on CBC's national news. She had died earlier that evening, without regaining consciousness. The next day, the flag at Ottawa's National Arts Centre flew at half mast in recognition that the voice that had defined Canadian music, the "common bond uniting one generation of Canadian musical life," had been silenced.

Family and friends organized a public memorial for Lois one month after her death, on March 19, 1997, at St. Andrew's Presbyterian Church, just across the street from Roy Thomson Hall in downtown Toronto. The proceedings, which included generous recorded samples of Lois's art, were broadcast that evening on CBC radio. Close friends, such as Monica Whicher, Carl Morey, and Walter Homburger spoke feelingly,

One of Lois's favourite publicity portraits from the mid-1960s.

Credit: From the collection of Kim Scott.

as did two of Canada's greatest singers, Ben Heppner and Jon Vickers. Lois's grand-niece, Sarah, read a poem she had written for her aunt. Stuart Hamilton, unavoidably out of town on the date, was relieved to be able to send a recorded message, relieved because he could not have trusted himself to say in person what he felt in his heart.

One time, on her farewell tour, she was absolutely transcendent. When I spoke to her about it afterwards she said, "You know Stuart, when everything is right for me, I feel that I am out there with the composers, among the spheres, and that is when I am happiest." Well, Lois, for those of us who knew you and loved you, and for the millions of people you touched with your art, you always were and always will be out there, with the composers among the spheres.

APPENDIX A

Many standard reference works, including the *Encyclopedia of Music in Canada*, record the story that Lois began voice lessons with Weldon Kilburn at age twelve. *Lois Marshall: A Biography* places the beginning of her voice lessons with Weldon in January 1940, when she would have been fourteen years old, about to turn fifteen at the end of the month. This appendix outlines the evidence and the line of reasoning for proposing the later age.

Lois herself was negligent about dates in her personal history. Early references listed her birth date as January 29, 1924, when the correct year was 1925. This error is perpetuated in the *Encyclopedia of Music in Canada*. Lois's sister, Rhoda Scott, in interview with the author (August 1998), mentioned this discrepancy, and also her frustration that Lois never bothered to correct the error. Official documents, including Lois's application for an American Social Security number and the legal papers for Lois and Weldon's divorce proceedings, confirm January 29, 1925, as correct.

Lois's notes in her personal memoir are vague and uncertain with respect to dates. They do, however, outline a definite sequence of events that can help in establishing dates. According to her memoir, supplemented by the recollections of her sister Rhoda, Lois's first big musical achievement was winning the gold medal in the Toronto Schools' competition. Sometime thereafter, she performed at a Rotary Club function in Toronto (according to Rhoda, it was the club's Christmas party at the Royal York Hotel). As a result of that performance, the Rotarians decided to fund voice lessons for Lois. She was told about them by her mother as a Christmas surprise, with the lessons to start early in the new year. After only a few months, the lessons were placed in jeopardy when the Rotary Club withdrew funding in order to direct it to support for the "War Guests," children being evacuated from England to Canada after the outbreak of the war. The lessons continued, and Lois's breakthrough performance, the one that convinced Weldon she had a future as a musician, occurred when, some time after beginning lessons, she shared a Conservatory recital program with Irene McLellan, one of Weldon's piano students.

The dates of some of these events can be verified from independent sources. Lois won the gold medal in the Toronto Schools' competition in May 1939, and performed in the Massey Hall concert connected to this competition later in the same month, as reported in the *Toronto Star* of May 13, 1939. The *Star* reported (on December 18, 1939) that the Rotary Club had entertained three hundred "crippled children" at its annual Christmas party at the Royal York Hotel, held on December 16, 1939, and that children from the harmonica band of Wellesley Orthopaedic School provided entertainment. Lois's name is not mentioned in this account. On December 19, 1940, however, the *Star* announced that Lois would be performing at the Rotary Club Christmas party on December 21, 1940. Irene McLellan has provided me with an original copy of the program for her joint recital with Lois, which took place on June 20, 1941.

Based on this evidence, I believe that Lois began her voice lessons with Weldon Kilburn in January 1940. Only the date of her performance at the Rotary Club Christmas party causes any problem with this dating, but by assuming that she performed at the 1939 party (which children from her school did attend) without the newspaper reporting it, that inconsistency is resolved.

The sequence of events, then would be as follows:

May 1939 — Lois wins the gold medal (as reported in the *Star*);

December 1939 — Lois performs at the Rotary Club (conjecture);

Christmas 1939 — Lois receives news of voice lessons;

January 1940 — Lois begins voice lessons, still aged fourteen;

June 1941 — Lois's first recital, eighteen months later (concert program).

The proposed sequence also takes account of Lois's recollection that her early scholarship was withdrawn because of the "War Guests" evacuations, which occurred between 1940 and 1943. The above sequence and dating are therefore adopted in this biography.

Some early interviews and journalistic information further support this dating. Isabel LeBourdais ("They're Calling Her a Genius!" *Canadian Home Journal*, December 1950) refers repeatedly to the fact that Kilburn has been Lois's teacher for the past ten years (i.e., since 1939 or 1940). The *Time Magazine* profile on Lois (December 15, 1952) states that she "took her first music lesson from a Royal Conservatory of Music teacher when she was 14," (i.e., in 1939 or January, 1940). Margaret Aitken, in the *Toronto Telegram* of June 5, 1956, says Lois began lessons at age fifteen (i.e., in 1940). In his 1957 interview with Lois ("Magic on the Concert Stage," *Saturday Night*, March 16, 1957), Frank Rasky says she began her lessons when she was fourteen (as she would still have been in January 1940). Despite earlier inconsistencies on the subject, Lois herself, in a 1985 promotional interview with Stephen Godfrey for the Tri-Bach Festival in Edmonton (*CBC Radio Guide*, April 1985), is quoted as saying "when I first started studying music at fourteen," (i.e., in 1939 or in January 1940). In a CBC Radio Schools' Broadcast of April 30, 1963, Kilburn dates Lois's first recital, the one with Irene McLellan, as "some — oh — year and a half after you [Lois] began [lessons]." If she began in January 1940, as here proposed, the recital would have been exactly a year and half later.

The story of Lois's beginning lessons at age twelve appeared in a publicity flyer of the early 1950s from the Conservatory's Concert and Placement Bureau and seems to have been picked up and passed on from there. However, the evidence, as outlined above, points to the later age, as adopted here.

NOTES

Chapter One

Lois and her sister, Rhoda Scott, were sometimes vague about important family dates, and some inaccuracies have crept into the official record. For this biography, all dates and locations for the Marshall family history have been verified through official sources: the Canadian censuses of 1881, 1891, 1901, and 1911; registrations of marriage, birth, and death for the relevant years in the Archives of the Province of Ontario; copies of the Toronto City Directory for the relevant years in the Metropolitan Toronto Reference Library. Two human interest stories in newspapers provided valuable family history: "Lois Marshall's Mother and Father met here. Latter Native of District," the *Owen Sound Sun*, November 27, 1954, and "Visiting Soprano to see Relatives," *Regina Leader Post*, April 9, 1954. Interviews conducted by the author with Rhoda Scott from August to October 1998, provided much anecdotal information about Lois's childhood years. After her retirement, Lois, encouraged by her friend Carl Morey of the Faculty of Music at the University of Toronto, began work on an autobiography. She had little taste for the project and soon abandoned it, but left behind detailed descriptions of her early life, her musical training, and the major milestones of her career up to her appearance with Arturo Toscanini in 1953. I have relied on the testimony of this draft memoir heavily through the early chapters of this book.

Lois Marshall's birth date, which has been incorrectly reported as 1924 in some sources, is confirmed as 1925 by family sources, by information supplied in Lois and Weldon's divorce records (located in the City of Toronto Family Law Office), and by Lois's application for an American Social Security Number, filled out in her own hand. Details of Ruth Marshall's death are according to her death certificate, available in the Archives of the Province of Ontario. Fred Marshall's birth date is taken from his Social Security Number application; his death date is as provided in the Social Security Death Index, operated online at *http://ssdi.rootsweb.com*.

Two sources provided information on poliomyelitis in the Canadian context: Christopher J. Rutty's "The Twentieth-Century Plague," in the *Beaver* (April/May 2004), and "Conquering the Crippler: Canada and the Eradication of Polio," published as an insert to the *Canadian Journal of Public Health* by the Canadian Public Health Association in 2005. The family anecdote about Lois and the Bradford frame is recorded by Lois in her memoir, as is the detailed description of Lois's first round of surgery, its aftermath, and the subsequent surgeries that permanently fused her leg.

Wellesley Orthopaedic School was developed on the Bay and Wellesley site until 1953, when it moved to a site on Blythwood Road and was renamed Sunny View Public School. Information on the school's history was provided by the website of the Toronto District School Board, found at: *http://schools.tdsb.on.ca/sunnyview*, and by the author's interview with one of Sunny View's former students, Ute Gerbrandt (April 2003), who also provided background information on the involvement of service clubs in assisting the families of disabled children with their medical expenses in the period before OHIP and about Lois's cloakroom performances at Wellesley Orthopaedic. Another version of that story is reported by Hugh Thomson in "Acclaim Comes for Canada's Lois Marshall," the *Star Weekly*, May 26, 1956. The date of Lois's entry to Wellesley Orthopaedic School is established in an article in the *Toronto Star* on December 3, 1952, "Retired Teacher Shares Success of Lois — Principal." The same article provides useful information regarding Elsie Hutchinson and her support of Lois in her early years. See also "Lois Marshall Honoured by Education Board," *Globe and Mail*, December 19, 1952.

The newspaper record of Lois's childhood and teenaged appearances under Miss Hutchinson's tutelage is surprisingly extensive. See, for example: "Wellesley Orthopaedic Group View Interesting Pictures," *Globe and Mail*, January 17, 1939; "Empire Day Treat by Fessenden Unit," *Globe and Mail*, June 2, 1942; "Ethel McCordic Guest of Confreres," *Globe and Mail*, June 25, 1943.

Although the interior of the Church of the Holy Name was altered substantially in 1967, in accord with the reforms of the Second Vatican Council, the exterior still commands its stretch of Danforth Avenue as it originally did, and the interior retains the dramatic proportions of the church as Lois knew it. Architectural details are taken from a pamphlet, *A Brief history of Holy Name Catholic Church Danforth Avenue, to Commemorate the Occasion of its 90th Anniversary*, courtesy Church of the Holy Name. I am grateful to Miss Mary McDonald, who grew up in the parish, and to Mrs. Pamela Cobham, Parish Secretary, for arranging a tour so that I could see first-hand the church in which Lois sang as a child.

There are a few records of Fred Marshall's activities in the newspapers of the time. His performances at weddings are noted, for example, in the *Toronto Star* for July 27, 1937 ("Leonard Edward Johnson weds Winifred Smith") and July 3, 1940 ("G.J. Barrett weds Verna N. M'Lellan"); on June 10, 1938, the *Star* noted that Fred had sung at the closing meeting of the Wellesley Orthopaedic Home and School Association ("Garden Tea and Bridge for Magna Charta I.O.D.E.").

Many sources suggest that Lois began voice lessons at age twelve, but for various reasons they are unreliable. For a detailed discussion of the evidence establishing Lois's age when she began voice lessons, please see Appendix A.

The death notice for David Marshall appears in the *Toronto Star* of September 9, 1940. The account of his death was supplied by Rhoda Scott, who remembered that Lois had been away at a camp for crippled children when he died. A newspaper account in the *Globe and Mail* of January 17, 1939 ("Home and School Groups Enjoy Splendid Programs at Year's First Meetings") suggests that the camp in question was Blue Mountain Camp near Collingwood, opened in 1937.

Chapter Two

The various homes that the Conservatory has occupied are described in Ezra Schabas, *There's Music in These Walls: A History of the Royal Conservatory of Music* (Toronto: Dundurn Press, 2005). Background on St. Alban the Martyr Cathedral Church comes from the Province of Ontario Conservation Review Board documentation regarding the intention to designate the property, dated January 17, 1992, which can be found online at *www.crb.gov.on.ca/stellent/idcplg/webdav/Contribution%20Folders/crb/english/toronto_howland100-112.pdf* (accessed December 22, 2009).

The standard biography for Sir Ernest MacMillan is by Ezra Schabas, *Sir Ernest MacMillan: The Importance of Being Canadian* (Toronto: University of Toronto Press, 1994). Basic information on Sir Ernest, as for most of the other musical figures discussed in this book, can also be found in the *Encyclopedia of Music in Canada*, now available online at: *www.collectionscanada.ca/emc/index-e.html*. The *Encyclopedia* has been used as the basic reference tool throughout this book. Much of the information on the Toronto Conservatory of Music, principally the annual yearbooks, is taken from records in the papers of the Royal Conservatory of Music housed at the University of Toronto Library, Archives and Records Management Services. See also Ezra Schabas, *There's Music in these Walls*.

I am grateful to Peter M. Kilburn for detailed genealogical information on the Kilburn family, and especially on Dr. Nicholas Kilburn, Weldon's great uncle. There are interesting internet resources on Dr. Nicholas as well, particularly the biography on the website of the Myers Project at: *www.seaham.i12.com/myers/famenewindex.html*, the same text that was formerly housed on the website of the British Library. Weldon Kilburn's arrival in Toronto has been variously reported as in 1926 or 1927. A passing reference in the *Edmonton Journal* ("Matters of Musical Moment," September 13, 1941) and an early biography Weldon used for his concert programs suggest that the correct date is 1927, when he was twenty-one. See also Blaik Kirby, "Kilburn's Musical Dynasty," *Toronto Star*, March 17, 1962. Additional information about Weldon Kilburn and about the life of the Conservatory when Lois studied there was supplied in interviews between the author and Kilburn's sons, Nicholas and Paul

(November 2005), Kilburn's former piano pupil, who shared the billing at Lois's first Conservatory recital, Irene McLellan (March 2006), and soprano Mary Morrison, a contemporary of Lois's at the Conservatory (March 2006). Miss Hutchinson's sponsorship of Lois's early singing lessons is mentioned by Isabel LeBourdais in "They're Calling Her a Genius!" *Canadian Home Journal*, December 1950.

The detailed description of Lois's first lesson and her responses to it comes from her personal memoir, supplemented by the author's interview with Rhoda Scott (August 1998). The description of Lois's voice as Kilburn first heard it is based on their descriptions of that event in a number of sources: June Callwood, "The Launching of Lois Marshall" (*Maclean's*, February 1, 1953); Margaret Ness, "Tribute to Talent and Drive" (*Saturday Night*, November 7, 1950); "How We Work," interview with A. Tumanov published in *Soviet Music* [1960?] (found in the Marshall Papers, Library and Archives Canada, Music Division); CBC Schools Telecast (April 30, 1963); interview between Weldon Kilburn and Carl Morey, 1983. The reference to Kilburn as a "dictator" and Kilburn's description of Lois's first recital, with Irene McLellan, are found in Frank Rasky, "Magic on the Concert Stage" (*Saturday Night*, March 16, 1957); the "ogre" reference is in the CBC Schools Telecast referred to above. The description of Kilburn in the studio, in later years, is based on the author's recollections of studying with Weldon Kilburn in 1969. The discussion of making vocal technique seem second nature is supported as well by comments Weldon Kilburn made in the interview in *Soviet Music* referred to above. Stuart Hamilton provided the anecdote about Lois leaving the room when talk turned to technical matters of voice production. Lois's description of herself as not having a technique and never having learned to sing is found in Thomas Hathaway, "What is a Song, how do You sing it and what is Tradition all About?: Lois Marshall and Greta Kraus on Music-Making" (*Queen's Quarterly*, 89/2 [Summer 1982]). Kilburn's characterization of Lois's musical personality as "turbulent" comes from the Callwood profile referred to above.

Lois spoke about her brother, Fred, in interview with Carl Morey in 1983, as did her sister Rhoda Scott, in interview with the author in 1998. Further details of Fred's wartime experiences come from an article by Dorothy Howarth, "First Canadian Singer to Capture 'Naumburg,'" published in the *Toronto Telegram* in April 1952.

The comparison of Lois's sound to that of earlier artists, including Lemnitz, was made by, among others, the Washington critic Day Thorpe in "Lois Marshall's Voice Rates Critical Acclaim," *Washington Sunday Star*, March 3, 1957.

A surprising number of Lois's wedding engagements, and some of her service club engagements, stretching from 1941 to as late as 1953, can be found documented in the wedding notices and the social pages for the period of the *Toronto Star* and the *Globe and Mail*. Lois's extravagant generosity to her family, especially once she started earning big fees, is commented on by Isabel LeBourdais in "They're Calling Her a Genius!" The date at which Lois left Wellesley Orthopaedic School is as noted in the *Toronto Star*, December 3, 1952, "Retired Teacher Shares Success of Lois — Principal."

More mature readers will remember the days, before Gilbert and Sullivan came out of copyright, when amateur performances were strictly regulated by the copyright holder and the D'Oyly Carte Opera Company soldiered on, performing every operetta exactly as it had been originally staged. In Canada, Tyrone Guthrie changed all that with his Stratford Festival production of *H.M.S. Pinafore* in 1960, which led the way in new stagings of the G & S repertoire. See also David Duffey, "The D'Oyly Carte Family," on the Gilbert and Sullivan Archive website: *http://math. boisestate.edu/gas/html/carte.html*. The added performances for *Princess Ida* in 1945 are documented in display ads in the *Globe and Mail*, March 17 and 22, 1945. Augustus Bridle's review, "'Princess' Fantasy Makes Debut Here," appeared in the *Toronto Star*, March 13, 1945.

The anecdotes about Lois's aloof stage presence and her occasional dilatoriness as a student come from June Callwood's profile, "The Launching of Lois Marshall," and from an interview conducted by the author with Irene McLellan (March 2006). Both Irene McLellan and Weldon Kilburn, in his interview with Carl Morey, remembered that Lois had sung in the choir at St. Alban's in her youth. Details of the development of the Conservatory in the 1940s come from the *Encyclopedia of Music in Canada* and from Ezra Schabas's two books, *Sir Ernest MacMillan* and *There's Music in these Walls*.

Information on the Senior School and the Opera School of the Royal Conservatory of Music, and on Lois's years in the Senior School, comes from a variety of sources in the papers of the Royal Conservatory (University of Toronto, Archives and Records Management Services); from interviews between the author and Mary Morrison (March 2006), Irene McLellan (March 2006), Stuart Hamilton (September 1999), Nicholas and Paul Kilburn (November 2005), and Jan Simons (April 2003); and from Lois's draft memoir. Published sources of information include the *Encyclopedia of Music in Canada*, *Sir Ernest MacMillan*, *There's Music in these Walls*, and Gwenlyn Setterfield's *Niki Goldschmidt: A Life in Canadian Music* (Toronto: University of Toronto Press, 2003).

The date for the 1947 performance of the Scarlatti *Christmas Cantata* is established in the concert program in the Greta Kraus papers, Library and Archives Canada. The Colin Sabiston review of the concert, "Mazzoleni Group 5 P.M. Program 'Beautiful' Music," appeared in the *Globe and Mail*, December 11, 1947. The other reviews cited in connection with this concert appeared in the *Toronto Star* ("Music, Art, Drama," December 20, 1947) and the University of Toronto *Varsity*, ("Bach, Scarlatti and Snow," December 12, 1947). The Rose MacDonald review is preserved in the papers of the Royal Conservatory of Music at the University of Toronto, Archives and Records Management Services, but without the date recorded. Details of the walk in the snow following this concert are from Lois's draft memoir. I am indebted to Irene McLellan for the suggestion that Kilburn's affections could be swayed by his musical enthusiasms.

Chapter Three

Biographical material on Emmy Heim comes from the *Encyclopedia of Music in Canada*, which lists her as a soprano, Lois's personal memoir, and the author's interviews with three other students of Emmy Heim, Jan Simons (April 2003), Irene McLellan (March 2006) and Joanne Mazzoleni (June 2006). Her career with the *Wiener Singakademie* is documented in the online archive of the *Akademie* at *www.wienersingakademie.*

at/archiv/programs.htm. Her connection to Martha Schlamme is noted in Schlamme's biography on the Jewish Music WebCenter site at *www. jmwc.org/Women/womens.html*. A copy of the recording of her interview with Ronald Hambleton is in the collection of the author. Kokoschka's 1916 lithograph of Emmy Heim is referenced in the *Encyclopedia of Music in Canada* article on "Art, Visual (Some Visual Art Inspired By Music and Musicians)." The online archive of the Arnold Schoenberg Center provides data for the first performance of "Verlassen" at *www. schoenberg.at/6_archiv/music/works/op/compositions_op6_e.htm*.

Lois's cancellation of her TSO debut is noted in Colin Sabiston, "School Concert by TSO Featured Amusing Works," *Globe and Mail*, February 11, 1948. June Callwood reports her tearful reaction in "The Launching of Lois Marshall." Details regarding Sir Ernest MacMillan's history of presenting the *St. Matthew Passion* in Toronto, the popular and critical response to these performances, and his eventual preference for Lois as his favourite soprano, are from Ezra Schabas's *Sir Ernest MacMillan*. The account of Lois's preparations for the *St. Matthew* is from her draft memoir and from her interview with Isabel LeBourdais, "They're Calling Her a Genius!" Lois's correspondence with Sir Ernest MacMillan is in the MacMillan papers in Library and Archives Canada. The size of the Mendelssohn Choir in 1948 is noted by Augustus Bridle in "A Big, Busy Choir" in "Music, Art, Drama," *Toronto Star*, January 24, 1948. In interviews with the author, both Stuart Hamilton (September 1999) and Mary Morrison (March 2006) recalled Sir Ernest's nickname of "Lord Largo." The negative critical responses to Sir Ernest's interpretations of Bach are cited by Schabas in connection with MacMillan's 1954 performance of the *St. Matthew* at Carnegie Hall in New York. Colin Sabiston reviewed Lois's 1948 performance in the *St. Matthew* in "New Laurels won by Great Choir in Bach Passion," *Globe and Mail*, March 24, 1948.

Lois's recollections of her Sundays at Bloor Street United and with the Silvester family are recorded in her personal memoir. The comments about her warm-up practices come from interviews between the author and Yehudi Wyner (August 2003) and Stuart Hamilton (September 1999). In interviews with the author, both Mary Morrison (March 2006) and Jan

Simons (April 2003) recalled the experience provided by the Department of Education sponsored tours of the late 1940s and early 1950s.

Biographical material on Nicholas Goldschmidt comes from Setterfield's *Niki Goldschmidt*. Additional material relating to Goldschmidt and his direct experience working with Lois comes from the author's interview with Goldschmidt prior to his death (September 1999).

Information about "Singing Stars of Tomorrow" comes from Lois Marshall's personal memoir and from the entry in the *Encyclopedia of Music in Canada*, with additional detail from Gordon Sinclair's columns in the *Toronto Star* of April 24, 1950 and June 24, 1950, and the author's correspondence with the late Lou Ann (Woods) Cassels, which included a copy of the program for the 1944 final concert. Lois's 1949 participation on "Opportunity Knocks" is recorded in Jack Karr's column in the *Toronto Star* for January 6, 1949. Doreen Hulme's career is summarized in the *Encyclopedia of Music in Canada*; the program for her February 1950 appearance with the TSO can be found in the program collection of the Music Division, Library and Archives Canada. Healey Willan's participation as a judge on "Singing Stars of Tomorrow" is noted by Isabel LeBourdais in "They're Calling Her a Genius!" Biographical information for Abramo Carfagnini appears in the Promenade Concert program for June 29, 1950, Varsity Arena, Toronto, the concert at which Lois and Abramo Carfagnini made their appearances as winners of "Singing Stars of Tomorrow." The program is in the private collection of Cindy Townsend. The letter of enquiry addressed to Lois c/o Singing Stars of Tomorrow (dated May 25, 1950) is in the Lois Marshall papers in the Music Division of Library and Archives Canada.

Eric McLean's letter to Paul Hume (July 11, 1950) is in the Paul Hume papers in the archives of the Georgetown University Library. In her autobiography, *Out of Character* (Toronto: McClelland & Stewart, 1986) Maureen Forrester recounts her first attempt at "Singing Stars" in the year before June Kowalchuk took first prize. Since Kowalchuk won in the 1950–51 season, Forrester must first have competed in the year of Lois's win. Weldon Kilburn recounted the story of urging Lois to try for the Eaton Scholarship in his interview with Carl Morey (March 1983). Lois's student relationship with Arnold Walter is described in her personal memoir and in Isabel LeBourdais, "They're Calling Her a Genius!" The announcement of the Eaton Graduating Scholarship appeared in the *Toronto Star* on June 6, 1950, and in the *Globe and Mail* on June 7. For historical detail on Eaton Auditorium, see Joan Parkhill Baillie, *Look at the Record: An Album of Toronto's Lyric Theatres 1825–1984* (Oakville, ON: Mosaic Press, 1985). Details of Lois's debut recital at Eaton Auditorium come from reviews by Hugh Thomson ("Lois Marshall wins big hand, Bouquets," *Toronto Star*, October 13, 1950) and Leo Smith ("Home Recognition to Lois Marshall is much Cherished Objective," *Globe and Mail*, October 13, 1950). Biographical detail on Leo Smith comes from the *Encyclopedia of Music in Canada*. Lois's experience after her Proms concert debut was reported in the *Toronto Star*'s gossip column, "Over the Teacups," on July 4, 1950.

Chapter Four

Lois's western Canadian tour of 1950 was described by Augustus Bridle in his column for the *Toronto Star*, September 23, 1950 ("Birds, Flowers Delighted Canadian Sculptor's Wife"). John Kraglund described the activities of the RCM concert bureau, using Lois's early tours as an example, in his "Music in Toronto" column for the *Globe and Mail*, September 8, 1955. Information on the Community Concerts organization comes from a variety of sources including: *The Encyclopedia of Music in Canada*; Schabas, *There's Music in These Walls*; J.V. McAree, "Obstacles Confront Canadian Musicians," *Globe and Mail*, July 5, 1949, and "Concert Group is Organized," *Globe and Mail*, December 7, 1954; author's interview with Jan Simons, April 2003. Full details on the legal proceedings against Community Concerts are in documents in the papers of the Peterborough Community Concerts Organization, Trent University Archives, Peterborough, Ontario. Schabas describes the network of examination centres that the Royal Conservatory of Music developed across Canada.

The comments on Lois's stage presence as a young performer come from a review in the *Moncton Transcript*, November 8, 1951; the

Vancouver Sun for January 24, 1951, recorded the broadcast delay caused by the prolonged applause for her performance. S. Roy Maley's comments on the emotional power of a Marshall performance occur in his review of an early concert in the *Winnipeg Tribune* (November 14, 1956) and in a fan letter to Marshall (June 17, 1970) preserved in her papers in the Music Division of Library and Archives Canada. The anecdote of Lois on a frigid train in western Canada is reported by Kay Rowe in the *Brandon Daily Sun*, February 22, 1958. John Beckwith reviewed Lois's performance of Elwell's "Pastorale" in the *Toronto Star*, January 31, 1962. An earlier story in the *Globe and Mail* (April 11, 1953) records Elwell's presentation of the autographed score to Lois.

For background on the opera festivals, see the entry under "Canadian Opera Company" in *The Encyclopedia of Music in Canada*. Additional information on the performance of *The Magic Flute* from the author's interviews with Mary Morrison (March 2006), Joanne Mazzoleni (June 2006) and Nicholas Kilburn (November 2005). Reviews of the production quoted in the text appeared in the *Globe and Mail* (February 23, 1952) and the *Toronto Star* (February 23, 1952). The Day Thorpe interview in which Lois discussed the Queen of the Night appeared in the *Sunday Star*, Washington, DC, on March 3, 1957; S. Roy Maley reported the possibility of a Glyndebourne Queen of the Night in the *Winnipeg Tribune*, December 17, 1960. Marjorie Laurence's operatic comeback after polio is recorded in many places, including Robert Tuggle, "A Season of Valkyries," *Opera News* (Vol. 70, No. 4, October 2005). The doubling of the Queen of the Night's role is confirmed by Ezra Schabas and Carl Morey in *Opera Viva: Canadian Opera Company, The First Fifty Years* (Toronto: Dundurn Press, 2000).

George Kidd's information on the Naumburg competition appeared in a feature story in the *Toronto Telegram*, December 2, 1952. Most of the other details of the Naumburg competition are taken from Marshall's draft memoir. Hugh Thomson reported Lois's triumphant return to Toronto in a front page story in the *Toronto Star* on April 2, 1952; the *Toronto Telegram* carried a full account with more family details on the same date.

June Callwood's detailed account of Lois's Town Hall debut appeared in *Maclean's* ("The Launching of Lois Marshall"), February 1, 1953; see also "Rave Notices Thrill Toronto Singer," *Globe and Mail*, December 3, 1952. Critical responses to the debut are recorded in "Critics Praise New York Debut of Lois Marshall" (*Globe and Mail*, December 3, 1952), *Musical America* (January 1, 1953), and George Kidd's "Critics, Opera Star rave over Toronto Girl's Voice" (*Toronto Telegram*, December 3, 1952). Personal reminiscences about the event come from the author's interviews with Rhoda Scott (October 1998) and Weldon Kilburn's interview with Carl Morey (March 1983). Some of the reactions of the Canadian press to Lois's New York success, as well as her work on behalf of children with disabilities, can be found in George Kidd, "Lois Marshall at new peak in Music Career" (*Toronto Telegram*, December 2, 1952); "Marshall, Bernardi Talents Fight Polio" (*Toronto Telegram*, April 29, 1953); and in "Lois Marshall Honoured by Education Board" (*Globe and Mail*, December 19, 1952).

A story in the *Ottawa Citizen* ("Lois Marshall Guest at Final Orchestra Concert," December 15, 1952) documents the timing of her contract negotiations with CAMI. Details of her fees for the period come from copies of her original contracts with CAMI (collection of the author) and from papers in the Royal Conservatory of Music files (University of Toronto Archives and Records Management Services), which also contain the detailed itinerary for Lois's 1953 Maritimes tour.

The accounts of the Toscanini audition, rehearsals, and performance are based on Lois's memoir; interviews by Carl Morey with Lois Marshall and Weldon Kilburn (March 1983); the following newspaper accounts: Paul V. Beckley, "Lois' Memory Startles even Fabulous Toscanini" (*Toronto Telegram*, March 27, 1953); John Kraglund, "Toronto Singer Chosen for Toscanini Program" (*Globe and Mail*, February 19, 1953) and "Lois Marshall Sings for the Maestro in Brilliant Triumph of her Young Career" (*Globe and Mail*, March 30, 1953); Hugh Thomson, "Lois Sings With Toscanini Passes Supreme New York Test" (*Toronto Star*, March 30, 1953); "Toscanini Chooses Lois to sing with Orchestra" (*Toronto Star*, February 19, 1953); and "Music News from NBC," (NBC Press Release, January 5, 1953, Toscanini Legacy Collection of the Performing Arts Library, New York Public Library). The standard biography of Toscanini is Harvey Sachs's *Toscanini* (London: Weidenfeld & Nicolson, 1978).

The cable from Nora Shea, confirming her engagement with Toscanini, is quoted in Lois's memoir. The estimate of Toscanini's radio audience is according to John Kraglund in "Lois Marshall Sings for the Maestro in Brilliant Triumph of Her Young Career" (*Globe and Mail*, March 30, 1953). Weldon Kilburn made the remark about Toscanini requiring no major changes of interpretation to his coaching of the score to the author in 1969, after one of our vocal coaching sessions that summer. The *Time* magazine review of the Toscanini *Missa* appeared in its issue of April 6, 1953.

Chapter Five

The British singer, Ian Bostridge, experienced in both recital and opera, commented on the practical advantages of a career in opera in "Unchained Melody," an interview with William R. Braun, in *Opera News*, Vol.70, No.8 (February 2006). In *Out of Character* (p.116), Maureen Forrester refers to the Ingrid Bergman example in discussing her motives for concealing her out-of-wedlock first pregnancy from the general public in 1955. Among the many honours bestowed on Lois during her career, she was named Woman of the Year by the Client Editors of the British United Press in 1953. Information on Lois's places of residence has been assembled from various items of correspondence and newspaper references, verified wherever possible in the Toronto City Directory for the appropriate year. Lois's impulsive generosity, legendary among her family and friends, is also chronicled by Isabel LeBourdais in "They're Calling Her a Genius!"

Lois mentioned her discomfort with Beethoven's Ninth in her interview with Carl Morey (1983); the annotated repertoire list from Columbia Artists is in Lois's papers in the Music Division of Library and Archives Canada. Details included in the description of the town of Kapuskasing are gleaned from its official website, *www.kapuskasing. ca*, accessed on February 13, 2006. The story of Gray Knapp's connection to Lois comes from personal correspondence with the author, May 4, 2003. Even Lois's pinch-hitting for bigger names was considered newsworthy in the early stages of her career. "Lois Marshall Subs for Pons" was the header for the item in the *Globe and Mail* (April 16, 1955) that reported both the Lily Pons and the Claudio Arrau substitutions. For a first-hand account of the early Stratford Music Festivals, see Louis Applebaum, "Stratford's Music Festival," in Peter Raby (compiler and editor), *The Stratford Scene: 1958–1968* (Toronto, Vancouver: Clarke, Irwin & Company Limited, 1968), 58–64. I have supplemented Applebaum's account with an interview with Jan Simons (April 2003), who sang with the Festival Singers at the 1955 opening concert, and with Ross Parmenter's review of that concert, "Stratford Opens Music Festival," *New York Times*, July 11, 1955.

June Callwood has documented Lois's reliance on Weldon during the preparation period for a major appearance in "The Launching of Lois Marshall." Ilona Kombrink, in interview with the author (March 2003) confirmed Weldon's absence from her wedding to Nicholas Kilburn. Lois's 1955 Town Hall recital was reviewed in the *New York Times* of January 24, 1955 and in the February 1, 1955 issue of *Musical America*. Writing shortly thereafter in the *Chicago Daily News* (March 16, 1955), Irving Sablosky reported that the New York recital had received "something like 17 curtain calls."

Statistics on the early performances of Orff's *Carmina Burana* are drawn from the official programs of the Cincinnati May Festival and the Chicago Symphony Orchestra. I learned about the Reiner anecdote in connection with *Carmina Burana* in interviews with Doreen Simmons (May 1997) and Monica Whicher (July 2004); Weldon Kilburn spoke briefly about the incident in his interview with Carl Morey (March 1983). Reviews of the Reiner performance of *Carmina Burana* appeared on March 18, 1955 in the *Chicago American* (Roger Dettmer); the *Chicago Daily News* (Irving Sablosky); the *Chicago Sun Times* (Felix Borowski); and the *Chicago Tribune* (Claudia Cassidy). Roger Dettmer's review of Lois's 1957 Orchestra Hall recital in Chicago appeared in the *Chicago American*, April 22, 1957.

Biographical information on Sir Thomas Beecham is from Alan Jefferson, "Beecham, Sir Thomas, Second Baronet (1879–1961)," *Oxford Dictionary of National Biography*, (Oxford University Press, 2004). Maureen

Forrester recounts the anecdote about Beecham's persecution of his recording companies in *Out of Character* (p.176). Beecham's audition comment about Lois's sight-reading is quoted in S. Roy Maley, "Top Names in Music Choose Canada's Lois," *Winnipeg Tribune*, November 13, 1956. Other details of the Beecham audition are from this interview with Lois and from Lois's interview with Carl Morey, (March 1983). A notice in the *Globe and Mail*, March 17, 1956, indicates March 27 and 28 as the dates of Beecham's Toronto engagement. Information on the history of the car industry is from the General Motors website, *www.gm.com/company/corp_info/history*, accessed February 21, 2006. Robert Donald, in interview with the author (March 2008), confirmed details regarding the options on Lois's cars and her vanity license plate. Lois recounted her anecdotes about the preparations for *The Abduction from the Seraglio* to Carl Morey in interview (March 1983) and in an article by Florence Schill, "Great Singer Finds Tour Taxing but Gratifying," in the *Globe and Mail* (January 1, 1957). Reviews of Lois's Festival Hall debut appeared on May 28, 1956, in the *London Times* and the *London Daily Telegraph*, and on May 29, 1956 in the *Edinburgh Scotsman*.

The most enthusiastic review of Lois's Hamburg recital appeared in the *Hamburger Abendblatt*, June 12, 1956. For readers able to understand German, the prose of the original conveys the reviewer's enthusiasm more graphically than any translation can. "… ein überwältigendes Erlebnis…. Eine vollkommene Naturbegabung verbindet sich mit untadeliger Technik und einer verschwenderischen Ausdruckskraft…. Etwas strahlendes … geht von dieser jungen Künstlerin aus … dass man Zeit und Raum vergisst." Details on Lois's 1956 schedule are found in the Columbia Artists' press materials in the "Lois Marshall" clippings file of the Performing Arts Division of the New York Public Library. Of particular interest is the letter from Columbia Artists to Leo Lerman, *Mademoiselle*, September 19, 1956, responding to an enquiry about Lois's popularity on the concert circuit. Lois saved the reviews of her Amsterdam debut until her death. "The Miracle," in *Trouw*, an Amsterdam paper, of December 22, 1956, is preserved in the Lois Marshall Papers in the Music Division of Library and Archives Canada.

Lois's projected appearances with the Washington Opera Society in 1958 were announced by Washington music critic Paul Hume in the *Washington Post and Times Herald*, September 22, 1957. The Washington *Così* was projected as her operatic debut in Columbia Artists' January, 1958 press book for Lois, preserved in the Lois Marshall clippings file at the New York Public Library (Performing Arts Division at Lincoln Center). Her conversation with Leslie Bell detailing the extent of her commitments in late 1957 appeared in his *Toronto Star* column for August 3, 1957.

CBC's 1959 *Peter Grimes* generated a large amount of advance press coverage, from which the details of the production are gleaned. For details, see: "Peter Grimes Telecast Split-Level Production," *Toronto Star*, January 10, 1959; and Gordon Sinclair, "Need 2 TV Networks to do 'Peter Grimes,'" *Toronto Star*, January 13, 1959. Lois defended the expenditure on the production in a later newspaper interview: "Lois Lauds CBC for Peter Grimes," *Toronto Star*, June 4, 1959. Franz Kraemer's anecdote about the production was televised on "Adrienne Clarkson's Summer Festival," on August 23, 1988; a copy of the videotape is located in Library and Archives Canada. Stuart Hamilton recalled the fall during *Peter Grimes*, and subsequent falls during Lois's career, in conversation with the author (August 2006).

Lois's operatic appearances in Boston were trumpeted as a major career shift for her in a story in the *Winnipeg Tribune*, December 5, 1959, which also provided details about the alternating performance weeks of Italian and English during the Boston run. A feature by Harold Rogers, "Operation Opera! A Pattern for Civic Opera Companies," in The *Christian Science Monitor*, September 1, 1959, provided many of the details of Sarah Caldwell's methods in setting up the Boston Opera Company. More information on Caldwell and her career can be found in Donal Henahan's profile, "Prodigious Sarah," in the *New York Times Magazine* for October 5, 1975. Lois told the story of Sarah Caldwell's joke about her disability on a CBC television interview, "Spectrum," broadcast December 10, 1980, a copy of which is preserved in Library and Archives Canada. In an interview with the author (September 1999), Stuart Hamilton commented on Caldwell's notorious body odour. Both

Lois and Weldon reminisced about Caldwell in their separate interviews with Carl Morey (March 1983). Lois revealed the secret of her body double for the leap from the parapet in *Tosca* during an interview with William Littler in the *Toronto Star* (October 16, 1976). Weldon's evaluation of Lois's acting in *Tosca* was quoted in the *Winnipeg Tribune* story of December 5, 1959.

Chapter Six

Blaik Kirby's article, "Kilburn's Musical Dynasty," appeared in the *Toronto Star* of March 17, 1962. The circumstances of family life in the Kilburn home are reconstructed from interviews with Ilona Kombrink (March 2003) and with Nicholas and Paul Kilburn (November 2005). The careers of both Nicholas and Michael Kilburn in the Toronto Symphony Orchestra are recorded in Richard S. Warren's *Begins with the Oboe: A History of the Toronto Symphony Orchestra* (Toronto: University of Toronto Press, 2002). Lois's agreement to purchase her house on Golfhaven Road, dated August 6, 1957, is preserved in her papers in the Music Division, Library and Archives Canada. Lois's estimated earnings for 1957 are from an article by Frank Rasky, "Persona Grata: Magic on the Concert Stage," in *Saturday Night*, March 16, 1957. Nicholas Kilburn believed that Weldon had left the family home to live with Lois in 1958, but the Toronto City Directory of 1960 is the first to list Marion as living alone at 64 Strathallan. Such a lag in reporting the change in Weldon's address for the City Directory would not be uncommon. Details on the purchase and furnishing of Lois's house are from an interview with Rhoda Scott (August 1998). In another feature article, "Lois Marshall Updated," in the *Toronto Star* of January 19, 1963, Blaik Kirby described the parties Lois liked to throw in the music room on Golfhaven.

In *Am I Too Loud? Memoirs of an Accompanist* (London: Hamish Hamilton, 1962), Gerald Moore provides accounts of early days at the Edinburgh Festival, where he appeared regularly, and describes his early years in Toronto. Paul Kilburn recalled Lois's 1957 Edinburgh recital in conversation with the author (November 2005). Stuart Hamilton

was one of Gerald Moore's piano students at his 1948 and 1949
Conservatory summer sessions and recalled, in conversation with the
author (September 1999) Lois's participation there, as does Moore in
Am I Too Loud?

Elly Ameling's recollection of hearing Lois sing in The Hague was
recorded in interview with Carl Morey in 1983. Gwenlyn Setterfield
recounts Niki Goldschmidt's creation of the Vancouver International
Festival in *Niki Goldschmidt: A Life in Canadian Music*. Paul McIntyre's
winning of the prize for Canadian composition at the VIF is documented in Setterfield and in the Bulletins of the Royal Conservatory of
Music, at the University of Toronto Archives and Records Management
Services. The 1956 video of Lois singing Puccini on the Jackie Rae Show
is in Library and Archives Canada. Keith MacMillan's comment about
the difficulty of recording Lois's voice occurs in a script for a radio interview with Carl Morey, "Lois Marshall: A Life in Music," kindly lent to
me by Carl Morey. The tape of Lois's interview with Pat Patterson is in
the CBC audio archives in Toronto.

Details of the negotiations for Lois's first Russian tour are from
an interview with Walter Homburger (June 1998) and from George
Kidd's column in the *Toronto Telegram* of January 4, 1958. David
Caute describes Leonard Bernstein's controversial behaviour in the
Soviet Union in 1959 in *The Dancer Defects: The Struggle for Cultural
Supremacy during the Cold War* (Oxford: Oxford University Press, 2003),
401. Details of Marshall's Moscow debut were provided in interviews
between the author and Peter Roberts (November 2002), Doris Crowe
(November 2002), and Alexander Tumanov (July 2003). Another
account of the Moscow debut was recorded by Mr. Tumanov for CBC
radio and broadcast on *Saturday Afternoon at the Opera* (June 14, 2003).
Peter Roberts, Doris Crowe, and Alexander Tumanov, all of whom were
present at Lois's Moscow debut, provided vivid first-hand accounts
of the second Moscow concert and the reception following it. Peter
Roberts also provided valuable commentary on the political situation
of the time. Lois's description of audience response to her first Moscow
appearance was quoted in an article by David Ghent in the *Toronto
Telegram* (October 14, 1958). Additional details about the Moscow

reception for Lois were provided by Naomi J. Roberts, who was married to Peter Roberts at the time, in a letter to her family immediately following the events, dated October 27, 1958 (by permission of Naomi Roberts). See also Peter Roberts, "The Night a Miracle Came to Moscow," *Globe and Mail*, March 20, 1997, and *Raising Eyebrows: An Undiplomatic Memoir* (Ottawa: Golden Dog Press, 2000). Mary Russell described Lois's experiences of Russian concert audiences in an article for the *Globe Magazine* (January 3, 1959), "In Russia, They Want Lois Marshall Back for Another Tour." The description of 1958 Soviet press coverage for artistic events was provided by Alexander Tumanov, who himself wrote for some of the Soviet journals before his immigration to Canada. Nina Dorliak's assessment of Lois's Moscow performance was quoted in "Soviet Ovation Concludes Tour of Lois Marshall," in the *Globe and Mail* immediately following her second Moscow concert (October 24, 1958). Lois described her 1960 Leningrad performance of Schubert's "Ave Maria" in one of her letters to the *Toronto Telegram*'s George Kidd, published February 15, 1960. Her experiences in Moscow and Riga that same year were also recounted in letters to Kidd, published on February 16 and 19, 1960. The note from the anonymous Russian admirer was quoted by C. Manson in a New Zealand newspaper, the *Weekly News*, on July 6, 1960. Weldon Kilburn told the story about the Russian cordial set in interview with Carl Morey (March 1983). Nicholas Kilburn, in interview with the author (November 2005), spoke about Weldon's attraction to one of their Russian interpreters while on tour.

Carl Morey's comment about the quality of Lois's sound is from an interview with the author (January 2003). The anecdote about Lois's teenage recording of Puccini is from her own memoir.

Margaret Cragg reported Lois's Dominion Day dinner and conversation with the Queen in the *Globe and Mail* (July 2, 1959). Nicholas Goldschmidt spoke in an interview with the author (September 1999) about Lois's substitution for Schwarzkopf at the Vancouver International Festival in 1959. Details of Lois's tour of Australia and New Zealand were reported in the *Globe and Mail* (February 4, 1960), by Jane Armstrong in the *Toronto Telegram* (February 8, 1960, which also records Lois's conversations with Covent Garden and the Metropolitan Opera), and by George Kidd, also in the *Telegram* (April 23, 1960).

Paul Malone's correspondence detailing his attempts to arrange the Australian tour for Lois are preserved in the External Affairs file on Lois Marshall in Library and Archives Canada. The criticism of Weldon's performance of the Moonlight Sonata appeared in the *New Zealand Herald* July 7, 1960. Irene McLellan, in interview with the author (March 2006) commented on Weldon's memory lapses in performance. The review in the *Auckland Star* (July 7, 1960) commented on the low turnout for Lois's recital there. Comments on Lois's stage deportment are from two unidentified clippings in the Marshall papers in Library and Archives Canada, one by L.B., "Marshall Recital," in an unidentified Sydney newspaper review of June 21, 1960 and another by Bob Hobman, "Singer Captivates Large Audience." The Australian press's comparisons of Lois to great sopranos, historical and contemporary, are culled from reviews in the Marshall papers in Library and Archives Canada.

Daniel J. Levitin's *This Is Your Brain on Music: The Science of a Human Obsession*, was published by Dutton in 2006, and appeared in a Plume paperback in 2007.

Chapter Seven

The website of the National Institute on Deafness and other Communication Disorders provides a brief, clear explanation of the functioning of the vocal cords at: *www.nidcd.nih.gov/health/voice/vocalabuse.asp* (accessed March 31, 2006). The Conservatory's annual prospectuses, which indicate Weldon's official titles and the length of his association with the Conservatory, are housed in the papers of the Royal Conservatory (University of Toronto, Archives and Records Management Services). A detailed description of the Brodie School of Music and Modern Dance appeared in the *Toronto Star* (June 3, 1961), "A Conservatory That's Creative." Irene McLellan and Mary Morrison (both interviewed in March 2006) provided anecdotal information about Weldon's status as a teacher of voice at the Conservatory. A display ad for Lois's International Artists appearance at

Massey Hall appeared in the *Globe and Mail* (November 17, 1960). Walter Homburger provided additional information about the series in interview with the author (June 1998). John Beckwith and John Kraglund reviewed the concert in the *Toronto Star* and the *Globe and Mail*, respectively, on November 19, 1960.

Lois spoke briefly about her dissatisfaction with the tour of *La Bohème* in an interview with the CBC's Pat Patterson, broadcast September 6, 1961. Reviews of the tour appeared in the *Toronto Star* of February 2, 1961 (Udo Kasemets, "In Canadian Stage Debut Marshall's Triumph a Miracle"); the Rockford, IL, *Register-Republic* of February 14, 1961 (Campbell Titchener, "Opera Group's 'La Boheme' Exciting, Tuneful Event"); the Greensboro, NC, *Daily News* of March 5, 1961 (Henry S. Wootton Jr., "'La Boheme' Gets Warm Reception"); and the *Christian Science Monitor* of March 16, 1961 (Louis Chapin, "Cast Projects Warmth of Puccini Masterpiece").

Information on Gold and Fizdale was gleaned from the *New York Times* obituary of Robert Fizdale (December 9, 1995) and from the liner notes to their recording of the Schumann and Brahms cycles, Columbia Masterworks MS 6461 and ML 5861. The re-release of this disc in the "Music from Marlborough" series was noted by William Littler in his column for the *Toronto Star* (February 16, 1985).

The recording history of Lois's collaboration with Glenn Gould has been detailed in "Lois Marshall + Glenn Gould," *Glenn Gould: A Publication of the Glenn Gould Foundation*, Volume 4/Number 1, Spring 1998. The aborted plans to record *Das Marienleben* are documented in correspondence in the Glenn Gould papers in the Music Division, Library and Archives Canada, which also contain his comments on the two versions of Hindemith's *Das Marienleben*. Lois commented on her collaboration with Gould in an interview on "Adrienne Clarkson's Summer Festival," broadcast August 23, 1988, a copy of which is housed in Library and Archives Canada; and in interview with Carl Morey (March 1983). Marshall's famous assessment of herself as "just a singer" was recorded in the same interview with Carl Morey, in preparation for his three-part CBC radio documentary, *Hark the Echoing Air*. The quoted passage was played at the memorial service in Marshall's honour,

held at St. Andrew's Presbyterian Church in Toronto on March 19, 1997
and broadcast nationally on CBC radio.

Details of the death of Florence Marshall are from the author's
interview with Rhoda Scott (August 1998). Mrs. Marshall's death
was announced in the *Toronto Star* of August 16, 1962; notice of Ilona
Kombrink's replacing Lois in Wisconsin appeared in the same newspaper (August 28, 1962).

Lois told Carl Morey in interview (March 1983) that hers had been
the first performances of Strauss's *Four Last Songs* in the Soviet Union.
Paul Kilburn, in interview with the author (November 2005) recalled
Lois's fondness for her Melodya recording of Schumann's *Frauenliebe
und Leben.*

Lois's Wagner concert with Heinz Unger was reviewed by John
Kraglund in the *Globe and Mail* (on January 23 and 24, 1963) and by Udo
Kasemets in the *Toronto Star* (on January 24, 1963). In interviews with
the author, both Rhoda Scott (September 1998) and Stuart Hamilton
(September 1999) provided details of Lois's bout with severe vocal strain
after the concert. Weldon Kilburn's comments on the subject are from
his interview with Carl Morey (April 1983). Lois herself spoke of the
event and its long-term effect on her singing in interview with Leslie
Thompson, in "Lois Marshall's Farewell Tour," *Music Magazine*, March/
April 1982. Beverly Wolter reviewed Lois's performance of *Messiah* in
the *Winston-Salem Journal* of December 2, 1963, comparing it to an earlier appearance by Lois in 1960. For details on the Toronto Symphony
Orchestra's New York engagement of 1963, see Warren, *Begins With the
Oboe.* Reviews of the TSO Carnegie Hall debut appeared in the *New
York Times* and *Herald Tribune* of December 5, 1963; Ralph Thomas's
account appeared in the *Toronto Star* of the same date.

Lois's letter to the editor in defence of Massey Hall's acoustics
appeared in the *Toronto Star* of February 5, 1964. Information on the
Coventry premiere of the *War Requiem* and the controversy surrounding
Vishnevskaya's proposed participation in it can be found in the *London
Times* (May 25 and June 1, 1962); the review of that performance appeared
in the *Times* on May 31. Reviews of Lois's performances in the *War
Requiem* in 1964 and 1969 appeared in the *Toronto Star* (November 11,

1964, and November 12, 1969) and the *Globe and Mail* of the same dates. Reviews of Lois's Toronto performance in Poulenc's *Gloria* appeared on October 21, 1965, in the *Toronto Star* and the *Globe and Mail*.

Lois's investiture in the Order of Canada was reported in the *Globe and Mail* (April 27, 1968). Details of Lois's fractured hip in 1966 came from the author's interview with Rhoda Scott (September 1998); from various newspaper accounts (the *Globe and Mail* of November 18, 1966 and January 2, 1967, the *Toronto Star* of December 30, 1966); and from Adrian Waller's "Lois Marshall: Canada's Queen of Song" (*Canadian Reader's Digest*, November 1978). John Kraglund reported the circumstances of Heinz Unger's death in the *Globe and Mail* of February 26, 1965. The death dates for Heinz Unger, Frederick C. Silvester, and Marion Wibby Kilburn are as reported in the death notices of the *Toronto Star* and the *Globe and Mail*.

Chapter Eight

Information on the Bach Aria Group comes from the author's interviews with Yehudi Wyner (August 2003) and William H. Scheide (June 2005), and from the entry for the Bach Aria Group on the Bach Cantatas website (accessed June 24, 2008) at *www.bach-cantatas.com/index.htm*, which includes the appreciation of Robert Bloom by Norman B. Schwartz. The inscribed copy of Scheide's book is in the Lois Marshall papers in the Music Division, Library and Archives Canada.

The audio transcript of the Centennial year television broadcast of the Beethoven Ninth is in Library and Archives Canada. Kenneth Winters' assessment of Weldon's playing in the Toronto City Hall recital appeared in the *Toronto Telegram* of July 5, 1967. The tape of that performance is in Library and Archives Canada. Biographical information on John Kraglund, Kenneth Winters, and William Littler comes from the *Encyclopedia of Music in Canada*. Irene McLellan, in interview with the author (March 2006), spoke about Weldon's general state of health in the 1960s. Donal Henahan's review of Lois and Weldon's Hunter College recital appeared in the *New York Times* of February 9, 1968.

Details of the wedding celebrations of Lois and Weldon were provided by Rhoda Scott in interview with the author (September and October 1998). The wedding was reported very briefly in the *Toronto Star* of September 10, 1968. The date and location of the ceremony were confirmed by the author from the records of the Anglican Diocese of Toronto. John Kraglund reported Weldon's heart attack, and Reginald Godden's substitution for him as Lois's accompanist, in his review of the York University concert in the *Globe and Mail* of October 7, 1968.

Professor Stephen Adams shared his student recollections of Lois's 1969 Hart House concert in email correspondence with the author (January 2003). Oskar Morawetz's letter to Lois regarding the premiere of *From The Diary of Anne Frank* (October 1970) is in the Marshall papers in the Music Division of Library and Archives Canada. Details of the opening night performance were recorded in "A Canadian Composer's Tribute to Anne Frank," *The Canadian Composer*, October 1970, and in Daniel Stoffman's "The Diary of Anne Frank Inspires Composer," *Toronto Star*, May 23, 1970.

Lois's frustrations at having to travel with Weldon on the 1971 tour of New Zealand were recounted by Doreen Simmons in interview with the author (June 1997). Dates relating to Lois and Weldon's divorce proceedings are from the Petition for Divorce and related papers consulted in the Family Law Office, City of Toronto. Monica Whicher recounted the story of *The Snow Goose* in interview with the author (July 2004). Nicholas Kilburn's recollection of Lois's comment after her separation from Weldon came in interview with the author (November 2005). The Peterborough Community Concerts Association papers are housed in the Trent University Archives, where Lois's 1972 last-minute substitution for another group is described in a letter from the Chair (February 1972). Stuart Hamilton's recollections of his association with Lois are from his interview with the author (September 1999).

Donal Henahan reviewed Lois's New York performance in *Rinaldo* in the *New York Times* of March 28, 1972. The anecdote about the post-performance party for *Rinaldo* comes from Stuart Hamilton in interview with the author. Doreen Simmons, in interview with the author, commented on Lois's slight prudery where sexual matters where concerned.

Maureen Forrester's recording of duets with Rita Streich was issued on the Etcetera label, as recorded live by Radio France at a concert on September 30, 1979. There is conflicting evidence about the year of Lois's residency at Ohio State University. The 1972–73 dates are supported by Stuart Hamilton's recollections of her final recital there, for which he was accompanist, and by the date of that recital, as confirmed by dated newspaper reviews and the concert program in the program collection of the Music Division of Library and Archives Canada. Details of her time in Columbus were recounted by Lois in interview with Carl Morey (March 1983), by Rhoda Scott in interview with the author (September 1998), and by Lois in an interview with Leslie Thompson in *Music Magazine* (March/April 1982). Lois's recital at Ohio State University was reviewed by Rosemary Curtin Hite in the Columbus *Citizen-Journal* of May 1, 1973. A review of Lois's performance of the Shostakovich Symphony No. 14, by Ronald Hambleton, appeared in the *Toronto Star* of April 29, 1974. William Littler and John Kraglund, respectively, reviewed the Janáček *Mša Glagolskaja* in the *Toronto Star* and the *Globe and Mail* of May 8, 1974. Kenneth Winters recounted the anecdote about Lois's telephone call to him in a telephone conversation with the author, October 18, 2005.

Financial information about salaries in the Bach Aria Group came from Yehudi Wyner in interview with the author (August 2003). Lois's application for an American Social Security number was dated March 3, 1953, using Columbia Artists Management as her American mailing address. Maureen Forrester describes some of her Bach Aria Group experiences in *Out of Character*. Additional comments about the relationship between Lois and Maureen Forrester came from the author's interviews with William H. Scheide (June 2005), Stuart Hamilton (September 1999), and Yehudi Wyner (August 2003). I am grateful to Yehudi Wyner for providing me with a copy of "Bach Aria Group Performs 69 S, Family Style." Information on the history and development of the Scheide Library comes from the New Jersey Public Television biography of William H. Scheide, posted on its website at *www.njn.net/artsculture/starts/season07-08/2603.html* (accessed June 25, 2008), from William H. Scheide, *For William H. Scheide: Fifty Years of Collecting* (Princeton, NJ: Princeton University Library, 2004), and from

Dinitia Smith's "A Curmudgeon's Priceless Trove," *International Herald Tribune*, June 13, 2002. Historical information on Schubert's "Die Sterne" is from Henry Pleasants' *The Great Singers: From the Dawn of Opera to Our Own Time* (New York: Simon and Schuster, 1966).

The end of Lois's association with Columbia Artists Management is confirmed from her contracts with CAMI. The progress of Maureen Forrester's concert fees and her use of a public relations agent to promote her career are documented in *Out of Character*. Lois recounted the anecdote about taking over for Helen Watts in El Paso in her interview with Carl Morey (March 1983). Additional detail came from the author's interviews with Yehudi Wyner (August 2003) and William H. Scheide (June 2005). William Littler also recounted the event in his music column in the *Toronto Star* of October 16, 1976.

Chapter Nine

Stuart Hamilton recounted Lois's warm-up comments about "I know that my Redeemer liveth" in interview with the author (September 1999). Mary Morrison remembered Patricia Rideout as the Festival Singers' original soloist in *In the Beginning*, in interview with the author (March 2006). The incident when Kuerti asked that children be removed from the audience occurred at a recital in Peterborough, Ontario, attended by the author. Kuerti discussed the collaboration with Lois, and her requests for transposition, in interview with the author (June 2006). Mary Morrison discussed Lois's characteristic sound in interview with the author (March 2006). The "Backstage" column of the *Globe and Mail* of November 20, 1976, reported the audience's impatience with the length of Kuerti's commentary for *Die Winterreise*. Lois's private feelings on the matter were conveyed to the author by Doreen Simmons, in email correspondence (June 4, 2006). The Hart House Schumann recital was reviewed by John Kraglund in the *Globe and Mail* on October 30, 1978, and by William Littler in the *Toronto Star* of the same date. Kraglund's review of *Die schöne Müllerin* appeared in the *Globe and Mail* of November 16, 1979.

Anton Kuerti recalled his role in persuading Greta Kraus to accompany Lois on the piano in interview with the author (June 2006). Kraus described her collaboration with Lois in interview with Carl Morey (March 1983). Doreen Simmons commented on Lois's initial nervousness in Greta Kraus's company, in interview with the author (June 1997). Kraus's notations on the Wolf recital program are preserved in the Greta Kraus papers in the Music Division of Library and Archives Canada. Arthur Kaptainis's review of the Hugo Wolf recital appeared in the *Globe and Mail* of March 16, 1981.

Lois's 1982 letter to Greta Kraus is in the Greta Kraus papers in the Music Division of Library and Archives Canada. Details of Lois's farewell tour are preserved in the Canada Council Touring Office files in Library and Archives Canada. Stuart Hamilton's reminiscence about accompanying Lois on the farewell tour came from his interview with the author (September 1999); Lois's thank-you letter to Stuart Hamilton is in his private collection. Catherine Robbin's recollection came from her comments at a concert tribute to Lois Marshall by the Aldeburgh Connection, broadcast on CBC radio, March 3, 1998. The *Glebe Report* account of Lois's Ottawa farewell (February 12, 1982) is in the Canada Council Touring Office files in Library and Archives Canada. The National Institute of Neurological Disorders and Stroke fact sheet is posted on their website at: *www.ninds.nih.gov/disorders/ post_polio/detail_post_polio.htm*, accessed July 2, 2008. Lois mentioned her battle with high blood pressure in an undated letter to Anton Kuerti (likely from 1979) in Mr. Kuerti's private collection.

Doreen Simmons described Lois's testiness about her wheelchair in interview with the author (June 1997). Ziggy Galko, one of the stagehands who assisted Lois during the NAC performances of *Eugene Onegin*, recounted their method of getting Lois onstage in interview with the author (April 2003).

The record of the Decree Absolute for Lois and Weldon's divorce is in the divorce records held at the City of Toronto Family Law Office. Lois's involvement with the March of Dimes was reported in the *Toronto Star* of January 17 and April 25, 1983; her appointment as the Honorary President of the Mendelssohn Choir was noted in the *Star* of July 5, 1984.

Information on Jon Donald comes from the author's interviews with Larry Pfaff (December 2007) and with Gayle and Robert Donald (March 2008); his dealings with Anton Kuerti are documented in letters from Lois to Kuerti (May to December 1979), in the private collection of Mr. Kuerti. Carl Morey spoke about the phone call between Lois and Weldon in interview with the author (January 2003). Weldon's death notice appeared in the *Globe and Mail* of March 7, 1986. Details about Lois's last appearance, in *Il Tramonto* at Walter Hall, were provided by Carl Morey in an email to the author (July 10, 2003) and by Monica Whicher in interview with the author (July 2004). The announcement for the concert, with Patricia Kern still listed as soloist, in the *Globe and Mail* of February 8, 1986, confirms the date of the event. The 1976 press release announcing Lois's appointment to the teaching staff of the Faculty of Music is in the Lois Marshall clippings file of the Metro Toronto Reference Library. Carl Morey discussed renovations to accommodate the disabled in the Edward Johnson Building and the circumstances of Lois's teaching there in interview with the author (January 2003). Monica Whicher's description of her first studies with Lois comes from her memorial tribute to Lois at St. Andrew's Presbyterian Church, March 19, 1997, later broadcast on CBC Radio.

Lois admitted to being "naïve and vague" about money in her 1979 correspondence with Anton Kuerti, in Mr. Kuerti's private collection. The anecdote about Lois trying to cope in the kitchen of the Castle Frank apartment comes from the author's interview with Doreen Simmons (June 1997). Other details of Lois's difficulty with the Castle Frank apartment are from the author's interview with Cindy Townsend (June 2003). Doreen Simmons, in an email on June 4, 2006, provided details about Lois's fall at her cottage. Rhoda Scott, in interview with the author (October 1998), recounted Lois's decision to abandon wearing a wig. Information on the financial support provided to Lois in the last years of her life came from the author's discussion with a member of the foundation providing the support (June 9, 2006). Details of Lois's recording for the Toronto Children's Choir come from the author's interview with Rhoda Scott (September 1998) and from Elizabeth MacCallum's "Lives

Lived" column about Lois, published in the *Globe and Mail* on February 25, 1997. Lois's obituary appeared in the *Globe and Mail* on February 21, 1997. Jean Ashworth Bartle speaking at the Memorial Tribute for Lois Marshall, recorded the fact that the NAC flag had been lowered to half-mast. The closing quotation by Stuart Hamilton is from his tribute at the same service.

SELECTED BIBLIOGRAPHY

Baillie, Joan Parkhill. *Look at the Record: An Album of Toronto's Lyric Theatres, 1825–1984.* Oakville, ON: Mosaic Press, 1985.

Caute, David. *The Dancer Defects: The Struggle for Cultural Supremacy during the Cold War.* Oxford: Oxford University Press, 2003.

Forrester, Maureen and Marci McDonald. *Out of Character: A Memoir.* Toronto: McClelland & Stewart, 1986.

Kallmann, Helmut and Gilles Potvin, eds. *Encyclopedia of Music in Canada.* Second edition. Toronto: University of Toronto Press, 1992. Also online at: *www.collectionscanada.gc.ca/emc/index-e.html.*

Kessler, Daniel. *Sarah Caldwell: The First Woman of Opera.* Lanham, MD: The Scarecrow Press, Inc., 2008.

Kilbourn, William. *Intimate Grandeur: One Hundred Years at Massey Hall.* Toronto: Stoddart Publishing, 1993.

Levitin, Daniel J. *This is Your Brain on Music: The Science of a Human Obsession.* New York: Dutton, 2006.

Moore, Gerald. *Am I Too Loud? Memoirs of an Accompanist.* London: Hamish Hamilton, 1962.

Neel, Boyd and J. David Finch. *My Orchestras and Other Adventures: The Memoirs of Boyd Neel.* Toronto: University of Toronto Press, 1985.

Nevins, Maureen, and National Library of Canada. *Sir Ernest MacMillan (1893–1973): Portrait of a Canadian Musician.* Ottawa: National Library of Canada, 1994.

Pitman, Walter G. *Music Makers: The Lives of Harry Freedman & Mary Morrison.* Toronto: Dundurn Press, 2006.

Pitman, Walter. *Elmer Iseler: Choral Visionary*. Toronto: Dundurn Press, 2008.

Pleasants, Henry. *The Great Singers: From the Dawn of Opera to our Own Time*. New York: Simon and Schuster, 1966.

Raby, Peter (compiler and editor). *The Stratford Scene, 1958–1968*. Toronto: Clarke Irwin, 1968.

Roberts, Peter. *George Costakis, a Russian Life in Art*. Ottawa: Carleton University Press, 1994.

Roberts, Peter. *Raising Eyebrows: An Undiplomatic Memoir*. Ottawa: Golden Dog Press, 2000.

Sachs, Harvey. *Toscanini*. London: Weidenfeld & Nicholson, 1978.

Sacks, Oliver W. *Musicophilia: Tales of Music and the Brain*. New York, Toronto: Alfred A. Knopf, 2007.

Schabas, Ezra. *Sir Ernest MacMillan: The Importance of Being Canadian*. Toronto, Buffalo: University of Toronto Press, 1994.

————. *There's Music in these Walls: A History of the Royal Conservatory of Music*. Toronto: Dundurn Press, 2005.

Schabas, Ezra and Carl Morey. *Opera Viva: Canadian Opera Company: The First Fifty Years*. Toronto: Dundurn Press, 2000.

Scheide, William H. and Princeton University Library. *For William H. Scheide: Fifty Years of Collecting:* Princeton, NJ: Princeton University Library, 2004.

Setterfield, Gwenlyn. *Niki Goldschmidt: A Life in Canadian Music*. Toronto: University of Toronto Press, 2003.

Toronto Mendelssohn Choir. *A Responsive Chord: The Story of the Toronto Mendelssohn Choir, 1894–1969*. Toronto: Toronto Mendelssohn Choir, 1969.

Warren, Richard S. *Begins with the Oboe: A History of the Toronto Symphony Orchestra*. Toronto: University of Toronto Press, 2002.

INDEX

Page numbers for photographs are in *italics*.

acoustics, 32, 36, 45, 79, 119, 208, 250, 254
Adams, Stephen, 232–33
Adaskin, John, 88
Adelaide Advertiser, 184
Adelaide Festival of the Arts, 182–84
Adelaide, Australia, 182
Aeroflot, 173–74
Agee, James, "Knoxville: Summer of 1915," 34
Aide, William, 255
Albany, Australia, 183
"Alice Blue Gown," 94–95
Ameling, Elly, 160, 268
Amici, 274
Amsterdam, 145
Ančerl, Karel, 208, 212, 238
Anderson, Marian, 92, 173
André Dorfman Scholarship in Voice, 63
Ann Arbor, Michigan, 128
Antonini, Alfredo, 128
Applebaum, Louis, 134
Arrau, Claudio, 133
Art Gallery of Ontario, 97
As You Like It, 274
Auckland, New Zealand, 183–84
Australian Broadcasting Corporation, 182
Aycock Auditorium (Greensboro), 191

Bach Aria Group, 221–24, 230, 232, 236, 239–40, 242–49, 251, 266

Bach Festival (Toronto), 89
Bach, Johann Sebastian, 49, 82, 134, 160, 221, 245–46, 252
    double violin concerto, 214
Baldwin-Wallace Bach Festival, 128
Barbirolli, Sir John, 145, 159, 163
Baron, Samuel, 223
Barrie, Ontario, 20, 120
Bartlett, Arthur, 82
Battle, Rex, 88
Bauer, Hans, 218
Bavarian Radio Symphony, 159
Bayreuth Festival, 103, 162
Beaudry, Jacques, 163
Beaux Arts Trio, 190, 223
Beckwith, John, 67, 101–102, 190
Beecham Choral Society, 141
Beecham in Rehearsal, 143
Beecham, Lady, 139, 141–42
Beecham, Sir Thomas, 52–53, 139–42, 144, 146, 176
Beethoven, Ludwig van, 245, 269
    "Moonlight Sonata," 183
    violin concerto, 214
Bell, Donald, 226
Bell, Leslie, 148
Berg, Alban, 71, 75, 134, 205
Bergman, Ingrid, 127
Berkshire Summer Festival, 128, 212, 234
Bernac, Pierre, 159

Bernard, Anthony, 144, 176
Bernardi, Mario, 114, 242
Bernini, *Ecstasy of Saint Teresa*, 225
Bernstein, Leonard, 163
Bing, Rudolf, 158
Bissell, Claude, 180, 240
Björling, Jussi, 52, 92
Bloom, Robert, 223
Bloor Street United Church, Toronto, 80–83, 88, 101, 120, 218
Bori, Lucrezia, 92
Boston Symphony Orchestra, 128, 151–52, 162, 191, 208, 212, 234
Boston, 128, 151, 181, 191, 214
Boult, Sir Adrian, 163
Bournemouth, England, 163
Bradford frame, 23
Brahms, Johannes, *Liebeslieder Waltzes*, 192
Brandon Daily Sun, 101
Braun, Victor, 209
Brevard Festival (North Carolina), 128
Bridle, Augustus, 67
Briggs, John, 112–13
Brisbane, 112, 183
British War Guests, 46
Britten, Sir Benjamin, 75, 92, 98, 209–12, 250
Brodie School of Music and Modern Dance, 189
Brodie, Paul, 188
Brodie, Rima, 188
Brott, Alexander, 204
Brown, Tom, 135
Brownlee, John, 52
Brussels, 173
Brymer, Jack, 161
Burlgano, Angelo, 88

Caldwell, Sarah, 150–53, 182, 191–92
Calgary, 96
Callwood, June, 109–10, 116–17
Camerata Bariloche, 236

Canada Council for the Arts, 169, 267
    Touring Office, 260–61, 263
Canadian Brass, 251
Canadian Broadcasting Corporation (CBC), 17, 19, 56, 64–65, 70–71, 84, 86–88, 91–92, 102, 134, 146–50, 156, 162–63, 177–79, 181, 205, 208, 214–15, 224, 227–28, 234, 237, 252, 255, 259, 267, 274, 276, 279
Canadian Embassy (Moscow), 166, 168–69, 171, 176
Canadian Home Journal, 58
Canadian Industries Limited (CIL), 88
Canadian League of Composers, 129
Canadian National Exhibition, 97, 205, *207*
Canadian Opera Company (*see also* Royal Conservatory of Music of Toronto, Opera Festival), 64, 84, 102
Canadian Physiotherapy Association, 114
Carfagnini, Abramo, 89–90
Carlu Centre (Toronto), 92
Carlyle, Trudy, 149
Carnegie Hall (New York), 95, 118–21, 123, 129, 202, 207, 238
Cassel, Walter, 147
Castle Frank Road, 274–75, 278
Cathedral Church of St. James (Toronto), 42, 44
CBC Chamber Orchestra, 161
CBC Opera Company, 84, 86–87
CBC Symphony Orchestra, 156, 181
Cedar Rapids, 133
Chabay, Leslie, 138
Charlottetown, 118, 263
Chatham, Ontario, 129
Chicago, 128, 137–38
Chicago American, 138
Chicago Daily News, 138
Chicago Symphony Orchestra, 129, 137
Christchurch, New Zealand, 183
Christian Science Monitor, 152–53, 191
Church of St. Andrew and St. Paul (Montreal), 263

Church of St. Mary Magdalene (Toronto), 43–44

Church of the Holy Name (Toronto), 20–21, 35, *36*, 42, 101

Church of the Messiah (Toronto), 80

Ciceri, Leo, 162

Cincinnati, 128

Cincinnati May Festival, 128, 137, 198

CJRT Orchestra, 251

Cleveland, 139, 147

Cleveland Symphony Orchestra, 200

Cliburn, Van, 163

Cohen, Nathan, 150

Columbia Artists Management, 96–97, 110, 114–19, 125, 128, 133, 145, 148, 151, 189, 191, 246–47

Columbus, Ohio, 241

Community Concert Associations, 96–97, 116–17, 129–30, 191, 236

Concert Hall (Stratford), 135

Concertgebouw, Amsterdam, 145

Concertgebouw Orchestra, 160

Convocation Hall (University of Toronto), 76, 79, 89, 132, 241

Cornerbrook, Newfoundland, 118

Costakis, George, 169

Council of Women of Toronto, 114

Coventry Cathedral, 209–11

Cram, Ralph, 42

Crawford, T.J., 57

Crooks, Richard, 37, 92

Crory, Neil, 267

Crowe, Doris, 166, 169–71

Crowe, Marshall, 168

Cunard, Lady, 139

Curtin, Phyllis, 147

Curtis Institute (Philadelphia), 136, 155

D'Oyly Carte, Dame Bridget, 58

D'Oyly Carte, Sir Richard, 58

David Haber Artists Management Inc., 260

Davies, Robertson, 136, 180

A Mixture of Frailties, 131–32

Davis, Sir Andrew, 208–209, 242

de los Angeles, Victoria, 52–53, 159, 185

della Casa, Lisa, 148

Department of Education of Ontario, 83

Dermota, Anton, 159

Destinn, Emmy, 113

Detroit, 101

Dettmer, Roger, 138–39

Diligentia, The Hague, 160

Donald, Jon, 267

Doráti, Antal, 128

Dorliak, Nina, 173

Dovercourt Citadel Salvation Army Band, 205, *206*

Dubrovnik, Yugoslavia, 230

Easter Seal campaign, 89

Eaton Auditorium, 57, 91–92, 112, 114, 133

Eaton Graduating Scholarship (*see* Royal Conservatory of Music of Toronto, Eaton Graduating Scholarship)

Eaton Operatic Society, 57, 92

Eaton's camp for girls, 56

Eaton's Department Store, 20, 33, 51, 56, 62, 91, 158, 274

Edinburgh International Festival, 158–59

Edinburgh Scotsman, 143

Edmonton, 43, 96, 117

Edmonton Symphony, 117

Edward Johnson Building, University of Toronto, 258, 269–72

Eglinton United Church (Toronto), 274

Eichendorff, Joseph Freiherr von, 72

El Paso, Texas, 247–48

Elgar, Sir Edward, 43, 78

Ellerbeck Street, 20–21, 34, 123, 246, 278

Elmira, New York, 133

Elwell, Herbert, 101–102

Encyclopedia of Music in Canada, 228

Erickson, Arthur, 208

Estevan, Saskatoon, 251

Faculty of Music (*see* University of Toronto, Faculty of Music)
Fairlawn movie theatre (Toronto), 88
Farrell, Eileen, 223
Farrow, Norman, 223
Feldbrill, Victor, 208
Festival Chorus, Stratford (*see* Festival Singers)
Festival Singers, 135, 242, 250–52
Firestone Library (Princeton University), 245
Fischer-Dieskau, Dietrich, 54, 159, 210, 254, 255
Five Piano Ensemble, 44
Flagstad, Kirsten, 92
Fleming, Renée, 53
"Ford Sunday Evening Hour," 27
Ford, John, 274
Forrester, Maureen, 19, 55–56, 91, 129, 139, 161–62, 166, 188, 217, 223, 226, 239–40, 243–44, 247–48, 251
Four Season's Hotel (Toronto), 275
Franca, Celia, 180, *181*
Frank, Otto, 234
Frankel, Max, 169
Fredericton, New Brunswick, 129
Freemason's Hall (Edinburgh), 159
Frick, Gottlob, 141

Gallico, Paul, *The Snow Goose*, 235–36
Garrard, Donald, 103
Gehman, Richard, 173–74
Geiger-Torel, Herman, 102
Gentry, Theodore, 251
German Lieder and Lieder singing, 53–54, 69–70, 72–74, 98, 252–59
Gignac, Marguerite, 84
Glanville-Hicks, Peggy, 112
Glebe Report (Ottawa), 263
"Glenn Gould on Strauss," 194
Glenn Gould Studio, Toronto, 274
Glick, Srul Irving, 252
Globe and Mail, 66, 79, 93, 104, 145, 150, 193, 198, 211–12, 214, 217, 227, 242, 251, 253–54, 259
Gluck, Christoph Willibald, *Alceste* ("Divinités du Styx"), 76
Glyndebourne Festival, 104
Godden, Reginald, 44, 231
Goethe, Johann Wolfgang von, 72
Gold, Arthur and Robert Fizdale, 192
Goldschmidt, Nicholas, 84–86, 101–102, 161, 180, 239, 267
Golfhaven Road, 157–58, 161, 175, 217, 235–36, 266
Golschmann, Vladimir, 147
Gosconcert, 164, 168, 175
Gould, Glenn, 19, 44, 56, 134, 147, 161, 163–64, 166, 193–96, 201, 230, 252
Governor General's Performing Arts Award, 267
Grace Church on-the-Hill (Toronto), 278
Gramm, Donald, 151–52
Grant Park Festival (Chicago), 183
Grant Park Symphony Orchestra (Chicago), 128
Great Hall of the Moscow Conservatory, 164–65, 168
Great Hall of the Philharmonic (Leningrad), 174–75
Greenhouse, Bernard, 190, 223
Greensboro, North Carolina, 191
Greensboro Daily News, 191
Guelph, Ontario, 240
Guelph Spring Festival, 239, 253
Guerrero, Alberto, 44
Guy, Elizabeth Benson, 84–85, 205

Hagen, Betty-Jean, 19, 106
Hallé Orchestra, 145, 159
Hambleton, Ronald, 70–72
Hamburg, Germany, 145
Hamburger Abendblatt, 145
Hamilton Philharmonic Orchestra, 201
Hamilton, Ontario, 109, 129, 191, 201

Hamilton, Stuart, 81, 149, 236–40, 243, 249, 253, 261–62, 265, 267, 275, 280–81

Hampson, Jean, 30, 63, 114

Handel and Haydn Society International Choral Festival (Boston), 214

Handel, George Frideric, 49, 82, 134
  Giulio Cesare, 247

"Hark the Echoing Air," 178, 267

Harper, Heather, 210

Harris, Lawren, 180

Harrogate Festival, 145

Hart House Orchestra, 134

Hart House (University of Toronto), 179, 232, *233*, 252–56, 258, 262–63

Hathaway, Thomas, 50

Hays, David, 191–92

Haywood, Lorna, 248

Heifitz, Jascha, 37

Heim, Emmy, 69–70, *71*, 72–75, 84, 113, 130, 225, 246, 255, 258

Heintzman Building, 56

Henahan, Donal, 229–30, 239

Heppner, Ben, 280

Hockridge, Edmund, 84

Hodgins, John and Mary, 81

Hoffmannsthal, Hugo von, 70

Hollweg, Ilse, 141

Hollywood Bowl, 128

Homburger, Walter, 164, 189–90, 279

Hopkins, John, 183

Horner, John, 184

Horowitz, Vladimir, 37

Horton, John, 193

Hospital for Sick Children, 23–27, 31, 59

Hulme, Doreen, 88

Humby, Betty (*see* Beecham, Lady)

Hume, Paul, 90, 190

Hunter College Playhouse, New York, 229–30

Hutchinson, Elsie, 30, *31*, 32, 37–38, 42–43, 46, 114

International Artists Greater Artists concert series, 164, 189–90

International Eisteddfod (Wales), 145

Iseler, Elmer, 135, 209, 213–14, 242, 250–51

Iturbi, José, 50

Ivey, Joanne, 103

"Jackie Rae Show," 162

Jochum, Eugen, 159, 161

Johnson, David, 168

Johnson, Edward, 92, 105–108

Johnson, Thor, 128

Judd, William, *115*, 116–17

Judson, Arthur, *115*, 117–18

Juilliard School of Music (New York), 223

Jurinac, Sena, 143

Kandinsky, Wassily, 70, 74

Kane, Peggy, 88

Kaptainis, Arthur, 259

Kapuskasing, Ontario, 129, 132

Kasemets, Udo, 133, 191–93, 199, 203

Kaunas, Lithuania, 251

Kern, Patricia, 268

Kidd, George, 106, 127, 175–76

Kiev, Ukraine, 167

Kilburn, Hilda, 117, 155

Kilburn, Marion, 127, 155–56, 158, 176, 219, 230

Kilburn, Michael, 156

Kilburn, Nicholas, 61, 136, 155–58, 176, 236

Kilburn, Nicholas (Dr.), 43

Kilburn, Paul 47, 49, 61, 156, 158, 159

Kilburn, Peter, 231

Kilburn, Weldon, 42–50, 52, 54, 58–62, 65–66, 68–69, 72–73, 75–77, 80, 83, 91–92, 98–99, *100*, 106–109, *110*, *111*, 112–14, *115*, 117, 119–21, 125–27, 129–30, 136–38, 140, 146, 152–53, 155–59, 161, 163, 165, 167, *168*, 170, *172*, 173–76, 178, 181, 183,

185, 188–90, 196–97, 200–201, 219, 225, 227–30, *231*, 232, *233*, 234–37, 239–42, 244, 250, 253, 255, 266, 268
King Edward Hotel (Toronto), 140
Kingston, Ontario, 129
Kingsway Hall (London), 141
Kirkland Lake, Ontario, 129
Kitchener, Ontario, 109, 128
Kiwanis Music Festival, 32
Klee, Paul, 70
Klemperer, Otto, 128–29
Knapp, Gray, 132–33
Kokoschka, Oskar, 70
Kombrink, Ilona, 136, 155–57, 196
Kondrashin, Kyril, 197
Kraemer, Franz, 149, 214
Kraglund, John, 150, 190, 193, 198–99, 203, 211–12, 227–28, 251, 253–54, 256
Kraus, Greta, 48, 64–66, 179, 257–60, 267, *272*
Krips, Henry, 183
Kuerti, Anton, 252–53, 255, 257, 267
Kunits, Luigi von, 208
Kurtz, Efrem, 181

La Scala, Milan, 163
Laidlaw Hall (Upper Canada College), 252
Lambert, George, 43
Landry, Rosemarie, 251
Latremouille, Jean, 261
Laurence, Margaret, *The Diviners*, 22
Lawrence, Marjorie, 104
Lawson, Hugh, 88
LeBourdais, Isabel, 58–61
Lehmann, Lotte, 92, 185, 253
Lemnitz, Tiana, 53–54, 73
Leningrad, 167–68, 234, 251
Leonard, Lawrence, 234
Leslie Bell Singers, 148
Lethbridge, Alberta, 238
Levitin, Daniel, *This Is Your Brain on Music*, 185

Lewis, Richard, 223, 244
Library and Archives Canada, 17, 132, 194, 204, 213–14, 225
Lieder (*see* German Lieder and Lieder singing)
Lifetime Achievement Award, 278
Littler, William, 212, 228, 253–54, 256
Lloydminster, Alberta, 43
Loew's movie theatre, 56
Lois Marshall Bursaries, 114
Loman, Judy, 250
London Daily Telegraph, 143
London Symphony Orchestra, 144, 176, 177
London Times, 142–44, 182, 210–11
London, George, 162
London, England, 142, 160, 163, 213
London, Ontario, 129, 274
Los Angeles Philharmonic Orchestra, 128
Los Angeles, 128
Ludwig, Christa, 253

MacDonald, Rose, 67
Macklem, Heloise, 57–58
Maclean's, 109–10, 116
MacMillan Theatre (University of Toronto), 258
MacMillan, Keith, 162
MacMillan, Sir Ernest, 42–43, 60, 69–70, 75–82, 89, 101, 113, 120–21, 129, 132, 180, 182, 202, 205, *207*, 208–209, 231, 241–42, 257, 270
Madison, Wisconsin, 157
Mahler, Gustav
   Symphony No. 9, 133, 199
   Kindertotenlieder, 72
Malcolm, Scott, 44
Maley, Roy, 101
Malko, Nicolai, 128, 183
Malone, Paul, 182
Manchester, 145
Mann, Thomas, 70
Maple Leaf Gardens (Toronto), 89

March of Dimes Ability Fund, 266
Marshall, David, 20–21, 26, 32–35, 39, 50, 196
Marshall, Florence (née O'Brien), 20–24, 26–27, 33, 35–39, 51, 58, 109, 128, 196–97, 241, 276
Marshall, Fred, 21, 36–37, 39, 41–42, 44, 50–51, 80, 109, 179
Marshall, James, 20
Marshall, Jean, 21, 35, 37, 39, 128
Marshall, June, 51
Marshall, Lois, *31, 38, 100, 103, 108, 110–11, 115, 168, 181, 206–207, 216–17, 231, 233, 272, 280*
    ancestry and birth, 20–21
    awards and distinctions, 33, 61, 63, 89, 91, 108, 189, 209, 216–17, 266–67, 278
    cars and driving, 140–41
    cats, 113, 240–41, 267, 276
    childhood, 21–29, 34–35
    disabilities, work in aid of, 114
    divorce, 235, 266
    early education, 29–32, 55, 62–63
    earnings, 55, 111, 115–16, 157, 175, 189, 201, 243, 246–47, 260, 266, 275
    effects of polio on career, 18, 24, 29, 33, 37, 58, 61, 63–64, 83, 93, 104, 106, 113, 116–17, 121–23, 126, 149–53, 165, 174, 213, 237, 264–66
    farewell tour, 260–64
    final illness and death, 278–79
    high blood pressure, 265
    hip fractures, 217–18, 224, 265, 276
    memorial tribute, 279–81
    Moscow debut, 163–73
    New York debut, 109–13
    opera, 63–64, 84, 146–53, 191–92, 265–66
    platform manner, 50, 59, 82, 100, 184–85
    polio, 22–26, 265

post-polio syndrome, 265
recording sessions, 122–23, 141–42, 144, 161–62, 176–79, 192, 197, 232, 250, 278–79
repertoire
    "Ae fond kiss," 18, 170, 178
    "Go Way from My Window," 233
    "Have You Seen but a Whyte Lilly Grow," 112
    "The Fairy's Lullaby," 32–33, 42, 45
    Arditi, Luigi, "Il Bacio," 45–46
    Bach, Johann Sebastian, 98–99, 161, 165, 213
        "Come Visit," 92
        Cantata No. 51 ("Jauchzet Gott in allen Landen"), 135, 205
        Cantata No. 78 ("Wir eilen mit schwachen doch emsigen Schritten"), 240, 248
        Cantata No. 202 (*Wedding Cantata*), 204
        Christmas Oratorio, 82, 241
        Mass in B Minor, 161, 201
        St. John Passion, 82, 88
        St. Matthew Passion, 76, 79, 88, 101, 109, 120–21, 132, 147, 202, 241, 257, 270
    Barber, Samuel, 111
        The Prayers of Kierkegaard, 137
    Beckwith, John, "Four Poems by e e cummings," 92–93
    Beethoven, Ludwig van, 75
        "Ah, Perfido," 183, 197
        Fidelio (Leonora), 85–88
        Fidelio ("Abscheulicher, wo eilst du hin?"), 86–87, 92–93, 101
        Missa Solemnis, 118, 163

Symphony No. 9, 129, 181, 226–27
Bellini, Vincenzo, *Norma* ("Casta diva"), 92–93, 177
Berg, Alban, 75
  Seven Early Songs, 134, 205
Berlioz, Hector, *Damnation of Faust*, 212–13, 234
  Les Nuits d'Été, 218, 230
Bissel, Keith (arr.), Folk Songs, 240
Brahms, Johannes, 75, 240
  Requiem, 82, 159
  Vier Ernste Gesänge, 99, 136, 146, 232
Britten, Sir Benjamin, English folk songs (arr.), 75, 92, 98
  Peter Grimes (Ellen Orford), 148–50, 279
  War Requiem, 209–12
Brott, Alexander, *Four Songs of Contemplation*, 129
Clari, 240
Copland, *In the Beginning*, 250–51
Debussy, Claude, *L'Enfant Prodigue* ("Air de Lia"), 183
Duparc, Henri, 232
Elgar, Sir Edward, *The Apostles*, 161
  The Kingdom, 163
Elizabethan songs, 111
Elwell, Herbert, "Pastorale for Voice and Orchestra," 101–102
Falla, Manuel de, "Seven Popular Spanish Songs," 98–99, 112, 144, 146, 171, 183, 233, 252
Fleming, Robert (arr.), Folk Songs, 240
French Art Songs, 98
Gilbert and Sullivan, *Princess*

Ida, 57, 92, 102
Gounod, Charles, *Faust* ("The Jewel Song"), 98, 202
Handel, George Frideric, 98–99, 165
  "German Arias," 190
  "So Shall the Lute and Harp," 92
  Judas Maccabaeus, 82, 180
  Messiah, 81, 101, 114, 117, 145, 158, 181, 198, 202, 209–10, 238
  Messiah ("I know that my Redeemer liveth"), 249
  Rinaldo (Almirena), 238–39
  Rinaldo ("Augelletti che cantate"), 239
  Rinaldo ("Lascia ch'io pianga"), 239
  Samson, 82, 180
  Solomon, 134, 139, 141, 180
Haydn, Josef, 99
  arias, 196
  Creation, 183
Hindemith, Paul, *Das Marienleben*, 134, 193–94
Janáček, Leoš, *Mša Glagolskaja* (Festival Mass), 242
Kennedy-Fraser, Marjorie (arr.), Folk Songs, 98
Mahler, Gustav, 75, 98, 165, 201
  "Um Mitternacht," 232
  Des Knaben Wunderhorn, 133, 251
  Lieder eines fahrenden Gesellen, 251
  Symphony No. 2, 133, 148
  Symphony No. 4, 133
Massenet, Jules, *Thérèse*, 265
McIntyre, Paul, *Judith*, 161
Mendelssohn, Felix, 99
  Elijah, 82, 109

Monteverdi, Claudio, "Interrotte Speranze," 240

Morawetz, Oskar, *From the Diary of Anne Frank*, 233–34, 238

Mozart, Wolfgang Amadeus, 75, 98
 Così fan tutte (Fiordiligi), 147–48
 Così fan tutte ("Come scoglio"), 213
 Davidde Penitente, 129
 Die Entführung aus dem Serail (Konstanze), 140
 Die Entführung aus dem Serail ("Martern aller Arten"), 140, 142–44
 Don Giovanni (Donna Anna), 84–86, 147
 Don Giovanni ("Non mi dir"), 177
 Don Giovanni ("Or sai chi l'onore"), 85
 Exsultate, Jubilate, 98–99, 101, 105, 142, 183, 197
 Il Re Pastore (aria from), 76
 La clemenza di Tito ("Parto, parto"), 177, 197, 228
 Mass in C Minor, 84
 Mass in C Minor ("Et Incarnatus Est"), 92, 111–12, 119
 Mass in C Minor ("Laudamus te"), 111, 119
 Requiem, 129, 141
 songs, 257
 The Magic Flute (Queen of the Night), 99, 102, *103*, 104, 182
 The Marriage of Figaro ("Non so più"), 206
 The Marriage of Figaro ("Voi, che sapete"), 206

Novello, Ivor, "The Little Damosel," 48

Orff, Carl, *Carmina Burana*, 129, 137–38

Poulenc, Francis, *Gloria*, 200, 213–14

Puccini, Giacomo, 98
 La Bohème (Mimi), 150, 152, 191–92
 La Bohème ("Musetta's Waltz"), 166–67, 190
 La Bohème ("Si, mi chiamano Mimi"), 179, 183
 Madama Butterfly ("One Fine Day"), 88
 Manon Lescaut ("Sola, perduta, abbandonata"), 101, 162
 Tosca (Floria Tosca), 147, 153, 181, 249
 Turandot ("In questa reggia"), 112, 138, 177, 183

Purcell, Henry, 98, 213, 238
 "Evening Hymn," 184
 "Hark the echoing air," 177, 232
 "The Queen's Epicedium," 138
 Dido and Aeneas, 200
 Divine Hymns, 136
 The Expostulation of the Blessed Virgin Mary, 224–25
 Ode on St. Cecilia's Day, 134

Ravel, Maurice, *Shéhérazade*, 129, 136, 183, 213

Respighi, Ottorino, *Il Tramonto*, 268–69

Ridout, Godfrey, *Two Mystical Songs of John Donne for High Voice and Orchestra*, 129, 202

Romberg, Sigmund, *The Desert*

Song (Romance), 90
Rossini, Gioachino, "Cat Duet,"
   240
   Petite Messe Solonnelle, 183
   The Barber of Seville ("Una
      voce poco fà"), 98, 131,
      138
Russell, Welford, "Come hither,
   you that love," 232
Rutter, John, *Brother Heinrich's
   Christmas* (Narrator), 278
Saint-Saëns, Camille, *Carnival
   of the Animals* (Narrator), 274
Scarlatti, Alessandro, *Christmas
   Cantata*, 64, 67, 69, 75–76,
   145, 257
Schmidt, Franz, *The Book With
   Seven Seals*, 129
Schoenberg, Arnold, 75, 201
   Gurrelieder, 129
   Pierrot Lunaire (Narrator),
      274
Schubert, Franz, 75, 111, 232
   "An die Musik," 232
   "Abschied von der Erde"
      (Narrator), 274
   "Ave Maria," 174
   "Gretchen am Spinnrade,"
      92
   "Im Haine," 92
   "Seligkeit," 92
   "The Shepherd on the
      Rock," 161
   Die schöne Müllerin, 179,
      256–58
   Die schöne Müllerin
      ("Ungeduld"), 257–58
   Die Winterreise, 252–56
Schumann, Robert, 75, 179, 240,
   256
   "Widmung," 72
   Dichterliebe, 232, 255
   Frauenliebe und Leben, 160,

190, 197, 230, 255, 262
   Frauenliebe und Leben
      ("Du Ring an meinem
      Finger"), 256
   Liederkreis, Op., 39, 255
   Spanische Liebeslieder, Op.,
      138, 192
Schütz, Heinrich, 240
Scott, Cyril, "The Blackbird's
   Song," 48
Shostakovich, Dmitri,
   Symphony No. 14, 242
Strauss, Johann, *Die Fledermaus*
   ("Adele's Laughing Song"), 98
Strauss, Richard, 165
   "Cäcilie," 194
   Ariadne auf Naxos
      (Ariadne), 147–48
   Four Last Songs, 134, 148,
      159, 163, 183, 197, 201,
      203, 205
   Four Last Songs ("Beim
      Schlafengehen"), 194
   Ophelia Lieder, 194, 230
Tchaikovsky, Peter Ilyich, *Eugene
   Onegin* (Nurse), 265–66
Verdi, Giuseppe, 90, 98
   Aida ("Ritorna vincitor!"),
      218
   Il Trovatore ("Pace, pace
      mio dio"), 98, 105, 202
   Il Trovatore ("Tacea la
      notte placide"), 177
   Requiem, 162, 205
Wagner, Richard, *Der fliegende
   Holländer* (Senta's ballad),
   198–99
   Die Meistersinger (Act III),
      129, 198
   Lohengrin (Elsa's dream),
      198–99
   Tannhäuser ("Dich theure
      Halle"), 105, 198–99

Tannhäuser (Elisabeth's prayer), 198

Walton, William, *Façade* (Narrator), 274

Weber, Carl Maria von, 90

Der Freischütz ("Leise, leise"), 105, 177

Willan, Healey, *A Song of Welcome*, 135

Wilson (arr.), "My Lovely Celia," 48

"Pastorale," 48

"Shepherd thy Demeanour Vary," 48

Wolf, Hugo, 75, 179, 258–59

"Abschied," 259

Zilcher, Hermann, *Rococo Trio*, 190

retirement, 264, 266

Toscanini audition, 119

tours and touring, 19, 77, 96, 101, 109, 117–18, 125, 127, 145, 157–58, 160–61, 163, 173–74, 180–83, 191, 194, 197, 199–200, 205, 218, 224, 230, 234, 236, 238, 240, 242–44, 251–52

vocal crisis and recovery, 133, 188, 198–205, 213

vocal range, 46, 59–60, 65, 70, 99, 143–44, 162, 201, 247–50

vocal training, 38, 44–50, 59–60, 62–64, 69–77

wedding, 230–31

wigs, 18, 215, 276

Marshall, Mary, 21, 39, 46, 51

Marshall, Patricia, 21, 157, 218, 230

Marshall, Rhoda, 20–21, 27–28, 34–35, 39, 45, 51–52, 55–56, 157, 200, 230, 274, 276, 278

Marshall, Rita, 21, 35

Marshall, Ruth, 21

Massey Hall (Toronto), 33, 37, 58, 87, 120, 133, 189–90, 198, 205, 208, 214, 218, 232

Masters from Soviet Russia, 214–15

Maynor, Dorothy, 185

Mazzoleni, Ettore, 60, 64–65, 67, 76, 149

Mazzoleni, Joanne (*see* Ivey, Joanne)

McCarthy, Pearl, 104

McCoy, Anna, 97

McGill Chamber Orchestra, 204–205

McIntyre, Paul, 161–62

McLean, Eric, 90–91, 130

McLellan, Irene, 48, 59, 62, 73

Mehta, Zubin, 231

Melbourne Symphony Orchestra, 183

Melbourne, Australia, 183

Mendelssohn, Felix, 78

violin concerto, 214

Meredith, Morley, 138

Merriman, Nan, 122

Metropolitan Opera, 37, 147–48, 151, 182

Miami, 218

Michener, Roland, *216*, 217

Milligan, James, 19, 95, 103, 109, 116, 161

Milstein, Nathan, 37

Minneapolis, 128, 140

Minneapolis Symphony Orchestra, 128

Moerike, Eduard, 72

Molson Music Prize, 266–67

Molyneaux, Anna, 106, 109–10

Moncton, New Brunswick, 100, 118

Montreal, 128, 130, 141, 204–205, 224, 232, 263

Montreal Daily Star, 90, 130

Montreux Festival, 163

Moore, Gerald, 159–61, 236

Moore, Trevor, 159

Morawetz, Oskar, 233–34

Morey, Carl, 52, 60, 66, 122, 178, 267–71, *272*, 273, 279

Morrison, Elsie, 139

Morrison, Mary, 61–62, 84, 99, 103–104, 229, 254, *272*

Moscow Philharmonic, 197

Moscow, 165, 167–68, 175, 197, 234, 251

Moses, Charles, 182

Mount Allison University, 267
Mount Hope Cemetery (Toronto), 196
Mozart, Wolfgang Amadeus, 49, 158
    The Magic Flute, 53
    Don Giovanni, 161
    Toy Symphony, 208
Mt. Orford, Quebec, 240
Munch, Charles, 128
Musical America, 110, 112–13, 137
Mustard, William (Dr.), 27

NAACP, Legal Defense Fund, 222
Nash, Heddle, 52
National Arts Centre Orchestra, 242
National Arts Centre (Ottawa), 265, 279
National Ballet of Canada, 260
National Ballet of Canada Orchestra, 156
National Concerts and Artists
    Corporation, 96–97
National Institute of Neurological
    Disorders and Stroke, 265
National Orchestra (New Zealand), 183
Naumburg competition and award, 105–
    109, 114
Naumburg, Walter, 105, 110
NBC Symphony Orchestra, 118, 223
Neel, Boyd, 128, 134
Netrebko, Anna, 53
New York City, 107, 136, 192, 202, 234,
    238
New York City Opera, 147, 151, 247
New York Handel Society, 238–39
New York Herald Tribune, 110, 112, 203
New York Philharmonic, 37, 117, 151, 163
New York Times, 110, 112, 136, 169, 203,
    229–30
Nipawin, Saskatchewan, 251
North American Night (Washington,
    DC), 90, 130, 182
Nourrit, Adolphe, 246
Nunes, Danny, 279

Oakville, Ontario, 129

Ohio State University, 240–41, 271
Oistrakh, David, 214
Oistrakh, Igor, 214
Opera Festival (*see* Royal Conservatory of
    Music of Toronto, Opera Festival)
Opera in Concert, 237, 265
"Opportunity Knocks," 88
Orchestra Hall (Chicago), 138
Orchestre Symphonique de Montréal,
    128–29, 231
Order of Canada, 217
Order of Ontario, 267
Orford Quartet, 268–69
Oriana Singers, 274
Orpheum Theatre (Vancouver), 162
Ottawa, 114, 129, 212
Ottawa Choral Union, 114
Owen Sound, Ontario, 20, 129, 276
Owen, Wilfred, 211
Ozawa, Seiji, 208, 212–13, 218, 226, 231,
    234

Palmateer, Mary, 82
Paris, France, 213
Park, Dorothy Allan, 43
Parmenter, Ross, 203
Parrott, Andrew, 78
Pasternak, Boris, 169, 172
Patterson, Pat, 163
Peaker, Charles and Marie, 81
Pears, Sir Peter, 209–12
Pedrazzoli, Eduardo, 177
Peerce, Jan, 92, 147
Pelligrini, Maria, 162
Peninsula Music Festival (Fish Creek,
    Wisconsin), 156, 196
Perli, Lisa, 52–53, 139
Perth, Australia, 183
Peterborough, Ontario, 129–30, 236–37,
    252
Peterborough Collegiate and Vocational
    School Auditorium, 130
Peterborough Examiner, 131

Philadelphia Orchestra, 117, 128
Piaf, Edith, 113
Pittsburgh Symphony, 162
Pons, Lily, 133
Poulenc, Francis, 159
Pressler, Menahem, 190
Princeton, New Jersey, 245
Princeton University, 222, 245
Promenade Concert (the Proms),
    (London, England), 163
Promenade Concerts (Varsity Arena,
    Toronto), 37, 88–90, 94
Puccini, Giacomo, 52, 88, 98, 101, 112,
    117, 138, 147, 150, 153, 162, 166, 177,
    183, 190, 205
Purcell, Henry, 49, 98, 134–38, 159, 177,
    184, 200, 213, 224–25, 232, 238, 261

Queen Elizabeth Theatre (Vancouver), 180
Quilico, Louis, 134

R.C.A. Victor, 119
Radio Canada International, 240
Redpath Hall (Montreal), 204–205
Regina, Saskatchewan, 23, 96, 129, 251
Rehfuss, Heinz, 159
Reiner, Fritz, 128–29, 137–38
Respighi, Ottorino, *Ancient Airs and
    Dances* and *the Fountains of Rome*,
    268
Rheinhardt, Emil, 70
Richard, Maurice, 180
Richardson, Bill, 274
Richter, Sviatoslav, 171, 173
Rideout, Patricia, 103, 251
Ridout, Godfrey, 268
Rifkin, Joshua, 78
Riga, Latvia, 167–68, 175, 234, 251
Rilke, Rainer Maria, 70–72, 193
Riversdale, Ontario, 20
Rix, Beverley, 263–64
Robbin, Catherine, 262–63, 273
Robert Shaw Chorale, 122

Roberts, Peter, 166, 169–71
Rogers, Harold, 152–53
Rose, Leonard, 134
Rosselini, Roberto, 127
Rostropovich, Mstislav, 210, 214
Rotary Club of Toronto, 38, 46
Roy Thomson Hall Award, 267
Roy Thomson Hall (Toronto), 208, 260,
    262, 278–79
Roy, Louise, 76, 85, 88
Royal Albert Hall (London), 145, 160,
    163
Royal Alexandra Theatre (Toronto), 84
Royal Conservatory of Music of Toronto,
    37, 41, 43–44, 47–48, 55, 60–64, 69,
    80, 86, 93, 97–98, 126, 132, 160, 188,
    189, 236, 267, 271, 273
    Concert and Placement Bureau,
      96–97, 115, 118
    Concert Hall, 64, 67
    Eaton Graduating Scholarship, 91,
      189, 270
    Opera Festival, 64, 84, 102
    Opera School, 60, 64, 84, 91, 102–104,
      146
    Royal Conservatory Opera Company,
      102
    Senior School, 60, 62–64, 69, 75, 77,
      83–84, 87, 91, 103, 270
    "Wednesday Five O'Clocks" concert
      series, 66
Royal Festival Hall (London), 142, 144, 161
Royal Opera House (Covent Garden,
    London), 93, 182
Royal Philharmonic Orchestra, 141–42,
    144
Royal York Hotel (Toronto), 38
Rubes, Jan, 84

Sabena Airlines, 174
Sabiston, Colin, 66–67, 79–80, 145
Sacks, Oliver, 74
Saint John, New Brunswick, 118–19

Sainte-Anne-de-Bellevue, Quebec, 129

Salle Claude Champagne (Montreal), 224

Salzburg Festival, 158

Salzman, Eric, 203

San Francisco, 128, 140, 198, 212

Saratoga Springs, New York, 212, 234

Sarfaty, Regina, 192

Sargent, Sir Malcolm, 160–61, 163, 183

Saskatoon, 251

Sault Ste. Marie, Ontario, 129

Sayão, Bidú, 92

Scarborough Town Mall (Toronto), 274

Schabas, Ezra, 97

Scheide Library (Princeton University), 245

Scheide, William H., 221, *222*, 223, 243–46, 248, 266

    The Virgin Birth: A Proposal as to the Source of a Gospel Tradition, 222

Schlamme, Martha, 70

Schmitz, Robert, 61

Schoenberg, Arnold, 70

    "Verlassen," 71

    Gurrelieder, 71, 129

Schonberg, Harold C., 136

Schubert, Franz, 71–72, 74, 258

    Eighth Symphony ("Unfinished"), 28, 72, 279

    "Gretchen am Spinnrad," 73

    "Die Sterne," 245–46

Schumann, Robert, 72, 258

Schwarzkopf, Elisabeth, 180

Scott, Rhoda (*see* Marshall, Rhoda)

Scott, Sarah, 274–75, 280

Scriabin, Alexander, 74

Seits, Ernest, 44

Serkin, Rudolf, 37

Shea, Nora, 118–19

Sheffield, England, 145

Sherbrooke, Quebec, 129

Shields, James, 84

Shumsky, Oscar, 134, 223

Sills, Beverley, 151, 188, 247

Silvester, Frederick C., 80–83, 218–19, 241

Simmons, Doreen Uren, 35, 234, 258, 274, *275, 276, 277*

Simon, Stephen, 238–39

Simoneau, Léopold, 19, 138, 141, 161, 192, 226

Simons, Jan, 72, 74–75, 135

"Singing Stars of Tomorrow," 87–90, *89*, 91, 95, 106, 189

Smith, Jane, *272*

Smith, Leo, 93, 227

Smith, Stephen, *272*

Smiths Falls, Ontario, 129

Smithsonian Institute (Washington, DC), 190, 223

Snell, Patricia, 105

Social Security benefits (U.S.), 243

Soviet Culture, 172

Soviet Ministry of Cultural Affairs, 163

Soviet Music, 172

Spectrum, 17

St. Alban the Martyr Cathedral Church (Toronto), 37, 42, 44, 60, 80

St. Andrew's Presbyterian Church (Toronto), 279

St. Anne's Anglican Church (Toronto), 250

St. Catharines, Ontario, 129

St. John's, Newfoundland, 118

St. Lawrence Centre Town Hall (Toronto), 242, 253

St. Louis, 147

St. Michael's Hospital (Toronto), 39

St. Paul's Anglican Church (Toronto), 57, 230

St. Petersburg (*see* Leningrad)

St. Thomas's Anglican Church (Toronto), 159

state dinner for Queen Elizabeth and Prince Philip, 180

Steinberg, William, 162–63

Steinway Building (New York), 107

Stephenville, Newfoundland, 118

Steuermann, Eduard, 70

Stokowski, Leopold, 117, 129, 202

Stratas, Teresa, 215

Stratford, Ontario, 128

Stratford Shakespearean Festival, 134–35, 156, 162, 193, 196, 200–201, 205, 223

Strauss, Richard, 133

Stravinsky, Igor, 212

Streich, Rita, 240

Sunny View Public School, 32

Supervia, Conchita, 185

Susskind, Walter, 202–203, 208–209

Sutherland, Joan, 53, 151, 161

Swift Current, Saskatchewan, 251

Sydney, Australia, 183–184

Sydney, Nova Scotia, 118

Sydney Symphony Orchestra (Australia), 183

synaesthesia, 74

Tafelmusik Baroque Orchestra, 78

Tallinn, Estonia, 251

Tanglewood (*see* Berkshire Summer Festival)

Tate, Nahum, 224

Taverner Consort, 78

Tchaikovsky Competition (Moscow), 163

tent theatre (Stratford), 134

Teyte, Dame Maggie, 92

The Hague, 160

Thomas, Ralph, 203–204

Thomson, Hugh, 92, 104

Thorpe, Day, 104

Thunder Bay, Ontario, 162

Thurber Theatre (Columbus), 241

Time Magazine, 122

Toowoomba, Australia, 183

Toronto Arts Award, 267

Toronto Board of Education, 32, 114

Toronto Children's Chorus, 278–79

Toronto City Hall, 227

Toronto Conservatory of Music (*see* Royal Conservatory of Music of Toronto)

Toronto Mendelssohn Choir, 42, 76, 78–80, 101, 120, 181, 209, 214, 226, 250, 266

Toronto Public Schools vocal competition, 32–33, 39

Toronto Star, 33, 67, 92, 104, 133, 148, 150, 156, 190, 193, 199, 203–204, 208, 212, 214, 228, 242, 253

Star Weekly, 173

Toronto Symphony Orchestra, 33, 42, 57, 75, 101–102, 139, 151, 156, 160, 164, 202–203, 207–209, 212–14, 218, 226, 234, 238, 242, 265

Toronto Telegram, 67, 106, 114, 127, 176, 227–28

Toscanini, Arturo, 118–20, 125, 128, 130, 223, 227

Missa Solemnis, 120–23

Tovey, Bramwell, 274

Town Hall (Adelaide), 184

Town Hall (New York), 105, 107, 135, 192

Townsend, Cindy, 274, 278–79

"Trans Canada Matinee," 163

Transposing, 229, 238, 253

Tredwell, Eric, 82

Trent University (Peterborough), 252

Truman, Margaret, 90, 91

Tumanov, Alexander, 166–67, 171

Turgeon, Bernard, 103

Ulanowsky, Paul, 223

Unger, Gerhard, 141

Unger, Heinz, 129, 133–34, 148, 198–99, 218

University of Toronto, 216–17
    Faculty of Music, 42, 60, 93, 255, 268, 270–72

University of Toronto Concert Choir, 270–71

University of Western Ontario, 200

University of Wisconsin, 157

Upper Canada College, 60, 64, 253

Valente, Benita, 248

van Beinum, Eduard, 128

van Renesse, George, 146

Vancouver, 96, 161, 180

Vancouver Civic Auditorium (*see* Queen Elizabeth Theatre)

Vancouver International Festival, 161, 180

Vancouver International Festival Chorus and Orchestra, 162

Vancouver Symphony Orchestra, 101

Varsity (University of Toronto student newspaper), 67

Verdi, Giuseppe, *Otello* ("Willow Song" and "Ave Maria"), 53

Verreau, Richard, 205

Vickers, Hetti, *272*

Vickers, Jon, 19, 95, 109, 116, 151, 162, *272*, 280

Victoria, British Columbia, 96

Vincent d'Indy School of Music (Montreal), 224

Vinci, Ernesto, 61–62, 65, 69, 189

Vishnevskaya, Galina, 210

"Voice of Firestone," 37

Waddington, Geoffrey, 129

Wagner, Richard, 198, 245

Walter Hall (University of Toronto), 268–70

Walter, Arnold (Dr.), 60, 63–64, 84, 91, 146

Walter, Bruno, 161

Warfield, William, 192

Washington, DC, 90, 147, 190, 234, 238

Washington Opera Society, 148

Washington Post, 90, 190

Washington Sunday Star, 104

Watts, Helen, 247–48

Webern, Anton von, 70–71

Welland, Ontario, 129

Wellesley Orthopaedic School, 29–30, 32–35, 39, 47, 55, 63, 114

Home and School Association, 32

Wellington, New Zealand, 183

Western Ontario Conservatory of Music, 267, 274

Weyburn, Saskatchewan, 251

Whicher, James, 149, 270, 279

Whicher, Monica, 235–36, 270–71, 273–74, 279

Whitehead, Albert, 43

Wichita, Kansas, 147

Wiener Singakademie, 70

Wilks, Norman, 60

Willan, Healey, 43–44, 80, 89

Willauer, Marguerite, 148

Winnipeg, Manitoba, 105, 162, 181, 198, 205

Winnipeg Symphony, 105

Winnipeg Tribune, 101, 153

Winston-Salem, North Carolina, 202

Winston-Salem Journal, 202

Winters, Kenneth, 227–28, 242

Wolf, Hugo, 71–72

Women's College Hospital (Toronto), 279

Woods, J.D., 88

Wreszynski, Ernst Moritz (*see* Vinci, Ernesto)

Wry, Gordon, 135

Wyner, Yehudi, 81, 223, 240, 243–45, 248

Yale University, 223, 243

York Concert Society, 129, 133, 198, 205, 218

York Knitting Mills, 88

York University (Toronto), 231

Of Related Interest

Elmer Iseler
Choral Visionary
by Walter Pitman
978-1-55002-815-7
$40.00

In a career that spanned five decades, Elmer Iseler was
pivotal to the development of choral music in Canada.
After founding Canada's first professional choir in 1954 he
became artistic director and conductor of the Toronto Mendelssohn Choir. In
1979 he established Canada's leading chamber choir, the Elmer Iseler Singers.
He also conducted more than 150 performances of Handel's *Messiah* with the
Toronto Symphony Orchestra.

    Iseler made an impact that will continue undiminished through his many
recordings, the Elmer Iseler Singers, the Elmer Iseler Chair in Conducting,
and the Elmer Iseler National Graduate Fellowships in Choral Conducting at
the University of Toronto.

John Arpin
Keyboard Virtuoso
By Robert Popple
978-1-55002-866-9
$26.00

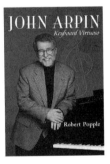

Born and raised in Port McNicoll, John Arpin discovered
his musical talents early: at the age of four he could pick
out tunes on the piano that he had heard on the radio; by
ten he had been identified as a child prodigy by a Royal
Conservatory of Music adjudicator. He would go on to become one of Canada's
finest keyboard virtuosos, playing at concert halls around the world. Equally at
ease performing solo piano concerts, being accompanied by a full symphony
orchestra, jamming with jazz greats, or accompanying opera singers, he was,
perhaps, best known as the premier ragtime pianist of his day.

    This authorized biography is based on more than 40 hours of conversation
during the last four years of John's life and supported by extensive research.

Available at your favourite bookseller.

DUNDURN PRESS
www.dundurn.com

What did you think of this book?
Visit *www.dundurn.com*
for reviews, videos, updates, and more!